INTERFACING
YOUR
MICROCOMPUTER
TO VIRTUALLY
ANYTHING

Other TAB Books by the Author

No. 901   *CET License Handbook—2nd Edition*
No. 1070   *Digital Interfacing With An Analog World*
No. 1152   *Antenna Data Reference Manual—including dimension tables*
No. 1194   *How To Troubleshoot & Repair Amateur Radio Equipment*
No. 1224   *The Complete Handbook of Radio Transmitters*
No. 1230   *The Complete Handbook of Amplifiers, Oscillators and Multivibrators*
No. 1250   *Digital Electronics Troubleshooting*
No. 1271   *Microcomputer Interfacing Handbook: A/D and D/A*
No. 1290   *IC Timer Handbook . . . with 100 projects and experiments*
No. 1346   *The Radio Hobbyist's Handbook*
No. 1396   *Microprocessor Interfacing*
No. 1436   *104 Weekend Electronics Projects*
No. 1550   *Linear IC/OP Amp Handbook—2nd Edition*
No. 1636   *The TAB Handbook of Radio Communications*
No. 1643   *8-Bit and 16-Bit Microprocessor Cookbook*
No. 1650   *CMOS/TTL—A User's Guide with Projects*
No. 1690   *Designing and Building Electronic Gadgets, with Projects*

No. 1890
$21.95

INTERFACING YOUR MICROCOMPUTER TO VIRTUALLY ANYTHING

BY JOSEPH J. CARR

TAB **TAB BOOKS Inc.**
BLUE RIDGE SUMMIT, PA 17214

FIRST EDITION

FIRST PRINTING

Copyright © 1984 by TAB BOOKS Inc.

Printed in the United States of America

Reproduction or publication of the content in any manner, without express permission of the publisher, is prohibited. No liability is assumed with respect to the use of the information herein.

Library of Congress Cataloging in Publication Data

Carr, Joseph J.
    Interfacing your microcomputer to virtually anything.

    Includes index.
    1. Computer interfaces.   I. Title.
TK7887.5.C376   1984   001.64′4   84-8709
ISBN 0-8306-0890-7
ISBN 0-8306-1890-2 (pbk.)

Contents

Introduction   vii

1 It's an Analog World   1
Analog Signals—Sampled Signals—Digitized Signals

2 Electrodes and Transducers   6
Electrodes—Transducers

3 Linear IC Basics   40
Semiconductor Theory—Linear ICs

4 Operational Amplifiers: The Basic Building Block   64
Ideal Operational Amplifiers—Operational Amplifier Problems

5 Other Linear IC Amplifiers   85
Current Difference Amplifiers—Operational Transconductance Amplifiers

6 Analog Signal Processing Circuits   100
Comparators—Integrators—Differentiators—Log-Antilog Amplifiers

7 Reference Sources for Data Acquisition   109
Zener Diodes—Precision IC References—Precision Current References

8 Sample-and-Hold Circuits   128
Ideal S/H Circuits—Sampling Errors

9 Number Systems and Binary Codes for Data Acquisition 142
Number Systems—Conversion between Systems—Binary Arithmetic—Logical Operations—Digital Codes

10 Data Conversion 161
Types of Signal—Conversion Time—Aperture Time—Settling Time

11 Digital-to-Analog Converter Circuits 170
Fundamentals—Full-Scale Output Voltage—Amplifier Settling Time

12 Analog-to-Digital Converter Circuits 181
Integration—Parallel—Binary Ramp—Successive Approximation

13 Microcomputer-Compatible DAC Circuits 203
Ferranti ZN425E—DAC-08

14 Microcomputer-Compatible ADC Circuits 223
Application—8-bit Binary ADC—8-bit Successive Approximation ADC—Ferranti ZN432—Intersil ICL7109—Analog Devices AD7570—Hybrid ADCs

15 Interfacing to Microcomputers 249
DAC Interfacing—ADC Interfacing

16 Microcomputer Control of External Circuits and Devices 274
Relay Controls—SCR Controls—Motor Control—Controlling Small Dc Motors

17 Projects 289
Single-Ended Amplifier—Differential Amplifier—Instrumentation Amplifier—ECG Bioelectric Amplifier—Another ECG Bioelectric Amplifier—Wheatstone Bridge Transducer Amplifier—Universal Rear-End—Universal Instrumentation Power Supply—Precision 10.00 Volt Reference Power Source

Appendix 315

Index 321

Introduction

Your average computer hacker will tell you that "analog is dead."
The implication is that the programmable digital computer can do
anything that an analog circuit can do—only better. Don't you
believe it! Analog electronics is not dead, and the companies that
supply analog circuits are not out of business. There has been some
realignment in the marketplace, but the changes are generally for
the better. Those companies specializing in analog circuits are now
producing integrated circuits and hybrids that far outdistance components sold only a few years ago. In some cases, especially where
the computer is limited, the analog solution may be the best solution
to a circuit problem.

Another reason for denying the death of analog electronics is
given as the title of Chapter 1—It's an Analog World. Most signals
that occur naturally and most transducers produce outputs that are
either currents or voltages are analogous (guess where the term
analog comes from?) to some physical event.

No, analog electronics is not dead, and the computer instrument designer who ignores analog circuit design is in for a rude
surprise. That might mean a less than effective overall design
despite the brilliance of the computer hardware and software implementation.

In this book I will discuss analog circuits and data conversion
circuits (both A/D and D/A). You will learn how to design these
circuits and how to specify others. For those who would like to

examine this subject deeper, please let me recommend two of my other books: *Microcomputer Interfacing Handbook: A/D & D/A* (TAB Book No. 1271) and *Linear IC/Op Amp Handbook—2nd Edition* (TAB Book No. 1550).

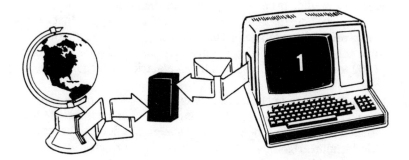

It's an Analog World

The digital electronics revolution has produced a myriad of new electronic applications and greatly simplified other applications. The immense range of applications for microprocessors, microcomputers, and other digital devices has yielded an attitude that *analog is dead*. Not so! If you examine the product lines of the major semiconductor/hybrid houses, you will find that they are *increasing* their analog product lines, not decreasing them as might be expected if the analog market was drying up.

There are two reasons why analog circuitry is needed in many microprocessor-based instruments. First, we have to recognize that *it is an analog world*. Most signals which are acquired will be either from natural electrical sources (biopotentials such as the ECG or from devices such as thermocouples), or from transducers that produce an electrical output that is proportional to some non-electrical parameter such as force, pressure displacement, etc. The second reason is the possibility of either processing speed or memory size limitations on the selected microcomputer that force us to perform certain signal processing chores in the analog sub-system rather than in software. If it is not economical to use a more capable machine, then these functions may well be candidates for analog processing. If we are using a relatively slow (i.e., 1 μs) cycle time, and 1 K of memory, we may elect the operational amplifier integrator in lieu of the more satisfying software integration.

In modern jargon, it is common to refer to any continuous

range, continuous domain voltage or current as *analog.* Thus, an audio signal used in a CB microphone speech amplifier or a public address amplifier is an *analog signal.* In the more rigorous sense, however, we note the similarity to the word *analogous.* In that case, analog refers to a voltage or current analog, or representation, of some non-electrical physical parameter. Thus a pressure range of 0 to 500 torr may be represented by an electrical analog of 0 to +5 volts.

Before going any further in the discussion, some of the signals that you will encounter need defining. Although some people are satisfied with intuitive definitions, it sometimes helps to become a little bit more rigorous. This allows you to more clearly see the function and limitations of various types of circuits.

ANALOG SIGNALS

Figure 1-1 shows the three types of basic signal which you will encounter. Although there are several subclasses that become important in certain instances, these are representative of most.

The basic analog signal is shown in Fig. 1-1A. Notice one fact about this signal. It can take on *any value in either range or domain.* While there may be limits imposed on the permissible end points of both range and domain, the signal can take on any value within that set of limits. You might, for example, label the arbitrarily selected point at which you become interested in the signal. The units to the right of zero, then, will be time units since the beginning of your interest. The range will be some voltage region. In some cases, the low end limit will be zero volts, while in others, it is some negative value set from design considerations. You might find that the signal has any value within the limits of the range. The resolution and accuracy of knowledge of the actual voltage present at any given instant of time is limited only by technology: i.e., that set of techniques which we might use to measure the potential.

Analog signals may be either voltages or current. In many cases, when one type signal is discussed, the opposite signal type may also be inferred as obeying the same rules.

SAMPLED SIGNALS

If an analog signal is allowed to exist only at certain discrete instants in time, then the signal is the sampled version of Fig. 1-1B. The voltage or current may take on any value within the range, but the domain is considered at only specific points. In the case of most electronics applications, the domain will be time, so the value of the

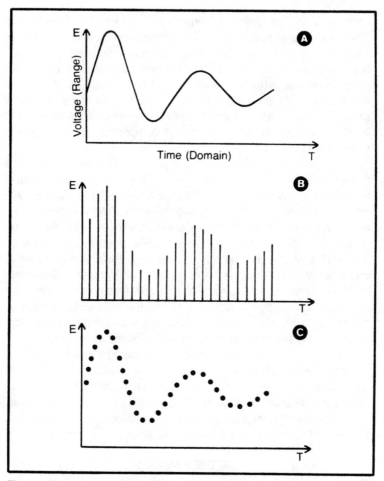

Fig. 1-1. Three types of signal A) continuous analog, B) sampled, C) digital.

signal is known precisely only at certain instants in time. The sampled signal might be measured once every millisecond, or 1000 samples per second.

Sampled signals are not without difficulty. There are certain rules regarding the rate at which the signal is sampled. If you fail to sample the signal often enough, you will lose the overall waveshape.

Any continuous signal can be represented mathematically by a *Fourier series*. This is a series of figures that expresses the function (signal) as a summation of sine and cosine terms. There will be a fundamental, plus some number of odd, even, or odd-even har-

3

monics of the fundamental frequency. Coefficients of each term give us the amplitude. All such functions can be expressed by a Fourier series. The sine (or cosine) wave is expressed by only one term, so it has no dc component or harmonics. In other words, it is a pure waveform. All other waveforms contain some harmonics. If these harmonics are lost, it is impossible to reproduce the signal properly. The sampling rate of the data converter must be set to at least twice the highest frequency component present in the waveform being sampled.

In the human electrocardiograph (ECG), for example, a passband of 0.05 Hz to 100 Hz is needed for proper reproduction of the waveform. A physician reading the ECG requires a trace made on equipment with those limits before being able to properly diagnose problems. In cardiac computers, therefore, the analog-to-digital converter at the input must provide a sampling rate of at least 2×100 Hz, or 200 Hz (200 samples per second). This specification, incidentally, is minimal, not optimal. In actual practice, therefore, much faster sampling rates are often found. One coronary care unit computer samples at a rate of 1000 samples/second. The traces produced on the CRT graphics display are noticeably better than those from a system that samples at 256 samples/second.

A sampled signal can be produced by a *sample and hold* (S & H) circuit. These circuits will typically close a switch to admit the signal and then open it again after the signal is measured. In most cases, the instantaneous value of the signal is stored in a capacitor. A/D converters can also produce a signal that looks sampled, though. It is, however, truly a digital signal.

DIGITIZED SIGNALS

The sampled signal can take on any value within the limits imposed upon the range, but can take on only certain values in the domain. A truly digitized signal, on the other hand, must exist only in certain discrete values in both the range and the domain. For example, a digitized voltage, such as shown in Fig. 1-1C, can take on only certain values (five shown), and is known only at certain discrete instants of time. The A/D converter would produce a signal of this type. Although the values would not be voltages but rather binary words that represent the voltage at some given time. Voltage levels between the allowed levels are in error, but will be given whatever values are nearest the actual values.

When a continuous signal, such as an analog voltage or current, is converted into a signal that can take on only discrete values, the

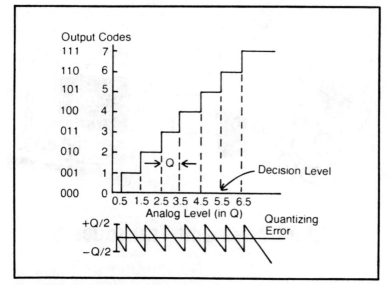

Fig. 1-2. Quantization error and its source.

signal is quantized. Figure 1-2 shows a quantizer transfer function. Note that an A/D converter is basically a quantizer. The analog input signal is plotted along the horizontal axis, and the permissible digital output codes are plotted along the vertical axis.

An error is inherent in the quantization process. Notice that the analog signal can take on any value between 0 volts and 7.0 volts. But the three-bit quantized output can only accommodate the specific values 0, 1, 2, 3, 4, 5, 6, and 7. If the value is, say, 2.56, then it will lay between two of the permissible output numbers (2 to 3). In this particular example, the output will show the binary code 111, indicating a decimal 3. If we denote the quantizing error by Q, then the error will be ±½Q at worst case, falling to zero only at those points where the analog input voltage exactly corresponds to the binary output number, or at 0, 1, 2, 3, 4, 5, 6, and 7 volts. An n-bit data converter will have 2^n possible discrete output states and 2^n-1 analog decision points (see Fig. 1-2).

Thus far we have discussed three different ways to represent the same physical parameter: analog voltage or current, sampled signal, or discrete digital signal. The rest of this book is basically about the hardware needed to acquire and/or process these signals. Before proceeding further, however, it is appropriate that we discuss at length the *sources* of analog signals: electrodes and transducers. They are, indeed, the *front-end* of the analog subsystem.

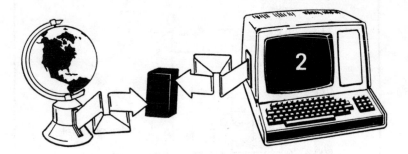

Electrodes and Transducers

I n the first chapter we learned that electronic instruments exist in an analog world. In this chapter, we will discuss various methods of acquiring the analog voltages and currents that are eventually digitized and input to the microcomputer. Some signals, such as biomedical body potentials, are generated by the signal source so only *electrodes* are needed. In other cases (e.g., temperature, pressure, or displacement) the phenomenon being measured are not electrical in nature, so a *transducer* must be used to generate an electrical analog of the measured parameter. Thus, electrodes and assorted transducers can be a part of a microcomputer's analog subsystem. These sundry devices are the computer's interface to an analog world.

ELECTRODES

For our discussion of electrodes we will pick biomedical electrodes. There are several sources of electrical current in the body including the heart (ECG or EKG), brain (EEG) and skeletal muscles (EMG). These signals can be picked up via surface electrodes attached to the patient's skin. Several problems must be overcome, however, before these signals can provide usable information.

One such problem involves the impedance of human skin. The impedance is not only very high for an alleged *voltage source*, but is also a complex impedance (i.e., it contains a capacitive reactance). The resistive component of the skin-electrode impedance can vary over 1 kohm to 10 kohm for moist skin to over 500 kohm for dry, scaly or diseased skin. Because this R-component is so high, the input impedance of the amplifier must be very high. Ordinarily, a 10X rule is followed, so we specify the input of impedance of biopotential amplifiers as not less than 5 megohms.

Figure 2-1 shows an equivalent circuit which models the skin-electrode impedance existing when metallic electrodes are applied to human skin. Note that there are resistances (R1A and R1B and R2A and R2B) and capacitances (C1A and C1B) associated with *each* electrode, plus a *mutual* resistance (R3) *between* the electrodes.

Perhaps the most startling features of Fig. 2-1 are the batteries. These batteries represent *half-cell potentials* formed by the interaction of metallic electrodes and electrolytic skin. The interface point of such a situation forms a miniature battery. The voltage produced can be as high as ±3 volts, but for most metals it is less than ±2 volts. In most biomedical applications, the electrodes are made of *silver-silver chloride* (Ag-AgC1) because that material provides a reasonably stable half-cell potential.

The biggest problem with these half-cell potentials is that they are essentially offset voltages for very low-level analog signals. An ECG signal is roughly 1 mV in amplitude. It would be buried in a 2000 mV half-cell offset potential! This problem could be overcome

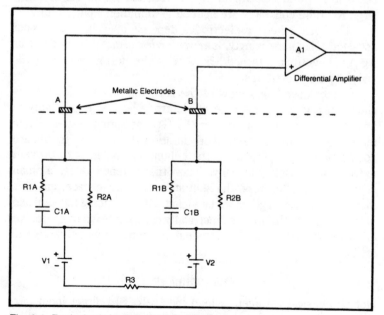

Fig. 2-1. Equivalent circuit for metallic electrodes.

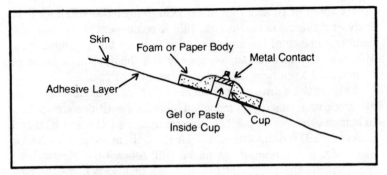

Fig. 2-2. Column electrode.

by using a differential amplifier (see Chapter 3) if V1 = V2. But in practical situations, the difference potential (V1 = V2) can be the full range of the amplifier input. Thus, the half-cell potential may *easily* saturate the amplifier!

Because of the half-cell potential, it is common practice on bioelectric amplifiers to ac-couple the input stage. On some amplifiers, however, the −3dB point in the frequency response requirement is so low that it is very near dc. For an ECG amplifier, for example, the frequency response requirement is 0.05 Hz to 100 Hz. The low-end −3dB point is 0.05 Hz, almost dc. As a result, large RC time constants are needed in amplifier input circuits.

The form taken by electrodes depends upon use. The most usual form, not surprisingly, is a *circular disc* of metal (either gold or Ag-AgC1) with an attached lead wire. Other forms include *needle* and *flat-plate* electrodes.

A cross-sectioned view of the *tower* or *column* electrode is shown in Fig. 2-2. This type of electrode is used extensively in hospitals for electrocardiogram (EKG) monitoring, especially in intensive care areas where short duration strap-on electrodes are not suitable. The purpose of the column electrode is to prevent movement artifact. Normally, when the patient moves, a small slippage occurs between the skin and electrode surface, and this movement causes a glitch in the signal. By interfacing the skin and metal electrode through an electrically conductive gel or paste, we allow a certain amount of electrode movement without creating the artifact.

TRANSDUCERS

Not all physical parameters lend themselves to direct input into electronic circuits or instruments. Unfortunately, electronic circuits operate only with inputs that are either currents or voltages. So when one is measuring nonelectrical physical quantities it becomes necessary to provide a device that converts physical parameters such as force, displacement, temperature, etc., into proportional voltages or currents. The transducer is such a device.

A *transducer* is a device or apparatus that converts nonelectrical physical parameters into electrical signals, i.e., currents or voltages, that are proportional to the value of the physical parameter being measured.

Transducers take many forms, and may be based on a wide variety of physical phenomena. Even when one is measuring the same parameter, different instruments may use a different type of transducer.

This chapter will not be an exhaustive treatment covering all transducers—the manufacturer's data sheets may be used for that purpose—but we will discuss some of the more *common types* of transducers used in scientific, industrial, medical, and engineering applications.

Strain Gauges

All electrical conductors possess at least some amount of electrical resistance. A bar or wire made of a conductor will have an electrical resistance that is given by:

$$R = \rho(L/A) \qquad \text{2-1}$$

where R = the resistance in ohms (Ω)
ρ = the reisitivity constant, a property specific to the conductor material, given in units of ohm-centimeters (Ω–cm)
L = the length of centimeters (cm)
A = the cross-sectional area in square centimeters (cm^2)

Example. A constantan (i.e., 55 percent copper, 45 percent nickel) round wire is 100 cm long and has a radius of 0.91 mm. Find the electrical resistance in ohms. (Hint: The resistivity of constantan is 44.2 × 10^{-6} Ω–cm).

$$R = \rho(L/A) \qquad \textbf{2-1}$$

$$R = \frac{(44.2 \times 10^{-6} \text{ ohm-cm}) \ (100 \text{ cm})}{\pi \left[0.01 \text{ mm} \times \dfrac{1 \text{ cm}^2}{10 \text{ mm}} \right]}$$

$$R = \frac{(4.42 \times 10^{-3} \text{ ohm-cm}^2)}{\pi \ (0.001 \text{ cm})^2}$$

$$R = \frac{(4.42 \times 10^{-3} \text{ ohm-cm}^2)}{\pi \ 10^{-6} \text{ cm}^2} = 1406 \text{ ohms}$$

Note that the resistivity factor (ρ) in Equation 2-1 is a constant, so if length L or area A can be made to vary under the influence of an outside parameter, then the electrical resistance of the wire will change. This phenomenon is called *piezoresistivity,* and is an example of a *transducible property* of a material. *Piezoresistivity* is the change in the electrical resistance of a conductor due to changes in physical dimensions (length and cross sectional area). In piezoresistive materials mechanical deformation of the material produces changes in electrical resistance.

Figure 2-3 shows how an electrical conductor can use the piezoresistivity property to measure *strain*, i.e., forces applied to it in compression or tension. In Figure 2-3 A, we have a conductor at rest, in which no forces are acting. The length is given as L_0 and the cross-sectional area as A_0. The resistance of this conductor, from Equation 2-1 is given by Equation 2-2.

$$R_0 = \rho(L_0/A_0) \qquad \textbf{2-2}$$

where ρ = the resistivity as defined previously
     R_0 = the resistance in ohms (Ω) when no forces are applied
     L_0 = the resting, i.e., no force, length in cm
     A_0 = the resting cross-sectional area in cm^2

But in Fig. 2-3B we see the situation where a compression force of magnitude F is applied along the axis in the inward direction. The conductor will deform, causing the length L_1 to decrease to ($L_0 - \Delta L$) and the cross-sectional area to increase to ($A_0 + \Delta A$). The electrical resistance decreases to ($R_0 - \Delta R$).

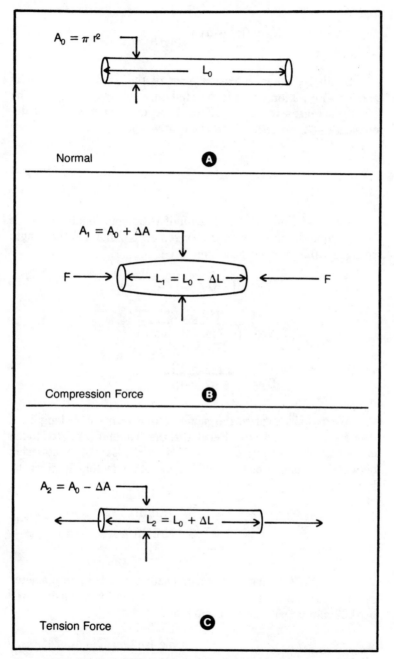

Fig. 2-3. Operation of piezoresistive strain gauge: A) at rest, B) in compression, and C) in tension.

$$R_1 = (R_0 - \Delta R) \ \frac{(L_0 - \Delta L)}{(A_0 + \Delta A)} \qquad \textbf{2-3}$$

Similarly, when a *tension force* of the same magnitude is applied—i.e., a force that is directed outward along the axis—the length increases to $(L_0 + \Delta L)$ and the cross-sectional area decreases to $(A_0 - \Delta A)$. The resistance will increase.

$$R_2 = (R_0 - \Delta R) \ \frac{(L_0 + \Delta L)}{(A_0 + \Delta A)} \qquad \textbf{2-4}$$

Example. Find the gauge factor of a 128-ohm conductor that is 24 mm long, if the resistance changes 13.3 ohms and the length changes 1.6 mm under a tension force.

$$S = (\Delta R/R) \ / \ (\Delta L/L) \qquad \textbf{2-5}$$

$$S = \frac{(13.3 \ /128)}{(1.6 \ mm/24 \ mm)}$$

$$S = \frac{1.04 \times 10^{-1}}{6.67 \times 10^{-2}} = 1.56$$

We may also express the gauge factor in terms of the length and diameter of the conductor. Recall that the diameter is related to the cross-sectional area (i.e., $A = d^2/4 = r^2$), so the relationship between the gauge factor S and these other factors is given by Equation 2-6.

$$S = 1 = 2 \ \frac{(\Delta d/d)}{(\Delta L/L)} \qquad \textbf{2-6}$$

Example. Calculate the gauge factor S if a 1.5 mm diameter conductor that is 24 mm long changes length by 1 mm and diameter by 0.02 mm under a compression force.

$$S = 1 + 2 \ \frac{(\ d/d)}{(\ L/L)} \qquad \textbf{2-6}$$

$$S = 1 + \frac{2[0.02 \text{ mm}) / (1.5\text{mm})]}{(1 \text{ mm}) / 24 \text{ mm}}$$

$$S = 1 + \frac{(2) (1.3 \times 10^{-2})}{(4.2 \times 10^{-2})}$$

$$S = 1 + (2) (0.31) = 1.62$$

Note that the expression $(\Delta L/L)$ is sometimes denoted by the Greek letter ϵ, so Equations (2-5) and (2-6) become

$$S = 1 + \frac{2(\Delta d/d)}{\epsilon}$$

$$S = \frac{(\Delta R/R)}{\epsilon}$$

Gauge factors for various metals vary considerably. Constantan, for example, has a gauge factor for approximately 2, while certain other common alloys have gauge factors between 1 and 2. At least one alloy (92 percent platinum, 8 percent tungsten) has a gauge factor of 4. Semiconductor materials such as germanium and silicon can be doped with impurities to provide custom gauge factors between 50 and 250. The problem with semiconductor strain gauges, however, is that they exhibit a marked sensitivity to temperature changes. Where semiconductor strain gauges are used, either a thermally controlled environment or temperature compensating circuitry must be provided.

Construction. Strain gauges can be classified as either *unbonded* or *bonded*. The categories refer to the method of construction used. Figure 2-4 shows both methods of construction.

The unbonded type of strain gauge is shown in Fig. 2-4A, and consists of a wire resistance element stretched taut between two flexible supports. These supports are configured in such a way as to place tension or compression forces on the taut wire when external forces are applied. In the particular example shown, the supports are mounted on a thin metal diaphragm that flexes when a force is applied. Force F_1 will cause the flexible supports to spread apart, placing a tension force on the wire and increasing its resistance. Alternatively, when Force F_2 is applied, the ends of the flexible

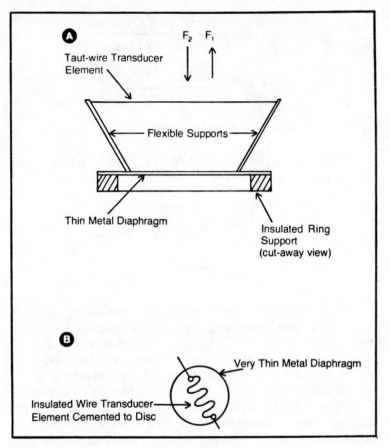

Fig. 2-4. Strain gauge, A) unbonded, and B) bonded.

supports tend to move closer together, effectively placing a compression force on the wire element, thereby reducing its resistance. In actuality, the wire's resting condition is tautness, which implies a tension force. So F_1 increases the tension force from normal, and F_2 decreases the normal tension.

The bonded strain gauge is shown in Fig. 2-4B. In this type of device a wire or semiconductor element is cemented to a thin metal diaphragm. When the diaphragm is flexed, the element deforms to produce a resistance change.

The linearity of both types can be quite good, provided that the elastic limits of the diaphragm and the element are not exceeded. It is also necessary to insure that the ΔL term is only a very small percentage of L.

In the past it has been the opinion of those who make purchasing decisions that bonded strain gauges are more rugged but less linear than unbonded models. Although this may have been true at one time, recent experience has shown that modern manufacturing techniques produce linear, reliable instruments of both types.

Circuitry. Before a strain gauge can be useful, it must be connected into a circuit that will convert its resistance changes to a current or voltage output. Most applications are voltage output circuits.

Figure 2-5A shows the half-bridge (so called because it is actually half of a Wheatstone bridge circuit) or voltage divider circuit. The strain gauge element of resistance R is placed in series with fixed resistance R1 across a stable and well-regulated voltage source E. The output voltage E_o is found from the voltage divider equation

$$E_o = \frac{ER}{R + R1} \qquad \text{2-7}$$

Equation 2-7 describes the output voltage E_o when the transducer is at rest, i.e., nothing is stimulating the strain gauge element. When the element is stimulated, however, its resistance changes by a small amount, ΔR. To simplify our discussion we will adopt the standard convention used in many texts of letting $h = \Delta R$.

$$E_o = \frac{E(R \pm h)}{(R + h) + R1} \qquad \text{2-8}$$

Another half-bridge is shown in Fig. 2-5B, but in this case the strain gauge is in series with a constant current source (CCS), which will maintain current 1 at a constant level regardless of changes in the strain gauge resistance. The normal output voltage E_o is calculated with Equation 2-9 for nonstimulated conditions and under stimulated conditions.

$$E_o = IR \qquad \text{2-9}$$

The half-bridge circuits suffer from one major defect: output voltage E_o will always be present regardless of the stimulus. Ideally, in any transducer system, we want E_o to be zero when the stimulus is also zero, and take a value proportional to the stimulus when the stimulus value is nonzero. A Wheatstone bridge circuit in which one or more strain gauge elements from the bridge arms has this property.

Figure 2-5C shows a circuit in which strain gauge elements SG1 and SG2 form two bridge arms and fixed resistors R1 and R2 form and other two arms. It is usually the case that SG1 and SG2 will be configured so that their actions oppose each other; that is, under

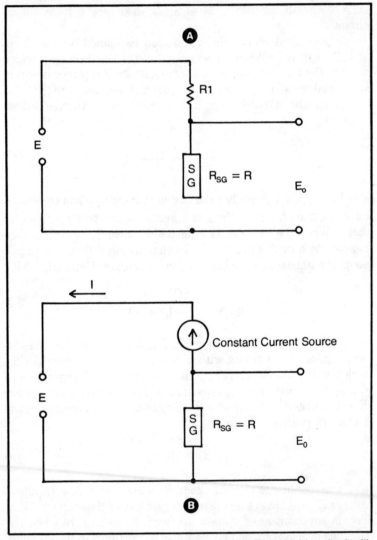

Fig. 2-5. Strain gauge circuits, A) half-bridge circuit, B) half-bridge circuit with constant current source (CCS).

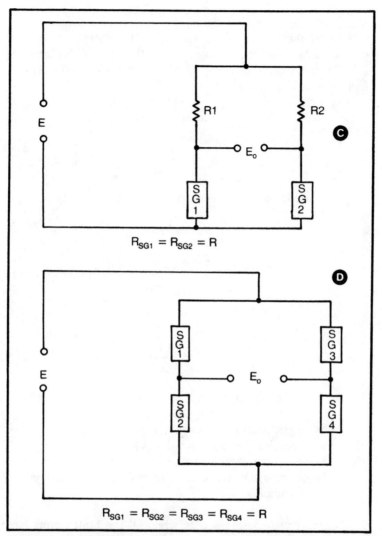

Fig. 2-5. Strain gauge circuits, C) full-bridge with strain gauge elements in two legs, D) full-bridge with strain gauge elements in all four legs. (Continued from page 16.)

stimulus, GS1 will have a resistance $R + h$ and SG2 will have a resistance $R - h$, or vice versa.

One of the most linear forms of a transducer bridge is the circuit of Fig. 2-5D in which all four bridge arms contain strain gauge elements. In most transducers like this all four strain gauge elements have the same resistance. R, which is a value between 100 ohms and 1000 ohms in most cases.

Recall that the output voltage from a Wheatstone bridge is the difference between the voltages across the two half-bridge dividers. The following equations hold true for bridges with one, two, or four equal active elements.

One active element

$$E_o = \frac{E}{4}\frac{h}{R} \qquad \text{2-11}$$

(accurate ± 5 percent, provided that h < 0.1)

Two active elements

$$E_o = \frac{E}{2}\frac{h}{R} \qquad \text{2-12}$$

Four active elements

$$E_o = \frac{Eh}{R} \qquad \text{2-13}$$

where, for all three equations,

E_o = the output potential in volts (V)
E = the excitation potential in volts (V)
R = the resistance of all bridge arms
h = the quantity ΔR, the change in resistance of a bridge arm under stimulus

These equations apply only when all the bridge arms have equal resistances under zero stimulus conditions.

Example. A transducer that measures force has a nominal resting resistance of 300 ohms and is excited by +7.5 volts dc. When a 980-dyne force is applied, all four equal-resistance bridge elements change resistance by 5.2 ohms. Find the output voltage E_o.

$$E_o = E(h/R) \qquad \text{2-13}$$
$$E_o = (7.5 \text{ V}) (5.2 \ \Omega/300 \ \Omega)$$
$$E_o = (7.5 \text{ V}) (5.2) / (300) = 0.13 \text{ V}$$

Sensitivity. (Ω). When designing electronic instrumentation systems involving strain gauge transducers, it is convenient to use the *sensitivity factor* (π), which relates the output voltage in terms of the excitation voltage and the applied stimulus. In most cases, we see a specification giving the number of microvolts or millivolts output per volt of excitation potential per unit of applied stimulus ($\mu V/V/Q_0$ or $mV/V/Q_0$).

$$\psi = E_0/V/Q_0 \qquad \textbf{2-14A}$$

$$\psi = \frac{E_0}{V \times Q_0} \qquad \textbf{2-14B}$$

where E_0 = the output potential
 V = one unit of potential or per volt
 Q_0 = one unit of stimulus

The sensitivity is often given as a specification by the transducer manufacturer. From it we can predict the output voltage for any level of stimulus and excitation potential. The output voltage is found from Equation 2-15.

$$E_0 = \psi EQ \qquad \textbf{2-15}$$

where E_0 = the output potential in volts (V)
 ψ = the sensitivity in $\mu V/V/Q_0$
 E = the excitation potential in volts (V)
 Q = the stimulus parameter

Example. A medical arterial blood pressure transducer uses a four-element piezoresistive Wheatstone bridge with a sensitivity of 5 microvolts per volt of excitation per torr of pressure ($5 \mu V/V/T$; 1 torr = 1 mm Hg). Find the output voltage if the bridge is excited by 5 volts dc and 120 torr of pressure is applied.

$$E_0 = EQ \qquad \textbf{2-15}$$

$$E_0 = \frac{5\mu V}{V \times T} \times (5\ V) \times (120\ T)$$

$$E_0 = (5 \times 5 \times 120)\ V = 3000\ \mu\ V$$

Balancing and Calibrating. Few Wheatstone bridge strain gauges meet the ideal condition in which four arms have exactly resistances. In fact, the bridge resistance specified by the manufacturer is a nominal value only. There will inevitably be an *offset voltage* ($E_o \neq 0$ when $Q = 0$). Figure 2-6 shows a circuit that will balance the bridge when the stimulus is zero. Potentiometer R1, usually a type with 10 or more turns of operation, is used to inject a balancing current, I, into the bridge circuit at one of the nodes. R1 is adjusted for zero output voltage with the stimulus at zero.

The best calibration method is to apply a precisely known value of stimulus to the transducer and adjust the amplifier following the transducer for the proper output for that level of stimulus. This approach may prove unreasonably difficult in some cases, so an artificial calibrator is needed to simulate the stimulus. This function is provided by R3 and S1 in Fig. 2-6. When S1 is open, the transducer is able to operate normally, but when S1 is closed it unbalances the bridge and produces an output voltage E_o that simulates some standard value of the stimulus. The value of R3 is given by Equation 2-16.

$$R3 = \left[\frac{R}{4Q\psi} - \frac{R}{2} \right] \qquad \text{2-16}$$

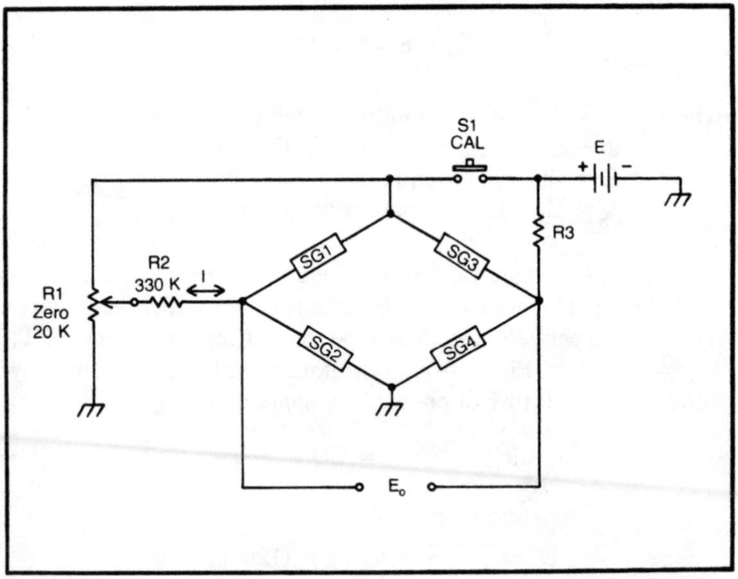

Fig. 2-6. Wheatstone bridge with offset/zero control and calibration circuit.

where   R3 = the resistance of R3 in ohms
     R = the nominal resistance of the bridge arms in ohms
     Q = the calibrated stimulus parameter
     ψ = the sensitivity factor in $\mu V/V/Q$ (note the difference in the units of : V instead of μV)

Example. An arterial blood pressure transducer has a sensitivity of 10 $\mu V/V/torr$ and a nominal bridge arm resistance of 200 ohms. Find a value for R3 in Fig. 2-6 to simulate an arterial pressure of 200 mm Hg (i.e., 200 torr).

$$R3 = \frac{R}{4Q\psi} - \frac{R}{2} \qquad \text{2-16}$$

$$R3 = \frac{200 \; \Omega}{4 \times \dfrac{10^{-5} \; V}{V - T} \times 200 \; T} - \frac{200 \; \Omega}{2}$$

$$R3 = \frac{200 \; \Omega}{(4)(10^{-5})(200)} - 100 = 24{,}900 \; \Omega$$

Temperature Transducers

A large number of physical phenomena are temperature dependent, so we find quite a variety of electrical temperature transducers on the market. In this discussion, however, we will discuss only three basic types: thermistor, thermocouple, and semiconductor pn junctions.

Thermistors. Metals and most other conductors are temperature sensitive and will change electrical resistance with changes in temperature. Equation 2-17 describes the relationship.

$$R_t = R_0 \left[1 + \alpha(T - T_0) \right] \qquad \text{2-17}$$

where R_t = the resistance in ohms at temperature T
     R_0 = the resistance in ohms at temperature T_0 (often a standard reference temperature)

T = the temperature of the conductor

T_0 = a previous temperature of the conductor at which R_0 was determined

α = the *temperature coefficient* of the material, a property of the conductor, in °C^{-1}

The temperature coefficients of most metals are positive, as are the coefficients for most semiconductors. Gold for example has a value of +0.004/°C. Ceramic semiconductors used to make thermistors can have either negative or positive temperature coefficients depending upon their composition.

The resistance of a thermistor is given by Equation 2-18.

$$R_t = R_0 e^{\left(\beta\left(\frac{1}{T} - \frac{1}{T_0}\right)\right)} \qquad \textbf{2-18}$$

where R_t = the resistance of the thermistor at temperature T

R_0 = the resistance of the thermistor at reference temperature (usually the ice point, 0 °C, or room temperature, 25 °C)

e = the base of the natural logarithms

T = the thermistor temperature in degrees Kelvin (°K)

T_0 = the reference temperature in degrees Kelvin (°K)

β = a property of the material used to make the thermistor

(Note: β will usually have a value between 1500 °K and 7000 °K)

Example. Calculate the resistance of a thermistor at 100°C if the resistance at 0°C was 18 kΩ. The material of the thermistor has a value of 2200°K. (Note: 0°C = 278°K, so 100°C = 373 °K).

$$R_t = R_0 \, e^{\beta\left(\frac{1}{T} \frac{1}{T_0}\right)}$$

$$R_t = (1.8 \times 10^4 \, \Omega) \, e^{\, 2200 \, °K \left(\frac{1}{373 \, °K} - \frac{1}{273 \, °K}\right)}$$

22

$$R_i = 1.8 \times 10^4 \ \Omega \ e^{-2.15} = 2089 \ \Omega$$

Equation 2-18 demonstrates that the response of a thermistor is exponential, as shown in Fig. 2-7. Note that both curves are nearly linear over a portion of their ranges, but become decidedly nonlinear in the remainder of the region. If a wide measurement range is needed, then a linearization network will be required.

Thermistor transducers can be used in any of the circuits in Fig. 2-5. They are constructed in many packaging arrangements.

The equations governing thermistors apply as long as *self-heating* of the thermistor is minimal. There are applications where self-heating is used, but in straight temperature measurements it is to be avoided. To minimize self-heating it is necessary to control the power dissipation of the thermistor.

Also of concern in some applications is the *time constant* of the thermistor. The resistance does not jump immediately to the new value when the temperature changes, but requires a small amount of time to stabilize at the new resistance value. This is expressed in terms of the time constant of the thermistor in a manner that is reminiscent of capacitors charging in RC circuits.

Thermocouples. When two dissimilar metals are joined together as seen in Fig. 2-8A, it is possible to generate an electrical

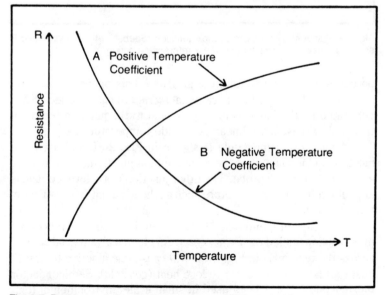

Fig. 2-7. Positive and negative temperature coefficient of resistance thermistor characteristics.

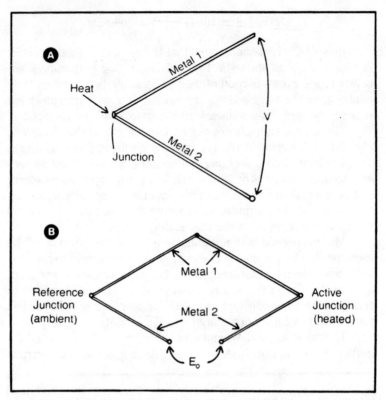

Fig. 2-8. Part A shows a thermocouple junction (Seebeck effect device) and B shows the use of thermocouple with a reference junction.

potential merely by heating the junction. This phenomenon, first noted by *Seebeck* in 1823, is called a *thermocouple*. Seebeck EMF generated by the junction is proportional to the junction temperature and is reasonably linear over wide temperature ranges.

A simple thermocouple is shown in Fig. 2-8B and uses two junctions. One junction is the measurement junction, and it is used as the thermometry probe. The other junction is a reference, and is kept at a reference temperature such as the ice point (0 °C) or room temperature.

Interestingly enough, there is an inverse thermocouple phenomenon, called the *Peltier effect*. An electrical potential applied across the terminals in Fig. 2-8B will cause one junction to absorb heat (get hot) and the other to lose heat (get cold). Semiconductor thermocouples have been used in small-scale environmental temperature chambers, and it is reported that one company researched the possibility of using Peltier devices to cool submarine equipment. Ordinary air conditioning equipment proves too noisy in submarines desirous of "silent running."

Semiconductor Temperature Transducers. Ordinary pn junction diodes exhibit a strong dependence upon temperature. This effect can be easily demonstrated by using an ohmmeter and an ordinary rectifier diode such as the 1N4000-series devices. Connect the ohmmeter so that it forward-biases the diode, and note the resistance at room temperature. Next hold a soldering iron or other heat source close to the diode's body and watch the electrical resistance change. In a circuit such as Fig. 2-9, the current is held constant, so output voltage E_o will change with temperature-caused changes in diode resistance.

Another solid-state temperature transducer is shown in Fig. 2-10. In this version, the temperature sensor device is a pair of diode-connected transistors. For any transistor, the base-emitter voltage, V_{be}, can be described by Equation 2-19.

$$V_{be} = \frac{kT}{Q} \ln\left(\frac{I_c}{I_s}\right) \qquad \textbf{2-19}$$

where V_{be} = the base-emitter potential in volts (V)
  k = Boltzmann's constant (1.38×10^{-23} J/°K)

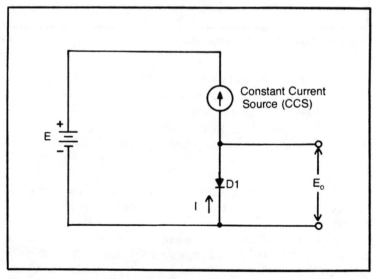

Fig. 2-9. Pn junction diode temperature probe.

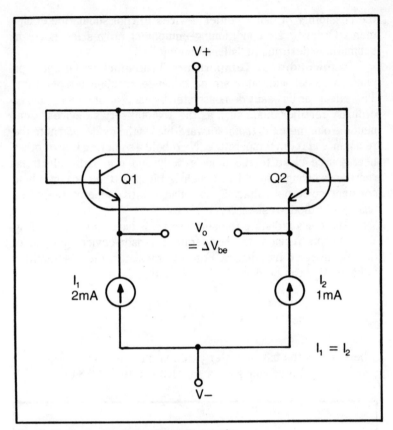

Fig. 2-10. Bipolar transistor temperature probe.

T = the temperature in degrees Kelvin (°K)
Q = the electronic charge (1.6×10^{-19} coulomb)
In = the natural logarithm
I_c = the collector current in amperes (A)
I_s = the reverse saturation current in amperes (A)

Note that the k and q terms in Equation 2-19 are constants, and both currents can be made to be constant. The only variable, then, is temperature.

In the circuit of Fig. 2-10, we use two transistors connected to provide a differential output voltage ΔV_{be} that is the difference between $V_{be(Q1)}$ and $V_{be(Q2)}$. Combining the expressions for V_{be} for both transistors yields the expression in Equation 2-20.

26

$$\Delta V_{be} = \frac{kT}{Q} \ln\left(\frac{I_1}{I_2}\right) \qquad \textbf{2-20}$$

Note that, since $\ln 1 = 0$, currents I_1 and I_2 must not be equal. In general, designers set a ratio of 2:1 ($I_1 = 2$ mA and $I_2 = 1$mA). Since currents I_1 and I_2 are supplied from constant sources, the ratio I_1/I_2 is a constant. Also, it is true that the logarithm of a constant is a constant. Therefore, all terms in Equation 2-20 are constants except temperature T. Equation 2-20, therefore, may be written in the following form:

$$\Delta V_{be} = KT \qquad \textbf{2-21}$$

where $K = (k/Q) \ln (I_1/I_2)$
$\qquad K = (138 \times 10^{-23}) / (1.6 \times 10^{-19}) \ln (2/1)$
$\qquad K = 5.98 \times 10^{-5}$ V/°K $= 59.8$ μV/°K

We may now rewrite Equation 2-21 in this form:

$$\Delta V_{be} = 59.8 \ \mu V/°K$$

Example. Calculate the output voltage from a circuit such as Fig. 2-10 if the temperature is 35 °C (Hint: °K = °C + 273).

$$\Delta V_{be} = KT \qquad \textbf{2-21}$$
$$\Delta V_{be} = \frac{59.8 \ \mu V}{°K} \times (35 + 372)°K$$
$$\Delta V_{be} = (59.8)(308) \ \mu V = 18,418 \ \mu V - 0.0184 \ V$$

In most thermometers using the circuit of Fig. 2-10 an amplifier increases the output voltage to a level that is numerically the same as a unit of temperature so that the temperature may be easily read from a digital voltmeter. The most common scale factor is 10 mV/°K, so for our transducer, the post-amplifier requires a gain of 167.

$$A_v = \frac{10 \ mV/°K}{59.8 \ \mu V \times \dfrac{1 \ mV}{10^3 \ \mu V}} = 167$$

27

Inductive Transducers

Inductance, L, and inductive reactance, X_L, are transducible properties because they can be varied by certain mechanical methods.

Figure 2-11A shows an example of an inductive Wheatstone bridge. Resistors R1 and R2 form two fixed arms of the bridge, while coils L1 and L2 form variable arms. Since inductors are used, the excitation voltage must be ac. In most cases, the ac excitation source will have a frequency between 400 and 5000 Hz, and an rms amplitude of 5 to 10 volts.

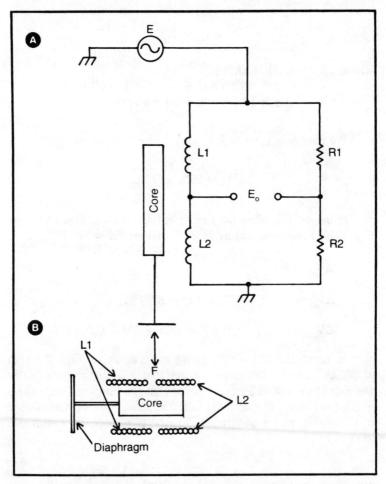

Fig. 2-11. An LVDT transducer is shown in A and the mechanical arrangement is shown in B.

The inductors are constructed coaxially, as shown in Fig. 2-11B, with a common core. It is a fundamental property of any inductor that a ferrous core increases its inductance. In the rest condition, or zero-stimulus, the core will be positioned equally inside of both coils. If the stimulus moves the core in the direction shown in Fig. 2-11B, the core tends to move out of L1 and further into L2. This action reduces the inductive reactance of L1 and increases that of L2, unbalancing the bridge.

Linear Variable Differential Transformers

Another form of inductive transformers is the linear variable differential transformer (LVDT) shown in Fig. 2-12. The construction of the LVDT is similar to that of the inductive bridge, except that it also contains a primary winding.

One advantage of the LVDT over the bridge-type transducer is that it provides higher output voltages for small changes in core position. Several commercial models are available that produce 50 mV/mm to 300 mV/mm. In the latter case, this means that a 1-mm displacement of the core produces a voltage output of 300 mV.

In normal operation, the core is equally inside both secondary coils, L2A and L2B, and an ac carrier is applied to the primary winding. This carrier typically has a frequency between 40 Hz and 20 kHz and an amplitude in the range 1 V rms and 10 V rms.

Under rest conditions the coupling between the primary and each secondary is equal. The currents flowing in each secondary, then, are equal to each other. Note in Fig. 2-12A that the secondary winding currents are equal, they will exactly cancel each other in the load. The ac voltage appearing across the load, therefore, is zero ($I_A = I_B$).

When the core is moved so that it is more inside L2B and less inside L2A, the coupling between the primary and L2B is greater than the coupling between the primary and L2A. Since this fact makes the two secondary currents no longer equal, the cancellation is not complete. The current in the load I_L is no longer zero. The output voltage appearing across load resistor R_L is proportional to the core displacement, as shown in Fig. 2-12C. The magnitude of the output voltage is proportional to the amount of core displacement, while the phase of the output voltage is determined by the direction of the displacement.

Position Displacement Transducers

A position transducer will create an output signal that is propor-

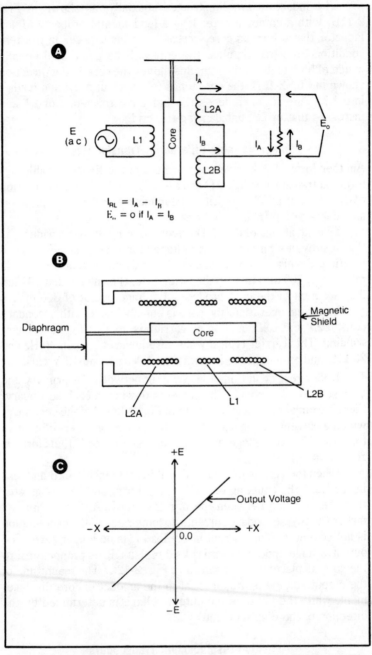

Fig. 2-12. LVDT circuit is shown in A with a cut-away view in B. Part C shows the LVDT transfer function.

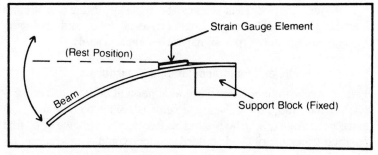

Fig. 2-13. Beam force-displacement transducer.

tional to the position of some object along a given axis. For very small position ranges we could use a strain gauge (as in Fig. 2-13), but note that the range of such transducers is necessarily very small. Most strain gauges are either nonlinear for large displacements or are damaged by large displacements.

The LVDT can be used as a position transducer. Recall that the output polarity indicates the direction of movement from a zero-reference position, and the amplitude indicates the magnitude of the displacement. Although the LVDT will accommodate larger displacements than the strain gauge it is still limited in range.

The most common form of position transducer is the potentiometer. For applications that are not too critical, ordinary linear taper potentiometers are sufficient. Rotary models are used for curvilinear motion, and slide models for rectilinear motion.

In precision applications, designers use either regular precision potentiometers or special potentiometers designed specifically as position transducers.

Figure 2-14 shows two possible circuits using potentiometers as position transducers. Figure 2-14A shows a single-quadrant circuit for use where the zero point, or starting reference, is at one end of the scale. The pointer will always be at some point such that $0 \leq X \leq X_m$. The potentiometer is connected so that one end is grounded and the other is connected to a precision, regulated voltage source V+. The value of V_x represents X, and will be $0 \leq V_x \leq$ V+, such that $V_x = 0$ when $X = 0$, and $V_x =$ V+ when $X = X_m$.

A two-quadrant system is shown in Fig. 2-14B. It is similar to the previous circuit except that instead of grounding one end of the potentiometer, it is connected to a precision, regulated negative-to-ground power source, V−. Figure 2-15 shows the output functions of these two transducers. Figure 2-15A represents the circuit of Fig. 2-14A, and Fig. 2-15B represents the circuit of Fig. 2-14B.

A four-quadrant transducer can be made by placing two circuits such as Fig. 2-14B at right angles to each other and arranging linkage so that the output signal varies appropriately.

Velocity and Acceleration Transducers

Velocity can be defined as displacement per unit of time, and *acceleration* is the time rate of change of velocity. Since both velocity (v) and acceleration (a) can be related back to position (s), we often find position transducers used to derive velocity and acceleration signals. The relationships are as follows:

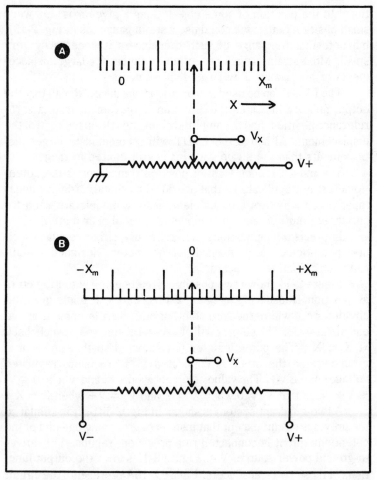

Fig. 2-14. Single-quadrant position transducer (A), and a two-quadrant position transducer (B).

$$v = \frac{ds}{dt} \qquad \textbf{2-22}$$

$$a = \frac{dv}{dt} \qquad \textbf{2-23}$$

$$a = \frac{d^2s}{dt^2} \qquad \textbf{2-24}$$

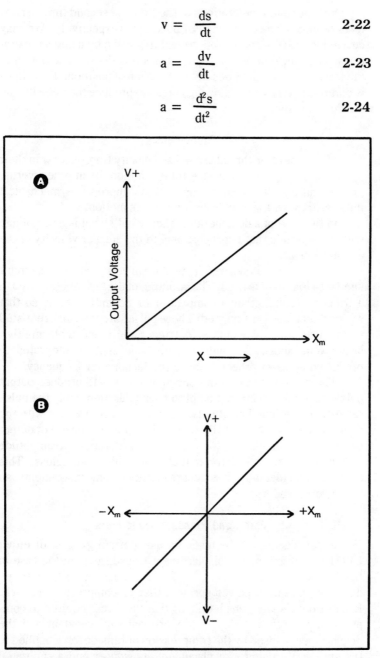

Fig. 2-15. The transfer function of single-quadrant transducer (A), and the transfer function of two-quadrant transducer (B).

Velocity and acceleration are the first and second time derivatives of displacement (change of position), respectively. We may derive electrical signals proportional to v and a by using an operational amplifier differentiator circuit (see Fig. 2-16). The output of the transducer is a time-dependent function of position. This signal is differentiated by the following stages to produce the velocity and acceleration signals.

Tachometers

Ac and dc generators are also used as velocity transducers. In their basic form, they will transduce rotary motion, or in other words, produce an angular velocity signal. With appropriate mechanical linkage, they will also indicate rectilinear motion.

In the case of a dc generator, the output signal is a dc voltage with a magnitude that is proportional to the angular velocity of the armature shaft.

If a dc output is desired instead of an ac signal, then a circuit similar to Fig. 2-17 is used. The ac output of the tachometer is fed to a trigger circuit (either a comparator or Schmitt trigger) so that squared-off pulses are created. These pulses are then differentiated to produce spike-like pulses to trigger the monostable multivibrator (one shot). The output of the one shot is integrated to produce a dc level proportional to the tachometer frequency.

The reason for using the one-shot stage is to produce output pulses that have a constant amplitude and duration. Only the pulse repetition rate (number of pulses per unit of time) varies with the input frequency. This fact allows us to integrate the one-shot output to obtain our needed dc signal. If either duration or amplitude varied, then the integrator output would be meaningless. This technique, incidentally, is widespread in electronic instruments, so it should be understood well.

Force and Pressure Tranducers

Force transducers can be made by using strain gauges, or either LVDT or potentiometer displacement transducers. In the case of the displacement transducer (Fig. 2-18A), it becomes a force transducer by causing a power spring either to compress or stretch. Recall Hooke's law, which tells us that the force required to compress or stretch a spring is proportional to a constant and the displacement caused by the compression or tension force applied to the spring. By using a displacement transducer and a calibrated spring, we are able to measure force.

34

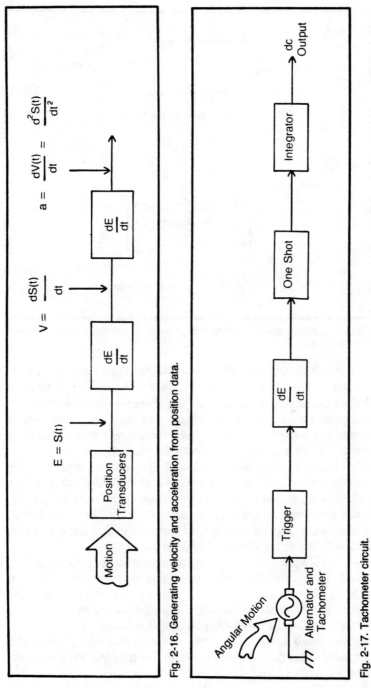

Fig. 2-16. Generating velocity and acceleration from position data.

Fig. 2-17. Tachometer circuit.

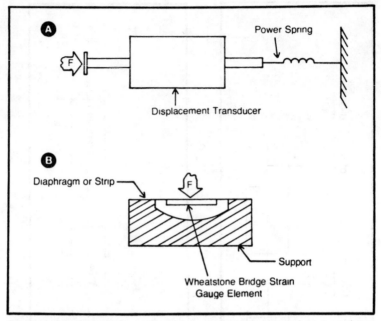

Fig. 2-18. A force-displacement transducer is shown in A and a force transducer is shown in B.

Strain gauges connected to flexible metal bars are also used to measure force, because it requires a certain amount of force to deflect the bar any given amount. There are several transducers on the market that use this technique, and they are advertised as *force-displacement* transducers. Such transducers form the basis of the digital bathroom scales now on the market.

Do not be surprised to see such transducers, especially the smaller types, calibrated in grams. We all know that the gram is a unit of mass, not force, so what this usage refers to is the gravitational force on one gram at the earth's surface, or roughtly 980 dynes. A one-g weight suspended from the end of the bar in Fig. 2-13 will represent a force of 980 dynes.

A side view of a cantilever force transducer is shown in Fig. 2-18B. In this device, a flexible strip is supported by mounts at either end, and a piezoresistive strain gauge is mounted to the underside of the strip. Flexing the strip unbalances the gauge's Wheatstone bridge, producing an output voltage.

A related device uses a cup- or barrel-shaped support, and a circular diaphragm instead of the strip. Such a device will measure *force per unit of area*.

36

Fluid Pressure Transducers

Fluid pressures are measured in a variety of ways, but the most common involves a transducer such as those shown in Fig. 2-19 and 2-20.

In the example of Fig. 2-19A, a strain gauge or LVDT is mounted inside a housing that has a bellows or aneroid assembly exposed to the fluid. More force is applied to the LVDT or gauge assembly as the bellows compresses. The compression of the bellows is proportional to the fluid pressure.

An example of the Bourdon tube pressure transducer is shown in Fig. 2-19B. Such a tube is hollow and curved, but flexible. When a pressure is applied through the inlet port, the tube tends to straighten out. If the end tip is connected to a position/displacement transducer, then the transducer output will be proportional to the applied pressure.

Figure 2-20 shows another popular form of fluid transducer. In

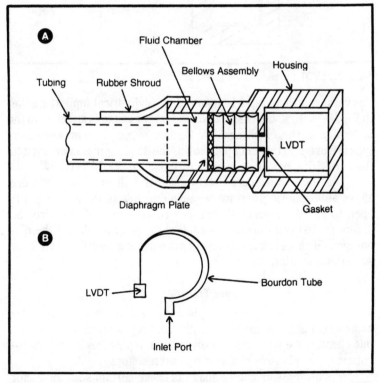

Fig. 2-19. Pressure transducer (A) and a Bourdon tube transducer for pressure (B).

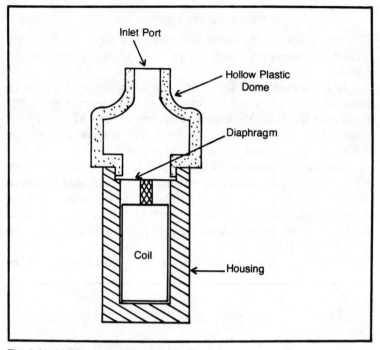

Fig. 2-20. LVDT pressure transducer.

this version, a diaphragm is mounted on a cylindrical support similar to Fig. 2-19. In some cases, a bonded strain gauge is attached to the underside of the diaphragm, or flexible supports to an unbonded type are used. In the example shown, the diaphragm is connected to the core drive bar of an inductive transducer or LVDT.

The fluid transducers shown so far will measure pressure above atmospheric pressure because one side of the diaphragm is open to air. A differential pressure transducer will measure the difference between pressures applied to the two sides of the diaphragm. Such devices will have two ports marked P1 and P2, or something similar.

Light Transducers

There are several different phenomena that can be used for measuring light, and they create different types of transducers. For this chapter, we will limit the discussion to photoresistors, photovoltaic cells, photodiodes, and phototransistors.

A photoresistor can be made because certain semiconductor elements show a marked decrease in electrical resistance when

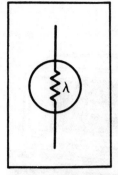

Fig. 2-21. Symbol for photoresistor.

exposed to light. Most materials do not change linearly with increased light intensity, but certain combinations such as cadmium sulphide (CdS) and cadmium selenide (CdSe) are effective. These cells operate over a spectrum from near-infrared through most of the visible light range, and can be made to operate at light levels of 10^{-3} to 10^{+3} footcandles (10^{-3} to 70 mW/cm^2). Figure 2-21 shows the photoresistor circuit symbol.

A photovoltaic cell, or solar cell, as it is sometimes called, will produce an electrical current when connected to a load. Both silicon (Si) and selenium (Se) types are known. The Si type covers the visible and near-infrared spectrum at intensities between 10^{-3} and 10^{+3} mW/cm^2. The selenium cell, on the other hand, operates at intensities of 10^{-1} to 10^2 mW/cm^2, but accepts a spectrum of near-infrared to the ultraviolet.

Semiconductor pn junctions under sufficient illumination will respond to light. Interestingly enough, they tend to be photoconductive when heavily reverse-biased, and photovoltaic when forward-biased. These phenomena have led to a whole family of photodiodes and phototransistors.

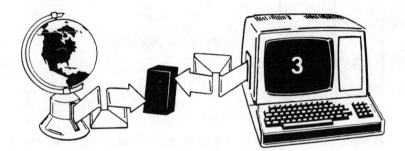

Linear IC Basics

The linear IC was first invented in the early sixties, and has gained in variety and complexity ever since. The first device was the Fairchild μA-703, a device with only a few transistors and was intended as an FM-IF stage or AM-IF/RF. Following that was the μA-709, the first IC operational amplifier. I can remember paying $10 a piece for the μA-703 and saw prices of $105 a piece for the μA-709. Today, of course, such garden variety devices cost pennies and ultra-premium devices only a few dollars. Before delving into the world of linear ICs, however, let's first discuss elementary transistor theory.

SEMICONDUCTOR THEORY

Semiconductors are the tetravalent elements from the central section of the Periodic Table of Elements. They are neither good conductors nor good insulators. Both silicon and germanium have found prominent use in transistor technology, but silicon is more prevalent in devices made in recent years.

To make a semiconductor element suitable for use in a solid-state electronic device it is necessary to add an impurity element. There are two types of semiconductors, made of either Ge or Si, differing mostly in the type of conduction created by the impurities. One type, called n-type, uses negative current carriers for conduction, while the other, p-type, uses a type of positive charge as the current carrier.

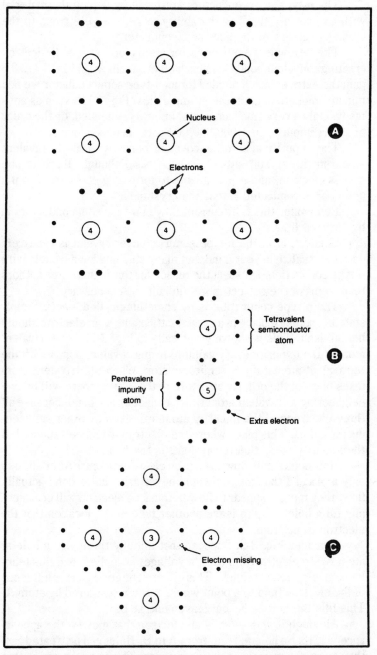

Fig. 3-1. At A, covalent bonding in a semiconductor crystal; at B, the effect of adding a pentavalent impurity; and at C, the effect of adding a trivalent impurity.

41

The n-type semiconductors are made by doping the material with an impurity that has the ability to add free electrons to the crystal structure of the pure semiconductor.

The tetravalent semiconductor atoms form crystal lattices by creating convalent bonds with each other, as shown in Fig. 3-1A. To gain the extra electron needed for an n-type semiconductor we add minute amounts of pentavalent impurities (Fig. 3-1B) such as antimony. Only a very small amount of impurity is needed, on the order of 1 part impurity in 1,000,000,000 parts semiconductor.

The impurity also forms covalent bonds with the tetravalent atoms in the crystal lattice. In each case, though, there is one excess electron, and it is available to form an electric current if a potential is connected across the crystal.

Remember this fact: current flow in n-type semiconductors is by electron flow.

Conduction in the n-type semiconductor crystal is relatively easy to visualize in your mind, but many students have trouble with p-type conduction. I suspect the reason for this is that some authors tend to make the subject more difficult than necessary.

The p-type conduction is by something called a *hole*. Simply stated, a hole is a place in a crystal lattice where an electron should be, but isn't. This is shown graphically in Fig. 3-1C. The trivalent atom of the impurity (e.g., gallium) forms covalent bonds with the tetravalent atoms of the semiconductor. When the trivalent atom takes place in the orderly structure of the lattice, there will be one neighboring tetravalent atom which cannot form a bond, because all three electrons of the impurity atom are taken by other semiconductor atoms. This place where the electron would be expected, if the impurity were also tetravalent, is the hole.

How does a hole flow to form an electric current? After all, it is only a place! I thought you would never ask—holes don't actually flow, they merely appear to flow because an electron will occasionally fill a hole, only to leave another hole in the location that the electron came from.

Consider Fig. 3-2. Suppose that initially there was a hole at atom A. An electric field (i.e., a voltage) is applied, and this tears loose an electron at atom B. This electron migrates under influence of the electron field to a point where it can be captured by atom A. This fills the hole at A, but leaves one at B.

Although it was actually an electron that moved, the appearance was that a hole moved, from A to B. Holes can be treated as if they were electron size positive charges. This is a convention that works most of the time, so accept it.

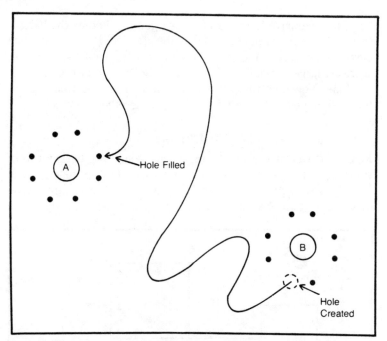

Fig. 3-2. Migration of an electron gives the appearance of hole movement.

PN Junctions

A diode is formed by joining together a section of p-type material and a section of n-type material. An example is given in Fig. 3-3. Please keep in mind that the manufacturers do not actually grab a chunk of p-type and another of n-type and unceremoniously throw them together, although history tells us that this is almost what the original inventors of the transistor were forced to do!

With the battery connected as shown in Fig. 3-3A, the (+) terminal is attached to the n-side, and the (−) terminal is connected to the p-side. The negative charges of the n-type. material are attracted to the positive terminal of the battery, while the positive charges (holes) are attracted to the negative terminal. This creates a wide depletion zone near the junction where there are no current carriers. Current would ordinarily flow across the junction by having electrons and holes combine to neutralize each other. When the depletion zone is wide, however, this cannot happen, so no current flows. Such a pn junction is said to be reverse biased.

Figure 3-3B shows a forward biased pn junction. In this case, the negative terminal of the battery is connected to the n-side of the junction, and the positive terminal is to the p-side.

Here we have the respective charges repelled by the battery terminals, so they tend to pile up at the junction. Here we find that current flow across the junction increases tremendously because there are large numbers of electrons and holes to come together and combine. New electrons are injected into the n-side from the battery, while new holes are created from the other terminal.

The Transistor

Figure 3-4 shows a schematic representation of two basic forms of transistors: npn and pnp. Both types consist of two pn junctions. In Fig. 3-4A we see the npn transistor in which a section of p-type material is sandwiched between two sections of n-type material. In

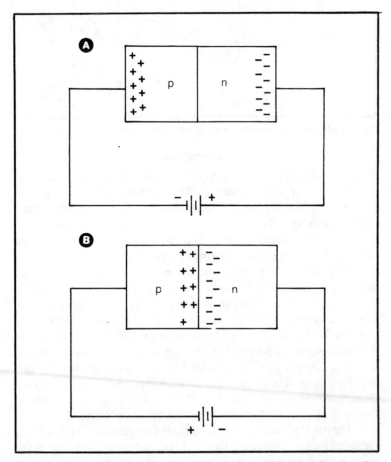

Fig. 3-3. Reverse biased pn junction (A), and forward biased pn junction (B).

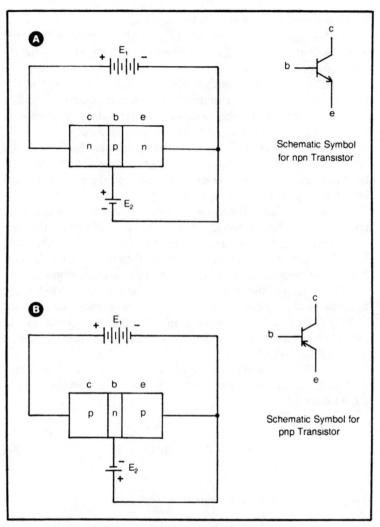

Fig. 3-4. Forward biased npn transistor (A), and forward biased pnp transistor.

the pnp transistor, just the opposite situation is found. A single n-type section is sandwiched between two p-type sections. These transistors are essentially the same except that the respective polarities are reversed.

Note that the power supply polarities are opposite for the two types. This is an immediate consequence of the opposite natures of the two respective types. In an npn transistor, the collector is positive with respect to both the base and the emitter, and the base is slightly positive with respect to the emitter.

In the pnp type of transistor of Fig. 3-4B, we find the collector more negative than the base and emitter, while the base is slightly more negative than the emitter.

The polarity relationships shown are found when the transistors are used in their normal mode of operation as amplifiers. You will, however, sometimes see other polarities when the transistor is being used as a switch, or for some special purpose.

Amplifiers. Amplification can be defined as the control of a larger current or voltage by a smaller current or voltage. Ideally, the waveshape of the smaller signal will be reproduced in shape, but larger in amplitude, at the output.

Most texts immediately label transistors as current amplifiers, but this is unfortunate because it fixes into people's minds the idea of current amplification at the expense of voltage amplification. Transistors may also be connected into circuits that will offer substantial amounts of voltage gain as well as current gain.

The base-emitter junction controls the current flowing in the collector-emitter path. Since the current flowing in the base circuit is only 2 percent to 5 percent of the current flowing in the collector-emitter path, it can be claimed that the transistor amplified the base current.

Gain is the measure of amplification in any type of amplifier device. In the simplest case, we could define gain as the ratio of output over input.

$$A_V = \frac{E_{out}}{E_{in}} = \text{voltage gain} \qquad \textbf{3-1}$$

$$A_I = \frac{I_{out}}{I_{in}} = \text{current gain} \qquad \textbf{3-2}$$

When talking in less generalized terms, however, we can further define gain for transistors. Two gain definitions are usually given: alpha, (α) and beta (β).

Consider Fig. 3-5. Here we see a simple transistor amplifier showing the respective base, emitter, and collector currents. Keep in mind that I_b is approximately $0.05I_e$, while I_c is approximately $0.95I_e$. By Kirchhoff's law, the following relationship is also true:

$$I_e = I_b + I_c \qquad \textbf{3-3}$$

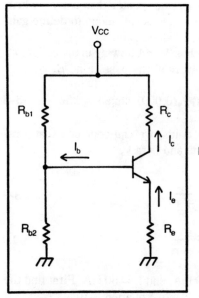

Fig. 3-5. Transistor bias network.

Alpha gain is defined as the ratio of collector current to emitter current, so by Equation 3-3, alpha will always be less than unity.

$$\alpha = \frac{I_c}{I_e} \qquad \textbf{3-4}$$

This will always be less than unity, and in our example above where $I_c = 0.95 I_e$ alpha would be exactly 0.95.

$$\alpha = \frac{I_c}{I_e} = \frac{0.95 I_e}{I_e} = 0.95 \qquad \textbf{3-5}$$

Example. An npn transistor has an emitter current of 25 mA and a collector current of 23 mA. What is the alpha gain?

$$\alpha = I_c / I_e = 23/25 = 0.92 \qquad \textbf{3-6}$$

Beta gain is defined in Equation 3-7.

$$\beta = \frac{I_c}{I_b} \qquad \textbf{3-7}$$

47

Beta gain will always have a value greater than unity—which may explain its popularity since it seems ridiculous to define gain with a number less than one, as in alpha gain.

Example. An npn transistor has 25 mA flowing in the collector, and 100 μA (microamperes) flowing in the base. Find β.

$$\beta = I_c/I_b = (0.025 \text{ amps}) / (0.0001 \text{ amps}) = 250 \qquad \textbf{3-8}$$

Since Kirchhoff's law still holds, we can conclude that a relationships exists between alpha and beta.

$$\alpha = \frac{\beta}{1 + \beta} \qquad \textbf{3-9}$$

$$\beta = \frac{\alpha}{1 - \alpha} \qquad \textbf{3-10}$$

Examples. Find β if $I_c = 49$ mA, and $I_e = 50$ mA. First find the alpha gain, and then substitute it into Equation 3-10.

$$\alpha = 49/50 = 0.98 \qquad \textbf{3-11}$$

$$\beta = 0.98/ (1 - 0.98) = 49 \qquad \textbf{3-12}$$

What is the alpha if a transistor has a beta of 250?

$$\alpha = \frac{250}{1 + 250} = 0.996 \qquad \textbf{3-13}$$

Voltage Amplification. A transistor is basically a current amplifier because a small base current can control a much larger collector current. The transistor can also be used as a voltage amplifier. A circuit that provides voltage amplification is shown in Fig. 3-6. Let us assume that E_o is equal to $V_{CC}/2$ when E1, the input signal is zero. Let us further assume that E1 is a sinewave.

When E1 goes positive, the transistor collector current increases. The voltage across resistor R_c increases. But V_{CC} is a constant, so according to Kirchhoff's voltage law $V_{CC} = E_2 + E$. We must, therefore, expect an increase in E_2 to cause a decrease in E_o. The minimum value of E_o occurs when E_1 is maximum.

Similarly, when E_1 goes negative, the transistor collector current tends to reduce. This reduces the voltage drop across R_c,

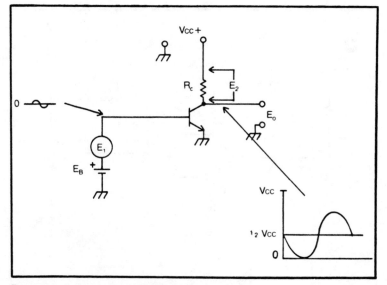

Fig. 3-6. Inverting voltage amplifier operation.

and increases E_o. The value of E_o may swing above and below $VCC/2$. $E_o = 0$ volts when the collector current is greatest and equals VCC when I_c is zero.

Biasing. Practical transistor circuits do not use batteries for both collector and base voltages. This is impractical. Most circuits use a single power supply that has a value between 1.5 volts and 28 volts, with 12 volts and 28 volts being very common. These limits, incidentally, are merely common, and you may find transistor circuits with potentials greater or less than the extremes presented.

Figure 3-7 shows four different methods for using resistors from a single VCC supply to bias the base-emitter junction. In each case the collector load is designated R_c, the base resistor is R_b, and the emitter resistor is R_e. The formulas that follow are approximations good only to about 100 kHz. At higher frequencies (rf) they tend to break down considerably.

The circuit of Fig. 3-7A is a simple resistor bias method in which a bias resistor is connected directly to VCC (+) power supply. The output impedance is approximately equal to the collector resistor, R_c, provided that the impedance of the power supply is less than about one-tenth of the value of R_c at the lowest frequency of operation.

The input impedance can be quite high, on the order of the product of the beta gain and the emitter resistor, or:

49

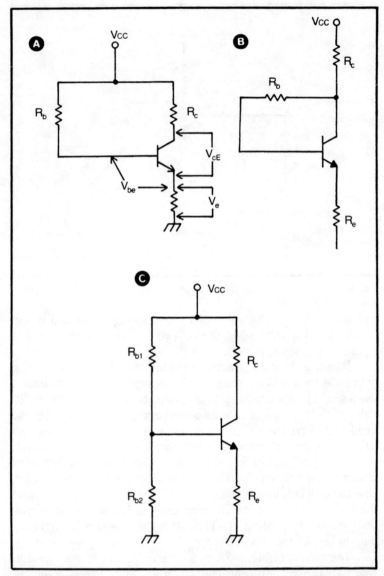

Fig. 3-7. Simple base bias (A) collector bias (B), and the most stable bias configuration (C).

$$Z_{in} = R_e \times \beta \qquad\qquad \textbf{3-14}$$

Two different figures are available for gain in this type of circuit: voltage and current. The current gain is simply the beta rating, often given as hfe in the transistor manufacturer's specification sheet. The voltage gain is given by Equation 3-15.

$$A_v = \frac{R_c \beta}{R_e}$$ **3-15**

The emitter resistor, R_e, is not actually necessary in all cases but is intended to provide an increase in thermal stability. Unfortunately, it also reduces gain. Designers must select a value for R_e that is a trade-off between thermal stability and gain. Note that R_e is in the denominator of Equation 3-15, so gain will reduce as it increases in value. Ordinarily, R_e will have a value betwen 50 ohms and 5 kilohms. Equation 3-16 shows an approximation of the value of R_e.

$$\frac{R_c}{20} < R_e < \frac{R_c}{5}$$ **3-16**

$R_c/10$ is very common, and easy to calculate in one's head.

The value of R_c is determined by computation and by consideration of the desired collector voltage and current. For most amplifier purposes, we set the voltage appearing between the collector and ground at approximately $V_{CC}/2$.

We may set the collector current at some convenient value less than the maximum current. One must consider not only the maximum collector current shown in the spec sheet but also the collector power dissipation (P_d) in general.

$$I_{c(max)} \times V_{ce(max)} = P_{d(max)}$$ **3-17**

The maximum allowable collector current may be less than that listed in the spec sheet because the product of maximum voltage allowed and the maximum collector current is often more than the maximum power dissipation. The maximum allowable collector current, which we will disignate I_c, is given by Equation 3-18.

$$I_c = \frac{P_{d(max)}}{V_{CC}(max)}$$ **3-18**

where P_d = the maximum collector power dissipation in watts

V_{ce} = the maximum allowable collector
potential

I_c = the maximum allowable current
in the collector

The base resistor value is determined by consideration of the required base current. The easiest way to approximate this current is:

$$I_b = \frac{I_c}{\beta} \qquad \text{3-19}$$

The beta (or hfe) is determined from the spec sheet for the transistor being used. We first determine collector current, and from that compute the voltage drop across the emitter resistor.

$$V_e = I_c R_e \qquad \text{3-20}$$

An approximation of the voltage drop across R_b is given by Equation 3-21.

$$E_{Rb} = (VCC - (V_{be} - V_e)) \qquad \text{3-21}$$

The value V_{be} is approximately 0.6 volts for silicon transistors, and 0.2 volts for germanium transistors. The base resistor can now be found by Ohm's law.

$$R_b = \frac{(VCC - (V_{be} + V_e))}{I_b} \qquad \text{3-22}$$

Substitute Equation 3-19 and 3-20 into Equation 3-22.

$$R_b = \frac{(VCC - (V_{be} + I_c R_e))}{\dfrac{I_c}{\beta}} \qquad \text{3-23}$$

$$R_b = \frac{\beta(VCC - (V_{be} + I_c R_e))}{I_c} \qquad \text{3-24}$$

Let me point out that these are approximations. They are to put you into the correct ballpark, but not necessarily to home plate. You should build the circuit on a breadboard or prototyping chassis and make adjustments in the values that give the results nearest the desired results.

Figure 3-7B is a variation in which the base resistor is returned to the collector instead of directly to the Vcc supply. The parameters for this circuit are essentially the same as for Fig. 3-7A, but the degenerative effect of the placement of the base register is said to improve stability. Keep in mind that the Vcc term in Equation 3-23 must be replaced by a lower potential found at the collector end of the resistor r. This potential (Vcc − $I_c R_e$).

Figure 3-7C shows what is probably the best as regards thermal stability, but sometimes at the expense of some input impedance. This circuit:

$$Z_{in} = R_{b2}(R_e \beta) \qquad \text{3-25}$$

The output impedance remains equal to R_c. Also different are the respective current and voltage gains.

$$A_I = \frac{R_b}{R_e} \qquad \text{3-26}$$

$$A_V = \frac{R_c}{R_e} \qquad \text{3-27}$$

Configurations. There are three basic transistor amplifier configurations: common emitter, common collector, and common base. These are shown in Fig. 3-8A, 3-8B and 3-8C, respectively.

The general properties shown in Table 3-1 hold true for these circuits.

These three circuits get their names from the element of the transistor that is common to both the input and the output circuit. In the common emitter circuit, the input signal is applied between the base and the emitter, while output is taken across the collector and the emitter.

Similarly, in the common collector circuit, input signal is applied across the base-collector junction, while output is taken from the emitter-collector junction. In the common base circuit, input signal is applied across the emitter-base junction, and output

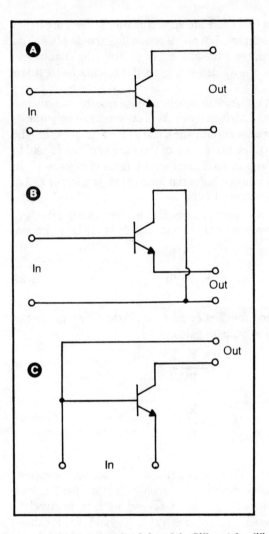

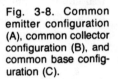

Fig. 3-8. Common emitter configuration (A), common collector configuration (B), and common base configuration (C).

Table 3-1. Relative Gains of the Different Amplifier Configurations.

Common Element	Relative Gain	
	Voltage	Current
Emitter	High	High
Collector	<1	High
Base	High	<1

54

is taken from the collector-base junction.

The output polarity in the common emitter amplifier stage is opposite the input polarity. As the input signal goes more positive, the output signal goes more negative. This is phase reversal, and the output is said to be 180° out of phase with the input. This is not true in the common collector and common base circuits. In those the output signal is in phase with the input.

Ac Amplifiers. A transistor ac amplifier is shown in Fig. 3-9. It is essentially the same as the dc amplifiers discussed earlier, except that capacitors have been added. Capacitors C1 and C2 are for dc blocking. They prevent the bias currents at the collector and base from affecting or being affected by the outside world. Capacitor C3 is a bypass capacitor. Its purpose is to place the emitter terminal at ac ground potential, while keeping the dc bias on the emitter at its proper value. This will increase the ac gain while preserving the benefits of dc stability provided by the emitter resistor.

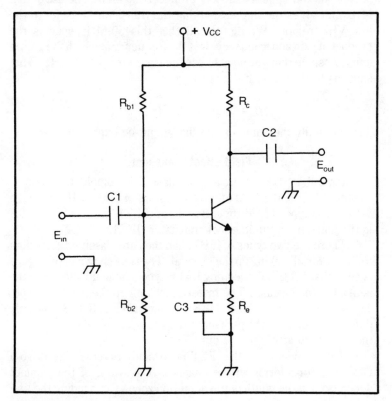

Fig. 3-9. Ac-coupled amplifier.

Transistors will not operate out to any frequency you select. They are rather narrow-minded in this respect, but then again, the device has yet to be invented that has a response from dc to light. There are several ways to specify transistor frequency response, and they must be understood before the devices can be properly applied.

Two of the frequency response measurements are based on the alpha and beta gains of the transistor. They are the points where the alpha and beta gains (respectively) drop to 0.707 times their values at some low frequency point, usually 1000 hertz. More often, though, we will see the gain-bandwidth product, designated F_t, as the frequency response parameter. The F_t is defined as the frequency where the gain (hfe or β) drops to unity. Although the F_t gives us a valid and highly valuable method for determining the range of applications for any particular transistor, it tends to be confusing. Let us take, for example, the case of a transistor with a beta of 300 and a gain-bandwidth product of 50 MHz. The use of that MHz unit gives the impression that the transistor is useful to the low VHF region. Wrong. Recall that this 50-MHz spec is the product of gain and frequency. It is the frequency at which the gain is unity. Assume that you want to use the transistor at 1000 kHz. What happens to the beta? It drops to

$$\beta = 50 \text{ MHz}/1\text{MHz} = 50$$

This is hardly the value of 300 that might be expected.

Field Effect Transistor

The npn and pnp transistors are of a class called bipolar transistors. Another class is the field effect transistors of Figs. 3-10A through 3-10D. The type of field effect transistor (FET) shown in Fig. 3-10A is the junction and field effect transistor (JFET).

There are two types of JFET, and they are classified according to the material making up the channel. The type shown in the figure is an n-channel JFET, meaning that n-type semiconductor material is used in the channel. The material making up the gate is p-type. The symbol for the n-channel JFET is shown in Fig. 3-10B. The only difference between the p-channel and the n-channel symbols is that the p-channel arrow points out.

The pn junction in the JFET is normally reverse biased, so a depletion zone forms in the channel. The width of the channel depends upon the width of the depletion zones surrounding the two gate sections.

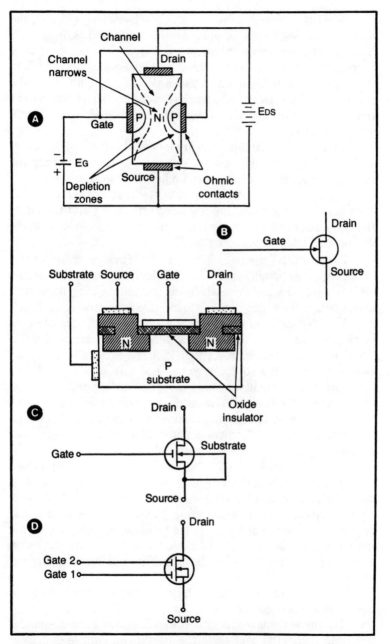

Fig. 3-10. At A, the structure of a junction field effect transistor; B JFET circuit symbol; C structure of a MOSFET or IGFET and circuit symbol for a single gate MOSFET; and D the circuit symbol for a dual-gate MOSFET.

When the reverse bias is low, the channel is wide, so the drain-source resistance is low. As the reverse bias increases, however, the channel width narrows, so the drain-source resistance becomes extremely high (as much as 100 kilohms to 1 megohm). In this respect the JFET is much like a pentode vacuum tube. The JFET channel acts as an electronically variable resistor which has a resistance proportional to the reverse bias applied between the gate and the source.

If the gate-source terminals are forward biased, a high current will flow that may well destroy the device. This is exactly the behavior expected of an ordinary pn junction, so be careful.

The other type of field effect transistor is shown in Fig. 3-10C. This is sometimes called the insulated gate field effect transistor (IGFET), but most frequently it is called the metal oxide semiconductor field effect transistor (MOSFET).

The MOSFET operates in either of two modes: enhancement or depletion. Although some MOSFET devices will operate in only one of these, there are some which will operate in either, depending upon whether the voltage applied to the gate is negative or positive.

The MOSFET does not have any actual gate region. The gate is merely a metal ohmic contact attached to the insulated oxide layer. It creates an electrostatic field in the substrate region between the drain and source regions. The gate is and acts like a capacitor. When a positive voltage is applied to the gate, conduction of electrons in the channel is enhanced. In the depletion mode, there will be a thin layer of conducting semiconductor material between the drain and source. A negative potential applied to the gate will create a depletion zone in this material.

These MOSFET devices which operate as depletion-enhancement field effect transistors have an intermediate value of current flow between full on and full off when the gate voltage is zero. Increasing the voltage in the positive direction turns the device on and allows operation in the enhancement mode. Increasing the voltage in the negative direction increases the depletion zone, so increases channel resistance. This will decrease channel current.

The JFET transistor can be handled just as you would handle any other semiconductor device, but the MOSFET is a bit sensitive. The metal oxide insulator between the gate electrode and the substrate channel is very thin. The breakdown voltage is usually less than 100 volts, but static charges that can build up on your body are usually a lot more than that. As a result, the MOSFET can be damaged by merely touching it! The MOSFET transistor should be handled with this in mind.

Some MOSFET devices use zener diodes inside the package to shunt excess voltages around the delicate gate insulator. An example of such a transistor is the RCA 40673. It is a dual gate MOSFET (see Fig. 3-10D), but each gate has a pair of back to back zener diodes to prevent damage from stray static charges.

Figure 3-11 shows a manner in which the JFET (and by implication the MOSFET) can be used as an amplifier. Bias to the pn junction forming the gate is indirectly created by the source resistor. The channel current flows through this resistor, so will cause a voltage drop that places the source at a slight potential that is positive with respect to ground. The current through the gate resistor is minimal because the junction is reverse biased. The voltage drop across R_g, therefore, is almost zero, certainly a lot less than the voltage across R_s. This places the gate at dc ground potential. The bias situation then, is the gate at ground potential and the source slightly positive. We want the gate slightly more negative than the source. Placing the source more positive than the gate is exactly the same thing.

The principal advantage of both types of FETs is an extremely high input impedance. The reverse biased junction of the JFET creates a depletion zone that has a channel-gate impedance well into

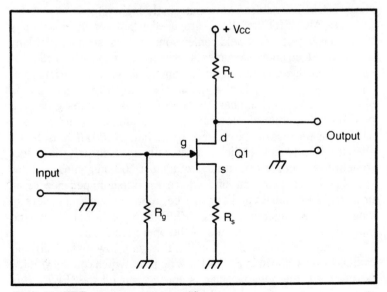

Fig. 3-11. JFET common-source amplifier.

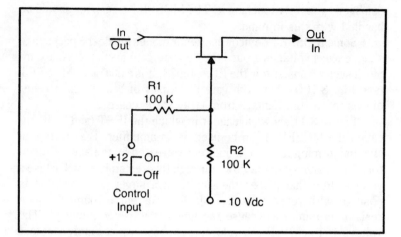

Fig. 3-12. JFET electronic switch.

the megohm region. Only a small leakage current flows across the barrier.

The MOSFET has even higher resistance because it has a capacitor for an input (the capacitance formed by the metallic contact of the gate and the substrate). This capacitor has a metal oxide insulator for its dielectric. Some of these devices have input impedances on the order of 10^{12} ohms (that's tetraohms!), and even cheap MOSFET devices have extremely high values.

The MOSFET and JFET are used wherever the extremely high input impedance would confer some special advantage. Many scientific electronic instruments are driven from electrodes or special transducers which have extremely high source resistances. This makes it mandatory that the amplifier input that receives the signal must be even higher, on the order of 10 times greater if possible. Biopotential electrodes, for example, typically have source impedances on the order of 10 kilohms to 100 kilohms. Some chemical electrodes (which are actually transducers, not electrodes) have source impedances of almost 100 megohms.

There are some circuits where the input impedance of an ordinary operational amplifier can be improved several orders of magnitude by connecting a pair of JFETS or MOSFETs between the input terminals and the inputs of the operational amplifier.

Another application of the JFET is as a low-loss electronic switch such as shown in Fig. 3-12. When the switch control voltage is zero (off), the negative bias is able to cut off the JFET. This effectively pinches off the JFET, and presents an extremely high

60

channel resistance. This allows no transmission of signal through the channel. When the control voltage is +12 volts, the effective bias on the transistor is forward bias, and the negative potential is overcome. In this case, the channel resistance is extremely low, the switch is on, and the signal is transmitted through the device.

These types of solid-state switches are bidirectional, so the terminals are marked in/out and out/in, respectively. Some manufacturers offer single or multiple JFET switches in a single IC package, known as multiple transmissions gates. The popular CD4016 IC is a quad electronic switch such as described here.

LINEAR ICs

In chapters to follow we will discuss linear IC devices, with special emphasis on the *operational amplifier*. We will discuss both basic theory and applications that are unique to the instrumentation and general computer industries.

There are several technologies used for creating transistors and other components on the semiconductor *substrate*. There may be several layers of material in the integrated circuit, of which the substrate is bottom-most. The usual substrate is approximately 6 mils thick, with a typical cross-sectional area being 50×50 mils and some up to 160×160 mils. In Fig. 3-13, the substrate is shown as p-type semiconductor material. The second layer is made of n-type material, but it is shown as an extension of the p-type substrate

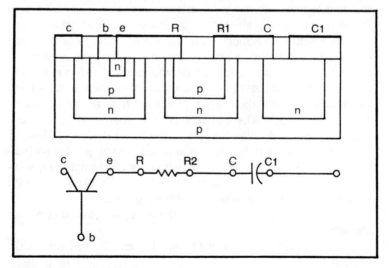

Fig. 3-13. Integrated circuit.

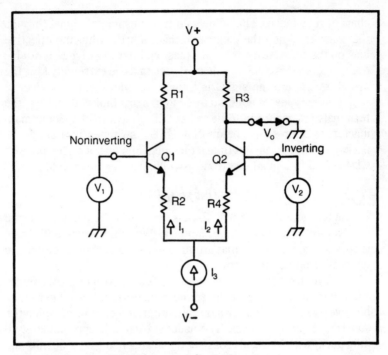

Fig. 3-14. Bipolar differential amplifier.

material. This pn junction must be maintained at a reverse bias, or the IC will be destroyed; a factor that affects some designers. This region is approximately 5 to 30 micrometers thick. The next region is of p-type material, while the uppermost is again n-type material.

Differential amplifiers were among the first integrated circuits. Even today, the differential amplifier is the basis for most IC linear devices. A sample differential amplifier is shown in Fig. 3-14.

The two transistors (Q1 and Q2) of the differential pair are connected such that their emitters are fed from a single *constant current source* (I_3). The constant current source will produce a constant current despite changes in the load resistance. Most IC constant current sources are bipolar transistors biased in a particular manner. Some discrete component operational amplifiers, however, may use a junction field effect transistor (JFET) operated with its source and gate terminals connected together. We can then take advantage of the saturation knee in the *voltage-vs-current* curve for the JFET.

The emitter currents of Q1 and Q2 are derived from CCS current I_3.

$$I_3 = I_1 + I_2$$

I_3 is a constant, thus, if either current is increased, the other must be decreased in order to maintain the above equality. Under the static condition where $V_1 = V_2$, we find that $I_1 = I_2$ and the output voltage is at the mid-point between V+ and V−; if V+ and V− have equal magnitude, then $V_o = 0$.

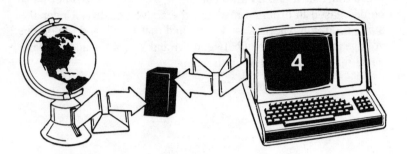

Operational Amplifiers:
The Basic Building Block

Basic to almost any analog circuit is the elementary voltage amplifier. Such amplifiers are used to scale signal levels, provide gain, and buffer devices against the outside world. An amplifier can be built from discrete transistors, but that is a difficult and time-consuming chore in most cases. A simpler approach is the IC operational amplifier. Because the IC op amp allows extremely simple circuit design (in addition to all the normal advantages of ICs), it has literally become the basic building block of the computer's analog subsystem.

The original operational amplifiers were discrete units built from vacuum tubes. Later versions were essentially discrete transistorized versions of the original designs. Such amplifiers were quite large by modern integrated circuit standards, but they did work quite well. The term *operational amplifier* came about because the original op amps were conceived to perform mathematical operations in analog computers. Today, many analog instruments still have op amps performing mathematical operations. These instruments are essentially little more than analog computers with a dedicated program. However, the main use of operational amplifier devices in modern data applications is in preamplifiers (ADCs) or post-amplifiers (DACs). They may also provide some signal processing, as in integration or logarithmic amplification. The nature of analog circuitry, however, is such that you should endeavor to perform most signal processing functions, other than amplification, in software rather than hardware. The only place where analog signal processing should be used in computer data crunching systems is where the software overhead for such processing is prohibitive.

The basic circuit symbol for an operational amplifier is shown in Fig. 4-1. It is the basic triangle symbol used for amplifiers in general. Note that there are two inputs shown. This in not strictly necessary; only the inverting (−) input is really necessary. The differential inputs are of such impressive utility, however, that all operational amplifiers have two inputs. The inverting input (−) will produce an output voltage that has the reverse polarity of the input signal voltage; there is a 180-degree phase inversion between input and output. The noninverting input (+) will produce an output that is in phase with the input signal. The phase reversal seen by the noninverting input is 360 degrees. The gain of the operational amplifier is quite high—at least 10,000 and many up to over 1,000,000! but each input, (−) and (+), sees the same open-loop voltage gain, A_{VOL}. This means that the two inputs will produce equal, but opposite polarity, effects on the output signal.

Notice also that there are two power supply terminals on the operational amplifier. The VCC supply is positive with respect to ground, while the VEE power supply is negative with respect to ground. There is no ground terminal on the operational amplifier. The output signal, however, is taken between the output terminal and the power-supply ground. The proper power-supply configuration for an operational amplifier is shown in Fig. 4-2.

The connections to the op amp are shown in Fig. 4-2A, and the basic functional power supply is shown in Fig. 4-2B. The batteries shown are merely representative, and in most cases will actually be

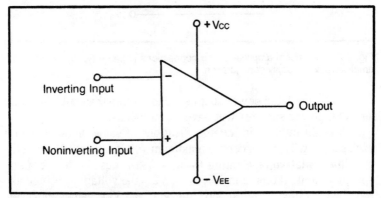

Fig. 4-1. Operational amplifier symbol.

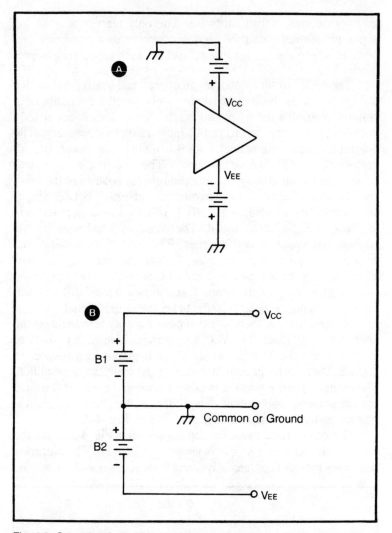

Fig. 4-2. Operational amplifier power connections (A), and typical operational amplifier power supply configuration.

electronic regulated power supplies. More often than not, the Vcc and Vee power supplies will have equal values.

A slight hitch is in the specifications of some units, though, each supply will have a certain maximum voltage rating. However, the differential voltage rating (Vcc − Vee) must be less than a specified limit. If this limit is less than 2× the voltage specified as the maximum for either supply, the Vcc and Vee values must be chosen carefully. For example, the 741 device usually has a specified maximum supply voltage for either VCC or VEE of 18 volts; i.e., VCC = +18 volts and VEE = −18 volts. But the same device has a differential supply voltage of only 30 volts. Note that +18 V −(−18V) = +36 volts, which is greater than the maximum. In the case of the 741, therefore, be careful in selecting the power supply potentials. For example, if VCC is selected to be the maximum (18V), then the VEE supply must be 30-18 volts, or 12 volts. In that case VCC = 18 volts, and VEE = 12 volts.

IDEAL OPERATIONAL AMPLIFIERS

The transfer of any electronic circuit is defined as the output function divided by the input function. For a voltage amplifier, then, the transfer function can be calculated by $E_{out}/E_{in} = A_v$. This is a way of expressing the gain (A_v) of the circuit. We can calculate the transfer function of any operational amplifier circuit from three basic principles: the properties of the ideal operational amplifier, Ohm's law, and Kirchhoff's current law.

The properties of the ideal operational amplifier are as follow:

Infinite input impedance ($Z_{in} = \infty$)
Zero output impedance ($Z_{out} = 0$)
Infinite open-loop voltage gain ($A_{VOL} = \infty$)
Zero internal noise generation
Infinite bandwidth
Differential inputs must be treated exactly the same

The last property means that anything that happens to one input will also happen to the other. In other words, if you apply a voltage to one input, you must treat the other input as if the same voltage were also applied to it. This is not some matter that works on paper only! If you apply a voltage to the inverting input, and then measure the potential at the noninverting input, you will find that both are at the same voltage.

There is one implication of the first property on our list that will be used in the creation of the transfer function for the various circuits. If the input impedance is infinite, the input current is zero. Remember that $Z_{in} = E_{in}/I_{in}$. The only way that Z_{in} can be infinite, then is for I_{in} to be zero. In general, therefore, the inputs of an operational amplifier will neither sink nor source current! Now let's see how these principles can be applied to solving a transfer equation.

Inverting Followers

Figure 4-3 shows one of the simplest operational amplifier circuits. It is the inverting follower circuit, or simply inverter. The noninverting input is grounded, so it will be at a potential of zero volts. Because of the last property just outlined, therefore, you must treat the inverting input as if it were also grounded. This concept is sometimes called a virtual ground, for the lack of a better word. Point A in Fig. 4-3 is, therefore, grounded for all practical purposes. In the analysis of the circuit, then, assume a ground is at point A.

Kirchhoff's current law tells you that the sum of all currents into and out of a junction must be zero. Because the first property of an ideal op amp tells you that the inverting input will neither sink nor source current, you must conclude that $I_1 + I_2 = 0$.

$$I_1 = -I_2$$

From Ohm's law, you know the following about currents I_1 and I_2:

$$I_1 = \frac{E_{in}}{R_{in}}$$

$$I_2 = \frac{E_{out}}{R_f}$$

If you substitute the two equations into the earlier one, you find the relationship in Equation 4-1.

$$\frac{E_{in}}{R_{in}} = \frac{-E_{out}}{R_f} \qquad \text{4-1}$$

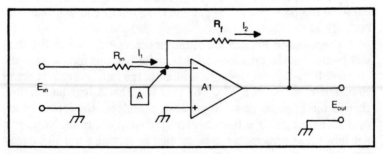

Fig. 4-3. Inverting follower.

This expression relates the input and output voltages to certain resistor values. Solve for the transfer equation and you will conclude that the gain is R_f/R_{in}.

$$A_V = \frac{E_{out}}{E_{in}} = \frac{-R_f}{R_{in}} \qquad \text{4-2}$$

This equation is the proper transfer equation for the inverting follower operational amplifier circuit of Fig. 4-3. This is not, however, the usual form in which the equation is presented. In most cases, you will see the rearranged versions.

$$E_{out} = -A_V E_{in} \qquad \text{4-3}$$

$$E_{out} = \frac{R_f E_{in}}{R_{in}} \qquad \text{4-4}$$

One of the beauties of the operational amplifier is that the voltage gain can be programmed with only two resistors, R_f and R_{in}. Figures 4-4 through 4-7 show several applications for the operational amplifier. The pinouts shown are sometimes called *industry standard*, but they are basically for the 741 device. In Fig. 4-4, the power supply terminals have been shown so that there is a reference for that device and any others based on the industry standard

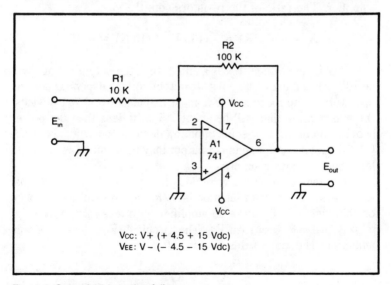

Fig. 4-4. Gain-of-10 inverting follower.

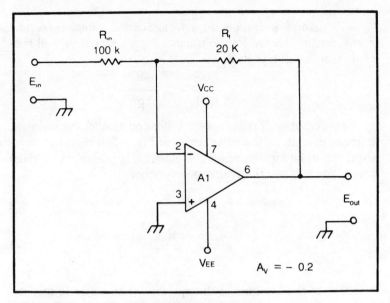

Fig. 4-5. Gain-of-0.2 inverting follower.

pinouts. In the later circuits, the standard practice of deleting the power supply terminals in order to simplify the drawing will be followed.

The circuit shown in Fig. 4-4 is a gain-of-10 inverting amplifier. The ratio of the resistors sets the gain.

$$A_V = -R2/R1 = -(100 \text{ K}) / (10 \text{ K}) = -10$$

If an input voltage, E_{in}, is applied, then the output voltage will be $10E_{in}$. The maximum allowable output voltage depends upon the operational amplifier used. For most manufacturers' 741 devices, the maximum output will be about 3.5 volts less than the power supply potential. For some modern devices, such as the RCA CA3140 device, the maximum output may be as much as 0.5 volts less than the power supply.

You may also obtain gains less than unity (1) in operational amplifiers. The transfer function is R_f/R_{in}, and no limits are placed on this function. To make an amplifier with less than unity gain, merely make R_f less than R_{in}. The circuit in Fig. 4-5 is such an amplifier. The gain of this circuit is 0.2.

$$A_V = -R_f/R_{in}$$

$$= -(20 \text{ K}) / (100 \text{ K})$$
$$= -1/5 = -0.2$$

This type of amplifier circuit is sometimes seen in cases where an ADC is being interfaced with an instrument or other voltage source that has a range greater than the ADC input range. You might, for example, have a 0-volt to 20-volt signal and a 0-volt to +2.5-volt ADC. In that case, set the R_f/R_{in} ratio to 2.5/20, or 1/8 (0.125).

You might also elect to provide gain trimming for the operational amplifier. If a precise gain is needed, then it might not be wise to trust the tender mercies of the resistor tolerances to set that gain. In such cases, you will want R_f to be a circuit such as shown in Fig. 4-6. In this amplifier, the feedback resistor is composed of two resistors, R1 and R2. If R2 has a total value that is approximately 10 percent of the total (R1 + R2), then you can trim the value of the gain quite neatly. This is especially true if the potentiometer is a 10-turn trimmer model.

It is sometimes desirable to make the overall gain of an amplifier quite high. However, certain problems with real operational amplifiers will limit the gain obtainable from a single stage. For these cases, a cascade amplifier is appropriate such as shown in Fig. 4-7. The total gain of the circuit is the product of the individual gains.

$$A_v = \frac{R2}{R1} \times \frac{R4}{R3}$$

$$= R2R4/R1R3$$

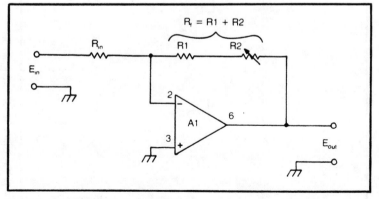

Fig. 4-6. Variable gain inverting follower.

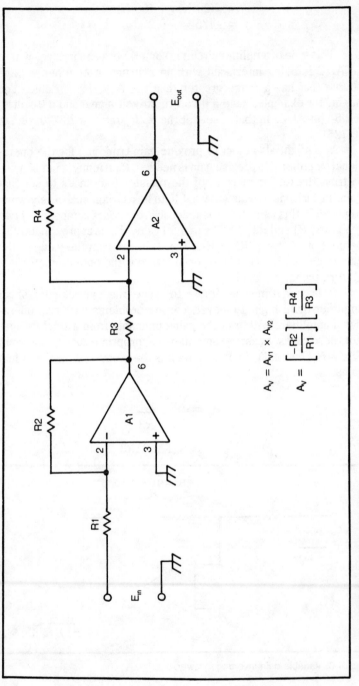

$$A_V = A_{V1} \times A_{V2}$$

$$A_V = \left[\frac{-R2}{R1} \right] \left[\frac{-R4}{R3} \right]$$

Fig. 4-7. Two-stage noninverting amplifier.

This circuit can also be used to provide a phase inversion of the output, so that the total phase shift will be 360 degrees (2 × 180) degrees. This means that the output signal E_{out}, will be in phase with E_{in} (360° = 0°).

The input impedance of the inverting follower is usually quite low. Because the inverting junction is essentially grounded, the input impedance seen by the signal is R_{in}. If R_{in} is low, then the input impedance is also low. You could try to force R_{in} to be high, but this limits available gain. There is a practical value to the maximum value that can be assigned to R_f. These problems are overcome by using the noninverting follower of the next section.

Noninverting Followers

The input impedance problems of the inverting follower can be overcome with one of the circuits shown in Figs. 4-8 and 4-9. These are noninverting followers. The feedback is still applied to the inverting input because degenerative feedback is desired. Applying the feedback to the noninverting input would result in regenerative feedback, and the circuit would likely oscillate. The signal, however, is applied to the noninverting input. Do you recall that first

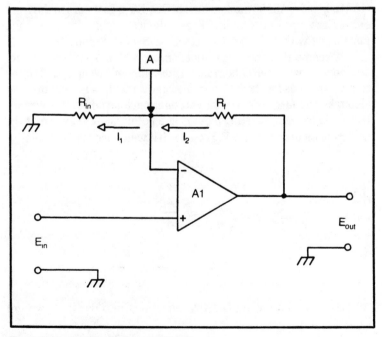

Fig. 4-8. Noninverting follower with gain.

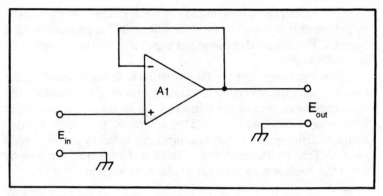

Fig. 4-9. Unity gain noninverting follower.

property? Infinite input impedance means that the signal source will see an infinite input impedance. In real operational amplifiers *infinite* might be a little optimistic; it exists only in idealized operational amplifiers. The approximations of infinity, however, can be quite exciting! Even rejected 741s will go over 500 Kohms, and most are in the megohm range.

Some of the newer op amps, such as the RCA CA3130, CA3120, and CA3160 models, use MOSFET transistors in the front end of the op amp circuit. These devices approximate infinite impedance with 1.5 *tetraohms* (that's 1.5×10^{12} ohms).

It seems that the input impedance problem has been solved, but what do we have? The transfer function will be analyzed in the same manner as for the inverter. You know that $I_1 = I_2$, but you must also take the last property into account once again. In this circuit, however, the noninverting input is at a potential of E_{in}, so treat the inverting input (point A in Fig. 4-8) as if it were also at potential E_{in}.

$$I_1 = I_2$$

$$I_1 = \frac{E_{in}}{R_{in}}$$

$$I_2 = \frac{E_{out} - E_{in}}{R_f}$$

By substitution the last two equations into the first, we get Equation 4-5.

$$\frac{E_{in}}{R_{in}} = \frac{E_{out} - E_{in}}{R_f} \qquad \textbf{4-5}$$

Solving for E_{out} and rearranging gives the normal transfer relationship in Equation 4-6.

$$\frac{R_f E_{in}}{R_{in}} = E_{out} - E_{in}$$

$$E_{out} = \frac{R_f E_{in}}{R_{in}} + E_{in}$$

$$E_{out} = E_{in}\left(\frac{R_f}{R_{in}} + 1\right) \qquad \textbf{4-6}$$

The last equation is the normal transfer equation for the circuit in Fig. 4-8: the noninverting follower with gain. For very high gain applications, the equation can be reduced to the equation for the inverting follower, but with a + sign. At lower gains, the +1 factor must be taken into consideration.

Figure 4-9 shows a special case of the noninverting follower in which the entire output signal is applied to the input. This reduces the gain to unity. This can be proven using ordinary feedback theory (which has not been used in this chapter), if you so desire.

The noninverting follower is used in buffer service and in impedance transformation between two circuits. A buffer is merely an isolation amplifier. It keeps load variation from affecting the driving circuit. In data converters unity gain followers are often seen in this application. Many ADC circuits have changing input impedance over the analog input signal voltage range. Many DACs will require a high impedance load in order to operate correctly, yet are already scaled to the correct voltage. In this cases, the unity gain, noninverting follower is the answer.

The noninverting follower circuits may be cascaded in the same manner as inverting amplifiers. Once again, the total gain is the product of the gains of all stages in cascade.

Positive-Negative Amplifier

It is sometimes appropriate to place a polarity switch in an amplifier

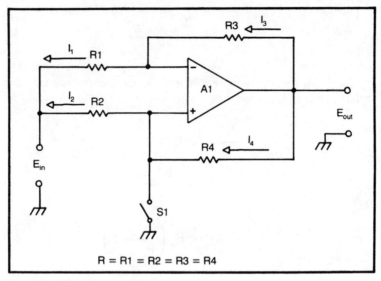

Fig. 4-10. Gain of ± 1 amplifier.

circuit so that the signal can be flipped over. In some applications, a circuit such as shown in Fig. 4-10 can be used to accomplish this purpose. When switch S1 is closed, the circuit operates as a unity gain (R_f/R_{in} = R3/R1=1), inverting follower. When switch S1 is open the circuit operates as a unity gain, noninverting follower; not the same as in Fig. 4-9, but unity gain nonetheless.

In most actual applications, it might be wise to make switch S1 an electronic switch. The circuit could then sense the polarity of the input signal and then open or close S1 as needed to make the signal proper for the data converter to follow. All resistors in this circuit have the same value. Resistance values in the 1 K to 10 K range are usually recommended.

Differential Amplifiers

The inputs of an operational amplifier are differential; the − and + inputs have equal but opposite effect on the output signal. There are actually three types of signal voltage that the op amp will respond to: single-ended input voltages, differential input voltages, and common-mode input voltages. A single-ended input voltage is the voltage appearing between the two input terminals. A common-mode input voltage is one that appears equally on both inputs. These signals are shown in Fig. 4-11. Voltages E_1 and E_2 are single-ended voltages. Voltage E_3 is common mode. The differen-

76

tial voltage (E_d) is the difference between the two single-ended input voltages; $E_d = E_2 - E_1$.

The operational amplifier is designed to reject the common-mode signal and amplify the differential signal. The ability of the amplifier to reject the CM signal is expressed in the *common mode rejection ratio* (CMRR). Most garden-variety, low-cost, op amps will boast common mode rejection ratios of around 60 dB, while premium models have CMRR figures as high as 120 dB.

The common mode rejection capability of the differential amplifier makes it primary for many instrumentation applications. Whenever there is a strong, outside, interfacing signal, the CMRR of the differential amp might eliminate the interference. Consider the case where an amplifier must be connected to its signal source through wires. These wires would have to be shielded in a single-ended circuit. Even then, some degree of 60-hertz interference from nearby power lines might be found. In the differential amplifier, the interfering field will affect both inputs equally so that the signal will cancel in the output. Remember the equal but opposite polarity effect on the output signal. The signals from a common mode source will tend to cancel algebraically in the output.

Figure 4-12 shows the simple dc differential amplifier using just one operational amplifier. Resistors R1 and R2 are input resistors, one to each input terminal of the op amp. It is necessary that R1 = R2. Similarly, feedback resistor R4 must equal grounded resistor R3. The voltage gain of this circuit is given in Equation 4-7 provided that R1 = R2 and R3 = R4.

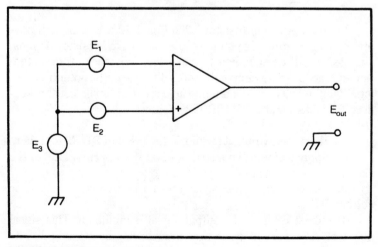

Fig. 4-11. Differential input signals.

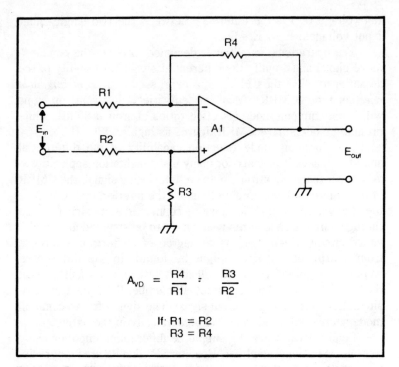

Fig. 4-12. Dc differential amplifier.

$$A_v = \frac{R4}{R2} = \frac{R3}{R2} \qquad \textbf{4-7}$$

In actual practice, resistor R3 in Fig. 4-12 will be potentiometer or a combination of a potentiometer and a fixed resistor. In most circuits, it will be sufficient to make the resistance of the potentiometer about 15 percent of the total. The use of the potentiometer for R3 will make a common-mode adjust control. The usual procedure for adjustment of CMRR is as follows:

1. Short the two input terminals (E_{in}) side of R1/R2 together.
2. Apply a sine wave signal of several volts amplitude to the shorted input terminals.
3. Examine the output signal on an oscilloscope or with an ac voltmeter.
4. Adjust R3 until the output signal is minimum. This signal may well drop very close to zero after having been several volts initially. It may, therefore, be necessary to readjust the sensitivity

of the output indicator progressively downward as the adjustment proceeds towards completion.

The simple circuit of Fig. 4-12 suffers from the same problem as the inverting follower: limited input impedance range. The solution to this problem is the use of the instrumentation amplifier circuit of Fig. 4-13. This circuit uses two input amplifiers in the noninverting follower configuration to drive a differential output stage. The voltage gain of this circuit is given by Equation 4-8 provided that R4=R5, R6=R7, and R2=R3.

$$E_{out} = \frac{2R2}{R1} + 1 \; \frac{R6}{R5} \; E_{in} \qquad \textbf{4-8}$$

It is interesting to note that making R2 = R3 will not materially affect the common-mode rejection ratio, although it will produce a serious gain error over that predicted by the last equation.

OPERATIONAL AMPLIFIER PROBLEMS

When we analyzed the various operational amplifier circuits, we assumed that they were ideal devices. Real operational amplifiers, however, only approximate the ideal parameters given earlier in the chapter. They will have some problems that can affect circuit operation, and these must be dealt with properly.

One of the problems is that the input impedance is not infinite. There will be a finite input impedance in real op amps. This means that a certain input current will flow either into or out of the junction. This current is an input offset current and is due to the bias currents needed to operate the input transistors. With some bipolar input devices, this current can be substantial, yet some MOSFET and superbeta (i.e., Darlington) input op amps have input currents measured in picoamperes.

The input bias current will cause an offset voltage to appear at the inverting input. The current will flow through the feedback and input resistors and cause this voltage drop. The voltage caused by the current will be equivalent to the voltage created if the current were flowing in a resistance equal to the parallel combination of R_f and R_{in}.

One low-cost solution to this problem is shown in Fig. 4-14. A compensation resistor, R_c, is connected between the noninverting input and ground. The same level of bias current flows in both inputs. If resistor R_c has a value equal to the parallel combination of R_f and R_{in}, the voltage applied to the noninverting input will be equal

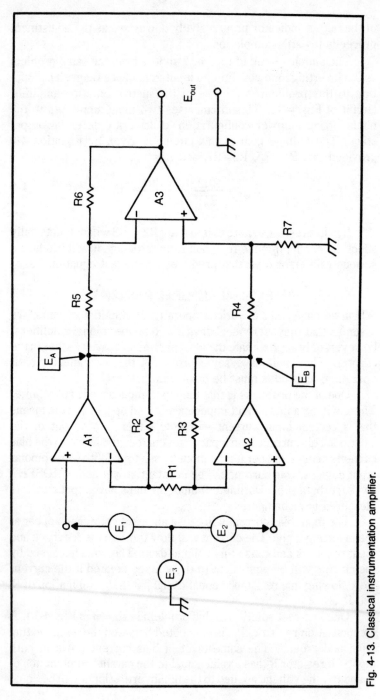

Fig. 4-13. Classical instrumentation amplifier.

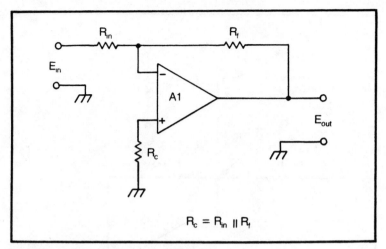

Fig. 4-14. Use of compensation resistor.

to that applied to the inverting input. This makes the differential offset voltage approximately zero, and the output offset is thereby nulled.

But several other forms of offset problems result in an output voltage that is not due to the input signal. There are several methods for nulling offset voltages. In Fig. 4-15, a pair of special offset null terminals found on some operational amplifiers is used. The ends of the potentiometer are connected to the offset null terminals, while the wiper is connected to the VEE negative power

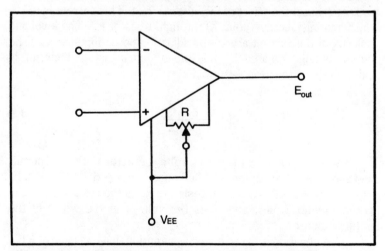

Fig. 4-15. Use of offset null terminals on operational amplifier device.

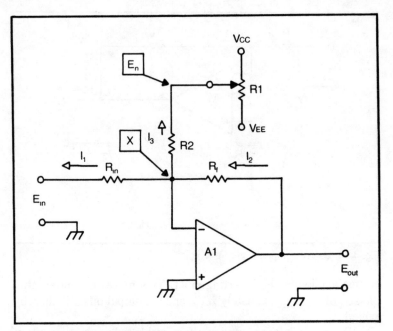

Fig. 4-16. Universal offset compensation circuit.

supply. The potentiometer is adjusted until the output offset potential, regardless of its cause, is nulled to zero.

A more universal circuit is shown in Fig. 4-16. In this case, a third current is summed with the input and feedback currents in order to cancel the effect of the output offset. This current is fed to the summing junction (point X) through resistor R2. The level and polarity of the current are set by adjusting potentiometer R1. The output voltage created by this offset null adjustment circuit is calculated by Equation 4-9.

$$E_{out} = \frac{R_f E_n}{R2} \qquad \textbf{4-9}$$

E_{out} is the component of the output voltage created by the null circuit and should not exceed the unnulled offset voltage (i.e., E_o when $E_n = E_{in} = 0$), R_f of the feedback resistor, R2 is the resistance to the potentiometer wiper, and E_n is the voltage at the wiper of the potentiometer.

This equation is based on the assumption that the value of R1 is small compared with the value of R2. In most cases, the value of R1

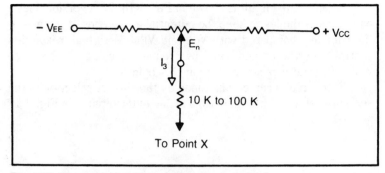

Fig. 4-17. Finer control version of compensation circuit.

will be from 0.1 to 0.2 of the R2 value. R2 will have a value in the 10 K to 100 K range.

It sometimes happens that a fine degree of control over current I_3 is needed. This occurs when the offset voltage is small and becomes especially acute when the voltage gain of stages to follow is very high. A small offset, say 10 mV, might not be much in some cases, but what happens if the stage is followed by stages with an overall gain of 1000 or more? Then the 10-mV offset of one early stage in the cascade chain becomes a 10-mV input signal amplified 1000 times. This means a 10,000 millivolt, or 10-volt, offset at the output of the chain. The circuits in Figs. 4-17 and 4-18 are designed to increase the resolution of the offset null circuit of Fig. 4-16. The version in Fig. 4-17 is designed with the potentiometer connected in series with two resistors. The resistance of the potentiometer should be approximately 10 percent of the total resistance. The two end resistors will have equal values in most circuits using this technique.

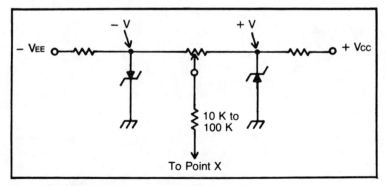

Fig. 4-18. Additional fine control compensation circuit.

An alternate circuit is shown in Fig. 4-18. This version uses a pair of zener diodes to keep the potential at the ends of the potentiometer low compared with VCC and VEE. Very high resolution control over the offsets could be created by using a 1.2 volt to 2.45-volt band-gap zener diode at this point.

Both circuits can be fine tuned by the correct selection of the series resistor (R2 in Fig. 5-16) and one of the circuits in Fig. 4-17 and 4-18.

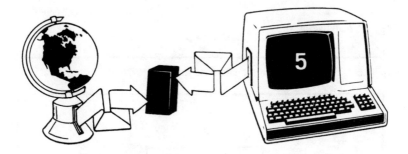

Other Linear IC Amplifiers

Although the operational amplifier is the basic workhorse of the analog subsystem, it is not the be-all and end-all for all possible applications. There are other linear IC amplifiers which may, on occasion, prove more useful than op-amps for specific applications. The current difference amplifier (or CDA), for example, may well be better suited than op-amps to certain mobile and portable applications in which only a single (monopolar) power supply is normally available. In this chapter, we will consider the CDA, and the operational transconductance amplifier (OTA).

CURRENT DIFFERENCE AMPLIFIERS

Until now the operational amplifiers, which we have considered have been classic voltage-difference devices. There is, however, a newer type not as well known but making significant inroads. This is the CDA, or *current difference amplifier*. The appropriate schematic symbol for the CDA or Norton amplifier (shown in Fig. 5-1) is the normal op amp triangle with the addition of a constant-current source symbol along the edge opposite the apex. Although it would not prove difficult to dissect the CDA relative only to itself, it might be easier to understand if we compared the CDA with the traditional operational amplifier.

Input Configuration

Figure 5-2A is a simplified version of the input stage of a classic

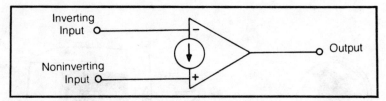

Fig. 5-1. Symbol for a current difference amplifier (CDA).

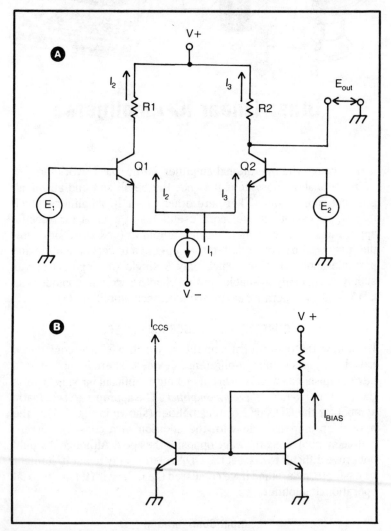

Fig. 5-2. Standard differential amplifier (A), and a bipolar transistor constant current source (B).

voltage-difference op amp. Together with a constant-current source (CCS), transistors Q1 and Q2, form a differential amplifier. The CCS is the circuit shown in Fig. 5-2B. It supplies the same value of I_1 regardless of the load conditions imposed by Q1 and Q2 of the op amp. Assuming Q1 and Q2 are so well matched that they are identical, currents I_2 and I_3 will be equal for equal value of E_1 and E_2. If E_2 is greater than E_1, current I_3 will increase. Since I_1 is a constant, and $I_1 = I_2 + I_3$, this can only result in less current being available for I_2. When E_2 is greater than E_1, voltage E_{out} will decrease. The base of Q2, therefore, can be used as the minus or inverting input.

The other alternative is for E_1 to be greater than E_2. Under that condition I_2 will be larger than I_3. Since this will cause I_3 to decrease relative to its quiescent value, E_{out} will increase. This makes for a handy noninverting input at the base of Q1. On that side of the differential amplifier, an increase of the input voltage will cause a corresponding increase in output voltage.

Figure 5-3 shows a simplified version of a typical CDA input amplifier stage. Transistor Q1 is a standard common-emitter stage while Q2 serves as an output buffer in an emitter-follower config-

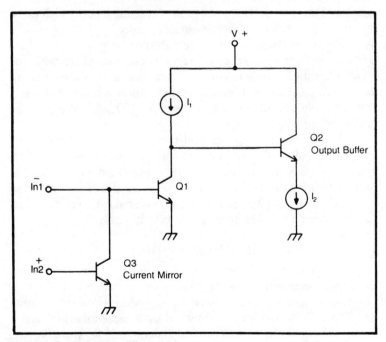

Fig. 5-3. Current mirror differential input.

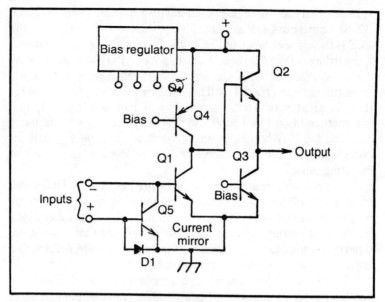

Fig. 5-4. Internal circuitry of a typical CDA.

uration. The base of Q1 serves as the inverting input, which is the normal situation for a common-emitter stage.

The noninverting input is through transistor Q5 (Fig. 5-4), a second common-emitter stage. This transistor, along with the diode shunting the base to emitter, form what is known as a *current mirror*. In most circuits, employing the typical CDA device there will be a permanent bias current of 5 to 100 μA flowing in the noninverting amplifier input.

Both the input amplifier and the output buffer derive their respective collector currents from constant-current sources. Figure 5-4 shows the same input stage expanded to include the constant-current-source transistors. Bias to the respective base terminals is from internally regulated reference power supplies. Current remains stable because the bias is stable.

Inverting Ac Amplifiers

Figure 5-5 shows the normal circuit for using a CDA as an inverting ac signal amplifier. Note that the external circuit configuration resembles that of a traditional voltage-difference operational amplifier. Dc to the input is blocked by a capacitor which has a reactance equal to about 10 percent the value of R_{in} at the lowest frequency of interest.

In a traditional op amp, voltage gain can be predicted with a fair degree of accuracy from the ratio of the feedback to input resistances; a fact that makes designers happy. This procedure retains some of its utility when CDA devices are used, but will yield only an approximate value for A_v:

$$A_v = R_f/R_{in} \qquad \text{5-1}$$

Several error terms are accounted for by the following equation for the quiescent output voltage level:

$$E_{out} = \left(\frac{E_{ref}R_f}{R_{ref}}\right) = +\left(1 - \left(\frac{R_f}{R_{ref}}\right)\right)\phi \qquad \text{5-2}$$

The term represents the normal junction potential of the input transistors. Since these are silicon, most CDA manufacturers recommend using a value of 0.7 for this when the device it is operated within normal temperature ranges. Figure 5-6 is a practical example of the former circuit offering a wide bandwidth (full audio spectrum) with a voltage gain of approximately 40 dB. Note that in both examples the noninverting input is returned to B+ through

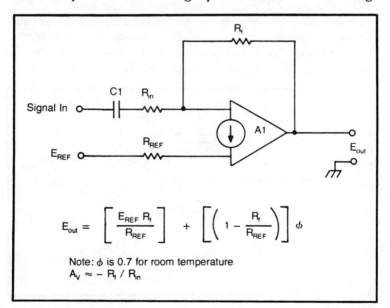

$$E_{out} = \left[\frac{E_{REF} R_f}{R_{REF}}\right] + \left[\left(1 - \frac{R_f}{R_{REF}}\right)\right]\phi$$

Note: ϕ is 0.7 for room temperature
$A_v \approx - R_f / R_{in}$

Fig. 5-5. Ac-coupled CDA.

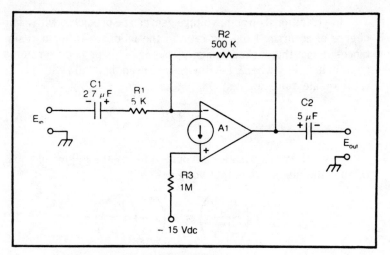

Fig. 5-6. Forty dB gain ac-coupled amplifier.

resistor R_{ref}. The value of this resistor is set so that a current between 5 μA and 100 μA will flow.

Noninverting Amplifiers

The circuit of Fig. 5-7 shows the noninverting configuration for a CDA. In this case, the signal is input through a current mirror. Note the major difference between this circuit and a similar function using operational amplifiers: R_{in} is part of the plus input circuit instead of being connected from the minus input to common. The gain of a noninverting CDA is given by Equation 5-3.

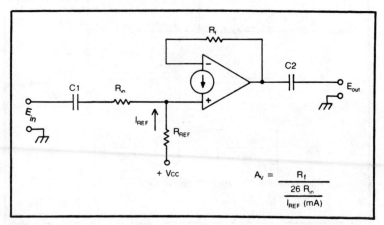

$$A_v = \frac{R_f}{\dfrac{26 R_{in}}{I_{REF} \text{ (mA)}}}$$

Fig. 5-7. Noninverting amplifier.

90

$$A_V = \frac{R_f}{R_{in} \dfrac{26}{I_{ref}}} \qquad\qquad \textbf{5-3}$$

I_{ref} is in milliamperes. An example of a unity-gain noninverting amplifier is given in Fig. 5-8.

The first step in CDA design is to set the quiescent output conditions. During this part of the procedure, we will want to set the current flowing in the noninverting input to a value within the specified range of 5 to 100 μA.

For the majority of applications, it will be desirable to use one-half the supply voltage as the quiescent output voltage. Once a resistor is selected to supply the reference current in the plus input, choose one-half its value as the feedback resistance. Gain is selected through a consideration of the needs of the overall design. Once the gain figure is selected, however, we plug it and the value of R_f into either Equation 5-1 or 5-3, as appropriate, and solve for R_{in}.

Differential Amplifiers

In operational amplifier circuits, the device delivers an output which is proportional to the voltage gain factor times the difference between input voltages. In the CDA device, we will also make use of the two inputs to form a differential amplifier. In this case, though, the output voltage is proportional to the difference between

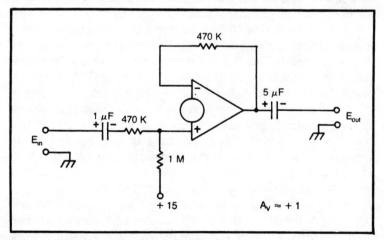

Fig. 5-8. Unity gain ac-coupled amplifier.

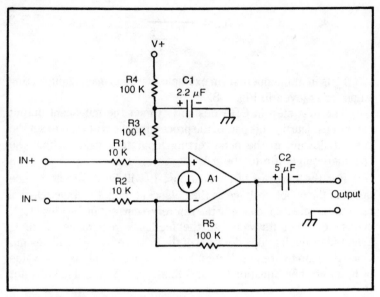

Fig. 5-9. Differential input CDA amplifier.

input currents. Figure 5-9 shows one form of CDA implementation of the differential amplifier idea.

Mixer Circuits

A linear signal mixer is a circuit which will combine analog signals from several sources into one channel without causing distortion to any of them.

The circuit in Fig. 5-10 uses one CDA as an output buffer amplifier fed by the output of several other CDA stages (only one channel is shown). This is a convenient arrangement, especially if only three channels are contemplated, since most CDA integrated circuits contain four amplifiers. One especially attractive feature of this circuit is the fact that any channel can be turned on or off simply by using a switch to ground the noninverting input bias current. It is generally agreed that signal switching is best handled by dc methods such as this, since switching audio and other ac signals can lead to interference problems, as well as mechanical problems resulting from the attempt at fixing interference!

The mixer of Fig. 5-11 is an ac OR gate. This circuit has simplicity of design as its main virtue. The gain seen by any one input is approximated by Equation 5-1; a fact which offers some intriguing possibilities for independent level controls.

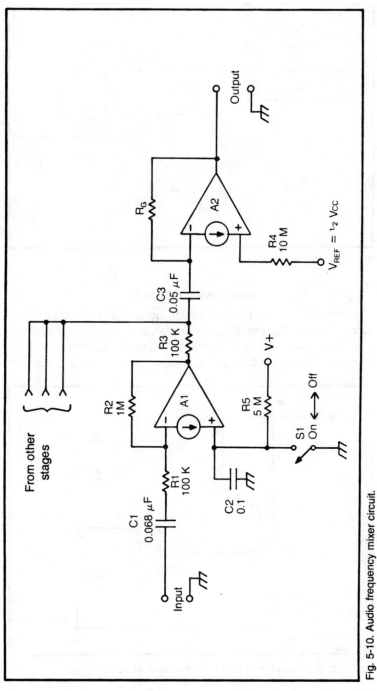

Fig. 5-10. Audio frequency mixer circuit.

93

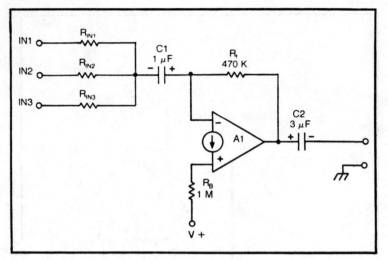

Fig. 5-11. Alternate mixer circuit.

Miscellaneous Circuits

Illustrations of assorted and miscellaneous CDA circuitry often succeed better than anything in demonstrating its utility of application. Figure 5-12 shows a method for using a CDA to regulate the reference bias of another CDA. In this circuit, potentiometer R3

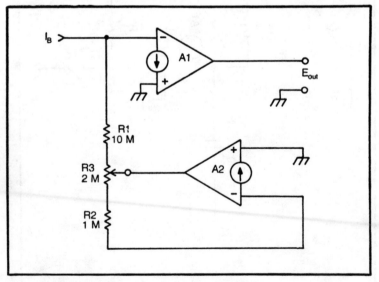

Fig. 5-12. CDA regulation of the bias of another CDA.

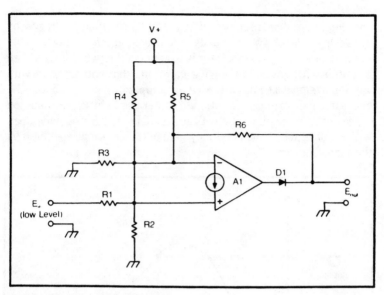

Fig. 5-13. Low-level CDA amplifier.

sets the current level (generated by amplifier A2) flowing into the input of the first amplifier.

Low-level dc signals are not easy to handle as larger high-level signals. This is probably because bias must be provided to the common-emitter input transistor. The circuit of Fig. 5-12 accomplishes this with an extra set of resistors.

A comparator circuit delivers an output that indicates either

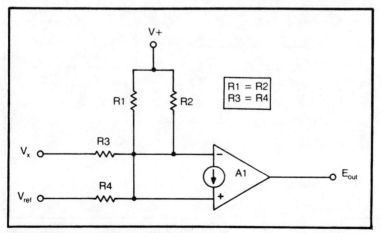

Fig. 5-14. Offset operation of CDA.

agreement or disagreement of two (or more) input voltages by delivering one of two mutually exclusive output voltages. One method for making a comparator is to connect the two voltages to an amplifier with grossly excessive gain; one that will saturate with any input signal at all. In the CDA comparator of Fig. 5-14, the excessive gain criterion is satisfied rather easily by the elimination of the feedback resistor. In that case the CDA is running wide open with a gain equal to the open-loop gain of the device as specified by the manufacturer.

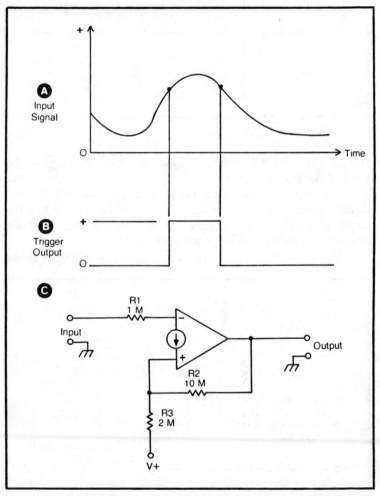

Fig. 5-15. Schmitt trigger operation A) signal, B) trigger output, C) CDA Schmitt trigger.

Assuming resistor equality is maintained, we will generate a zero output when $V_x = V_{ref}$. This situation causes the two inputs to see equal currents which will, therefore, have equal but opposite effects on the output voltage. A difference in the two input voltages, however, causes one input to have a greater effect on the output, resulting in amplifier saturation due to the high gain. The polarity will depend upon the polarity of the input difference voltage.

A Schmitt trigger is a circuit used to square an input waveform. It maintains a zero output until such a time when the input voltage exceeds a predetermined threshold value. At that instant, the output snaps to some high (in our case positive) value. The output will remain at that level until the input falls back to the threshold level. This is shown in Fig. 5-15 A and B. Schmitt trigger circuits exist using almost every form of active electronic device (transistors, op amps, plus several digital logic IC families), so why not the CDA? Figure 5-15C is respectfully submitted.

One major application of the Schmitt trigger is the conversion of sine waves or irregular electrical signals into nice, clean square pulses which digital circuitry can process. In fact, equipment such as digital counters require square waves for proper and accurate operation; a situation that calls for a lot of Schmitt triggers.

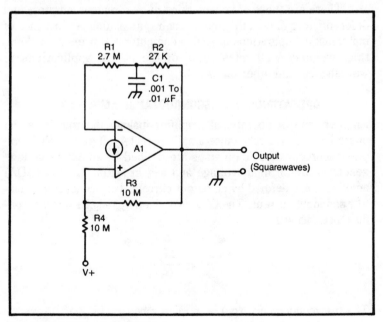

Fig. 5-16. Astable multivibrator.

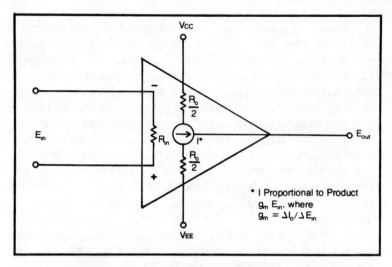

Fig. 5-17. Operational Transconductance Amplifier (OTA) model.

The multivibrator of Fig. 5-16 adds frequency-selective feedback to the trigger forming a self-triggering circuit which produces a square wave. The frequency of the output wave is a function of the RC time constant of the feedback network.

There are those of us who think of electronic integrators and differentiators only in the light of their outstanding performance of mathematical operations in analog computers. However, by doing this, we may well miss some of the neater applications in waveshaping and other areas.

OPERATIONAL TRANSCONDUCTANCE AMPLIFIERS

Another type of operational amplifier making the rounds is the operational transconductance amplifier (OTA) offered by RCA and other sources. Classic op amps are defined by an output voltage generated by an input voltage and a gain factor. Norton (CDA) amplifiers are defined by an output current, transconductance factor, and input current. The OTA is defined by the classic transconductance formula.

$$g_m = \frac{\Delta I_{out}}{\Delta E_{in}} \qquad \text{5-4}$$

The transconductance (g_m) is in micromhos.

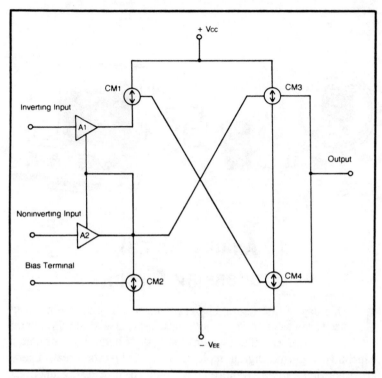

Fig. 5-18. OTA block diagram.

A symbolic representation is shown in Fig. 5-17 (the normal op amp symbol of a triangle is used in circuit diagrams), and Fig. 5-18 shows the block diagram of internal OTA circuitry. Note that the OTA will perform all, or at least most, of the usual op amp chores. There are, however, some functional differences.

For example, since the g_m is proportional to bias current, gain can be externally adjusted by varying the level of current applied to the bias terminal. The output voltage swing exhibited by the OTA is proportional to the product of the output current and the load resistance. That quantity, I_{out}, is set (for any specific bias current level) by the product of g_m and E_{in}.

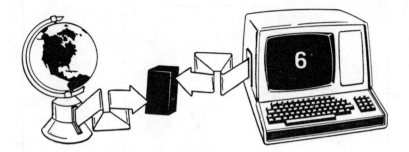

Analog Signal
Processing Circuits

I n this day of fast digital signal processors it may seem out of
place to speak of *analog* processors. Yet this is what this chapter
is about. There are times when the cost of additional computer
capability to permit digital implementation is just too great. There
are other times when a requirement for signals processing functions
comes along after the design of the computer is frozen. Alternatively, the best and most economical computer may be some
ready-made off-the-shelf model that would be too costly to modify.
There are even some cases where an analog signal processing
circuit will do a specific job better than the digital method.

We won't endeavor to cover all forms of signal processors in
this chapter—only a few of the most common. For a better overview
of what's possible, I recommend to you the catalogs of firms such as
Burr-Brown and Analog Devices.

COMPARATORS

A voltage comparator circuit is a differential operational amplifier
with no feedback. The gain of the circuit, therefore, is essentially
the open-loop gain of the operational amplifier. With real devices,
the gain will not be infinity of the ideal case, but will approach 10^6
routinely. Even the least expensive rejects sold by the dozen will
boast gains of 10^4 to 10^5. Figure 6-1 shows a typical op amp voltage
comparator. One input will be connected to one of the voltages,
while the other input receives the alternative voltage. The output

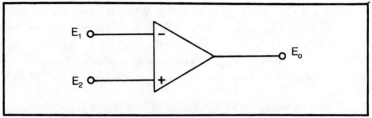

Fig. 6-1. Voltage comparator based on operational amplifier.

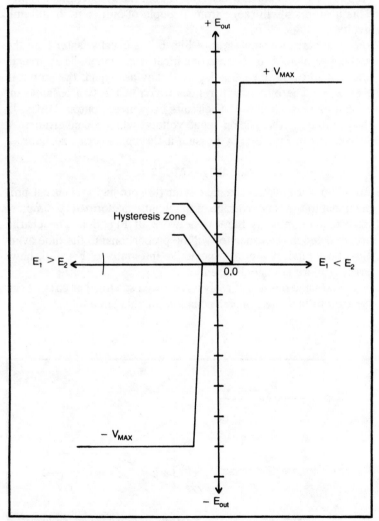

Fig. 6-2. Comparator transfer function.

transfer function is shown in Fig. 6-2. When the two voltages are equal ($E_1 = E_2$), the output voltage will be zero. But if E_1 is less than E_2, the output will be $V_{max(+)}$. On the other hand, if E_1 is greater than E_2, the output will be $V_{max(-)}$. The voltage comparator, then, will issue an output that indicates which voltage is higher, or that they are equal.

There is usually a small amount of hysteresis in comparators, however. This means that there is a small band of voltage difference around the zero point at which $E_1 \neq E_2$, but the output remains zero. This hysteresis will range from a couple of millivolts to 100 millivolts.

The current comparator of Fig. 6-3 is usually faster than the voltage version. The noninverting input is grounded. The currents are applied to the inverting input. If they are equal, the output is then zero. The output will reflect which of the two possible inequalities exist. Some ADC circuits use current output DACs. In those circuits, the analog input voltage will be converted to a current (as in Fig. 6-3) by passing it through a series resistor.

INTEGRATORS

An integrator is an electronic circuit that produces an output proportional to the time average of the input waveform. The simplest form of integrator is the RC network of Fig. 6-4. The charge accumulated in the capacitor will be proportional to the time average of the input potential. The active integrator of Fig. 6-5, however, is more commonly used.

The same method of analysis that we used in other circuits can be used to find the transfer equation for this circuit.

$$I_1 = I_2$$

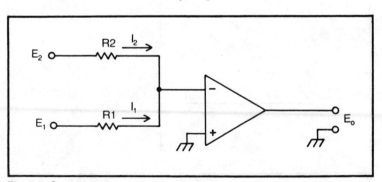

Fig. 6-3. Current-mode comparator.

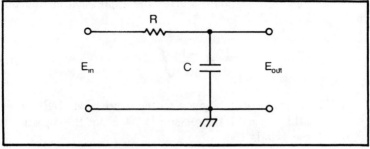

Fig. 6-4. RC low-pass filter/integrator.

$$I_1 = \frac{E_{in}}{R}$$

$$I_2 = C\left(\frac{dE_o}{dt}\right)$$

Substituting the last two equations into the first one gives Equation 6-1.

$$\frac{E_{in}}{R} = -C\frac{dE_o}{dt} \qquad \textbf{6-1}$$

You can simplify the equation by integrating both sides of this equation.

$$\int \frac{E_{in}}{R}\, dt = \int -C\left(\frac{dE_o}{dt}\right) dt \qquad \textbf{6-2}$$

$$= -CE_o \qquad \textbf{6-3}$$

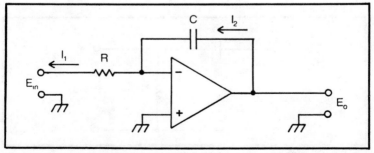

Fig. 6-5. Operational amplifier integrator.

Rearranging Equation 6-3 gives the expression in Equation 6-4.

$$E_o = \frac{-1}{RC} \int E_{in} dt \qquad \textbf{6-4}$$

The integrator gain is given by the expression, 1/RC. Consider what this means. If the resistor is 100 K and the capacitor is 0.01 μF, the gain is 1000.

$$A = -1/RC \qquad \textbf{6-5}$$
$$= -1(10^5 \text{ ohms}) (10^{-8}\text{F})$$
$$= -1/10^{-3} = 1000$$

If the input voltage is 10 mV, then the output will rise at a fast rate to the supply voltage (a 10−mV input produces a 10,000−mV output). Now consider what happens when the RC time constant is changed to $R=10^5$ ohms and $C=100$ pF. The gain becomes 100,000. This integrator will charge rapidly to the supply voltage just on the bias current of the operational amplifier!

DIFFERENTIATORS

A differentiator will output a signal that is proportional to the time rate of charge of the input signal; i.e., the derivative of the input signal. Figure 6-6 shows the usual RC integrator circuit, while Fig. 6-7 shows the active differentiator based on the operational amplifier. Again, use the same method of analysis.

$$I_1 = -I_2$$

$$I_1 = C\left(\frac{\cdot dE_{in}}{dt}\right)$$

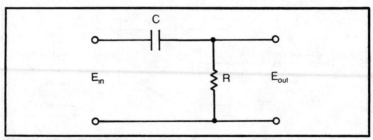

Fig. 6-6. RC high-pass filter/differentiator.

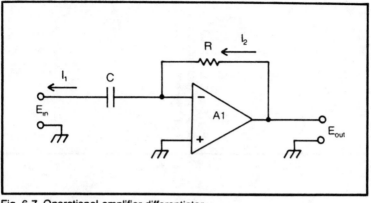

Fig. 6-7. Operational amplifier differentiator.

$$I_2 = \frac{E_o}{R}$$

By substituting the last two equations into the first, we get Equation 6-6.

$$C \left(\frac{dE_{in}}{dt} \right) = \frac{-E_o}{R} \qquad \textbf{6-6}$$

Rearranging this equation to solve for E_o gives us Equation 6-7.

$$E_o = -RC \left(\frac{dE_{in}}{dt} \right) \qquad \textbf{6-7}$$

The differentiator is basically a high-pass filter and is often used as such. To make a correct differentiator, however, the time constant of the RC network in the differentiator circuit must be short compared with the period of the input waveform. On the other hand, the integrator wants to see a time constant that is long relative to the input waveform. Figure 6-8 shows the frequency response plot of an operational amplifier differentiator that is compensated to produce a low-noise output.

LOG-ANTILOG AMPLIFIERS

An amplifier with a logarithmic transfer function is shown in Fig. 6-9. The collector current, I_c, of the transistor in the feedback loop has a logarithmic relationship to the base-emitter potential V_{be}:

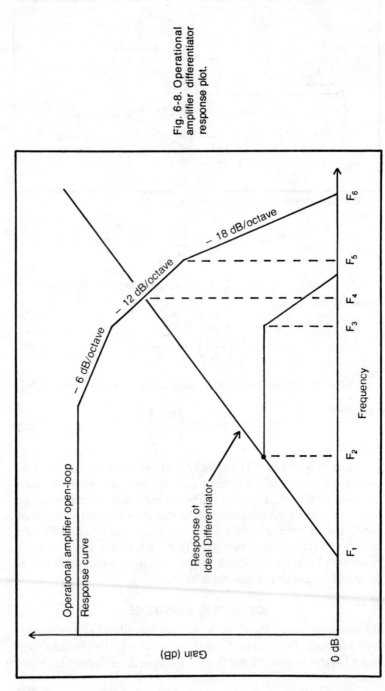

Fig. 6-8. Operational amplifier differentiator response plot.

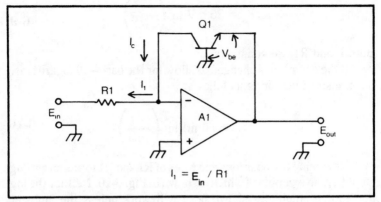

Fig. 6-9. Logarithmic amplifier.

$$V_{be} = \frac{kT}{q} \ln\left(\frac{I_c}{I_s}\right)$$

V_{be} is the base-emitter potential, k is Boltzmann's constant (1.38×10^{-23} joules/°K), and T is the temperature in degrees Kelvin, q is the electronic charge (1.6×10^{-19} coulombs), I_c is the collector current in amperes (A), and I_s is the reverse saturation current in amperes (A). At room temperature (300 °K), the term kT/q is equal to 26 mV/°K, so this equation can be rewritten as shown in Equation 6-8.

$$V_{be} = 26 \text{ mV } \ln(I_c/I_s) \qquad \textbf{6-8}$$

When analyzing the circuit in Fig. 6-9, the transfer equation is as follows:

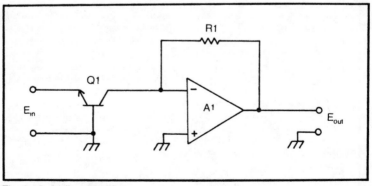

Fig. 6-10. Antilog amplifier.

107

$$E_o = 26 \text{ mV ln} \left(\frac{E_{in}}{I_s R1} \right) \qquad \textbf{6-9}$$

Both I_s and R1 are constants.

If the equation is changed to allow for the base−10 logarithms, the transfer function is as follows:

$$E_o = 60 \text{ mVln} \left(\frac{E_{in}}{I_s R1} \right) \qquad \textbf{6-10}$$

Reversing the positions and roles of R1 and Q1 forms an antilog amplifier, an example of which is shown in Fig. 6-10. Neither the log nor antilog amplifiers shown here will work unless the ambient temperature is held constant. Otherwise, you will have to modify the circuits to temperature-compensate them with additional circuitry.

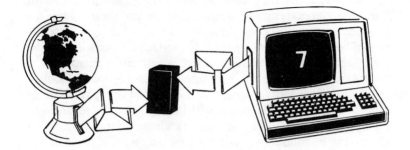

Reference Sources
for Data Acquisition

Perhaps the single most neglected subsection of the data converter (both DAC and ADC) is the analog reference source. Both DAC and ADC circuits are using comparison techniques in order to make the measurement or in the case of the DAC, produce an output. In all cases, they use some form of precision analog reference circuit to make this comparison with the analog input or output, as the case may be. **The data converter can only be as accurate as its analog reference.** Bit length means little if the reference does not have precision to match. For converts of less than 10-bit word length, we can be relatively modest as the requirements are more flexible for the reference source. But at word lengths over nine or 10 bits, the accuracy of the reference becomes even more acute.

Consider two cases, an eight-bit converter and a 10-bit converter. The resolution of the eight-bit model is 0.391 percent, while that of the 10-bit is 0.098 percent. These figures are the maximum permissible resolution based on bit length alone. What does this do to the reference source? If you want to maintain that accuracy, it is then necessary to have a reference source that is at least as good, preferably one order of magnitude better. If the latter criterion is followed, then reference accuracies of 0.0391 percent for the eight-bit case and 0.0098 percent for the 10-bit case are required. If the reference for both is to be nominally 10.00 volts, then, the actual voltages must be 10.00 ± 390 mV for the eight-bit and 10.00 ± 98 mV for the 10-bit case. If you wanted a reference for a 12-bit converter, the reference must then be 10.00 ± 24 mV.

Clearly, as the bit length increases, the strains placed on the reference source design are magnified. Note that these figures are minimums, and actual circuits may require even the tighter specifications because of other problems. In this chapter, we will consider the basic designs for reference sources that are compatible with most ADC and DAC designs presented in the rest of the book.

Until a few years ago, precision current and voltage references could be quite costly. But today, with integrated circuit technology, the situation is quite different. Circuits adequate for use with 10 or 12 bits can be routinely constructed for only a small amount, frequently for only a few dollars. There are several basic techniques used to generate reference sources, and they all have different classes of acceptable application in the data converter design business.

ZENER DIODES

The zener diode is a simple circuit element that can be made to regulate a dc voltage. A simple dc voltage regulator using a zener diode is shown in Fig. 7-1, and the transfer characteristic for a typical zener diode is shown in Fig. 7-2. It is the transfer characteristic that allows us to use the zener as a regular. Consider Fig. 7-2. The diode behaves like any other silicon diode in the forward bias region. At voltage levels less than some junction potential (0.6 to 0.7 volts in silicon devices), the *I vs. V* curve is quite nonlinear. But once the forward bias voltage exceeds this magic point, the

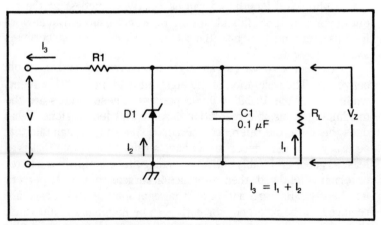

Fig. 7-1. Zener diode voltage regulator circuit.

current passed by the diode increases rapidly, limited mainly by the series resistances of the circuit. In the reverse bias region, however, things are a little bit different from ordinary diodes. For all reverse bias voltages ($-V$) less than some specified value, V_z, the reverse current through the diode is merely the reverse saturation leakage current. So far, it is exactly like other silicon diodes. But at certain value of $-V$, shown as V_z in Fig. 7-2, the diode avalanches. The current in the reverse direction increases rapidly. In fact, the increase is often much more rapid than the knee at 0.7 volts in the forward direction. Voltage V_z is called the avalanche potential, or zener voltage of the diode. Resistor R1 in Fig. 7-1 limits the value of

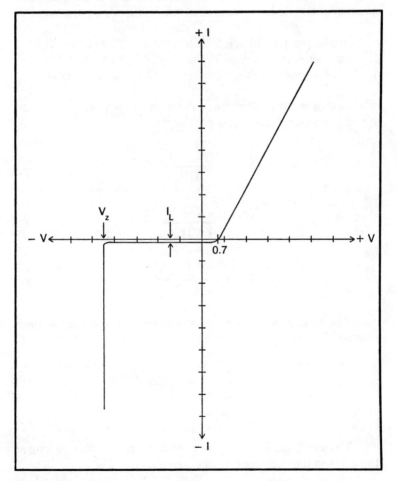

Fig. 7-2. Zener diode transfer function.

the reverse current to some specified zener current that is well within the safe range for that device.

The basic circuit shown in Fig. 7-1 is an example of a shunt regulator (the regulating device is in parallel with the load). Proper regulator action will occur if the current through the zener (I_2) is considerably greater than the current through the Load I_1. One common rule of thumb (something everybody does to keep from explaining why they do it) is to make current I_2 approximately 10 times I_1. If the load current remains a negligible percentage of the zener current, then regulation will result.

There are three conditions in which the circuit of Fig. 7-1 might be used. All three conditions might have slightly different problems, and do have somewhat different design equations.

☐ Variable supply voltage (V) and constant load current (I_2).
☐ Constant supply voltage (V) and variable load current (I_2).
☐ Variable supply voltage (V) and variable load current (I_2).

The design equations for these different classes of operation are given in the same order just presented.

$$R1 = \frac{V_{min} - V_z}{1.1(I_1)} \qquad \textbf{7-1}$$

$$R1 = \frac{V - V_z}{1.1(I1_{1max})} \qquad \textbf{7-2}$$

$$R1 = \frac{V_{min} - V_z}{1.1(I_{1max})} \qquad \textbf{7-3}$$

The power dissipation equations are the same in all three classes.

$$P_{di} \quad \frac{V_{max} - V_z}{R1} - (I_1 \times V) \qquad \textbf{7-4}$$

$$P_{R1} = P_{di} + (I_1 \times V_z) \qquad \textbf{7-5}$$

The zener potential, V_z, will remain constant only as long as the ambient temperature remains constant also. The actual value of V_z will, however, be slightly different, even among diodes of the

112

same voltage rating. The rating on most zener diodes is merely nominal. This means that a large number of zener devices will have values that tend to cluster around the V_z point in a bell-shaped curve.

When you build a precision reference source, two things must be kept in mind: temperature effects and calibration. For the former, you must either keep the ambient operating temperature constant or you must use some form of temperature compensated circuitry. In the latter, you must either hand select the proper voltage zener from a large collection or provide some means for adjusting the output potential.

Unfortunately, temperature cannot always be maintained constant in practical circuits. Unless cost is not a factor, you cannot always place the reference supply inside a temperature controlled oven, although that is done in high precision designs.

Figure 7-3 is an attempt at solving the temperature depen-

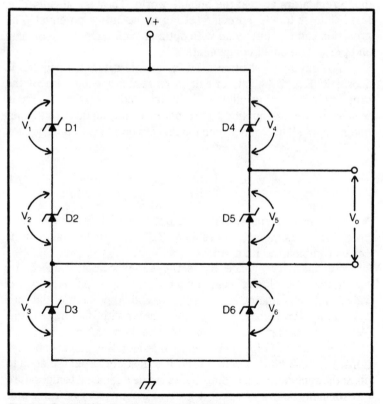

Fig. 7-3. Zener diode temperature compensation.

dence problem using several zener diodes to produce the desired V_o output voltage. The actual value of the output voltage is dependent upon the V_Z values of the individual diodes. These values will change with temperature, but if all of the diodes are in the same thermal environment, all of the diodes will change equally. The output voltage, which is the differential voltage between the two points shown, will remain relatively constant over a wide variation of ambient temperatures. The output potential of the zener stack shown is $V_o = (V_5 + V_v) - V_3$.

A major problem with circuits such as Fig. 7-3 is that the output voltage is not ground referenced; it is differential. If a grounded reference is required, then V_o should be applied across the input terminals of a differential amplifier. The op amp output potential would then be a product of the amplifier closed-loop gain, A_v, and the differential voltage, $A_v V_o$.

Operational amplifiers are frequently used to buffer zener diode regulators against the outside world. They are also used as level shifters to allow precise setting of the output potential. The precision can be quite good with optimum selection of the op amp and peripheral small components.

The circuit most often used for simple reference sources is shown in Fig. 7-4. This circuit is merely a special case of the ordinary noninverting follower circuit (common in op amp design) in which the voltage applied to the noninverting input is the zener potential, V_z. The voltage gain for this circuit is given by Equation 7-6.

$$V_o = V_z \left(\frac{R_A}{R1} \right) + 1 \qquad \textbf{7-6}$$

V_0 is the operational amplifier output potential, V_z is the zener potential, R1 is the value of resistor R1, and R_A is the value of the series combination R2 and R3.

Feedback resistance R_A is the series combination of two resistors, R2 and R3. It is generally the practice to make the overall value of potentiometer R3 between 10 and 20 percent of the total value of R_A. If R3 is a trimmer potentiometer with 10 or more turns, very close setting of the output potential is possible.

The circuit of Fig. 7-4 is useful for moderately precise applications, say for 8-bit data converters. It still suffers from the need to place the zener and other components inside a constant temperature environment before any real degree of stability can be achieved. Both the zener potential of the diode and the gain of the amplifier

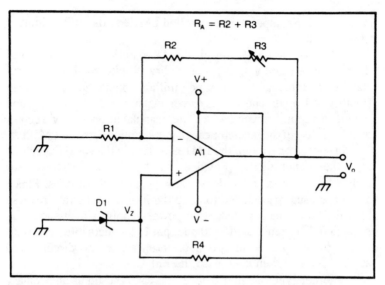

Fig. 7-4. Reference power supply.

might tend to drift with changes in ambient temperature. This circuit is used, however, in very precise applications. In those cases, the entire circuit, sometimes along with a preregulator for V+, are placed inside of a proportionally controlled constant temperature oven.

PRECISION IC REFERENCES

Among the newer developments in low cost reference supplies are precision IC voltage/current references. These circuits are quite good, performing almost as well as the best discrete component models. The National Semiconductor LM199 (and companion LM299 and LM399 devices) is shown in Fig. 7-5. This device contains a zener diode inside an IC that also contains a built-in conductor heater. The zener diode is buried in the same semiconductor die as the heater circuitry. The actual heater is not a resistance wire, as you might suppose, but rather a class-A amplifier with its input terminals shorted. The normal operation of a class-A amplifier is to dissipate a constant collector power under zero signal conditions. This constant power dissipation results in a constant die temperature once equilibrium is reached. Burying the zener in the die results in lower noise operation and provides the thermal stability by virtue of the constant temperature of the die. Ordinary discrete zener diodes will have a temperature change as great as 5

115

mV/°C, but in temperature controlled LM199s, the drift is limited to microvolts.

Although the LM199 terminal is rated initially as ±2 pecent of the nominally rated voltage, its stability is quite good. Long-term stability is rated at 20 parts per million (ppm), and short-term stability is 1 ppm. These figures correspond to 0.002 percent and 0.0001 percent, respectively. The manufacturer highly recommends the use of the insulator cap that is supplied with the LM199.

In normal operation, the LM199 is used in the same manner as any other zener diode, provided that the heater terminals are connected across a stable dc power supply of 9 to 40 volts. Pins 2 and 4 are usually grounded to keep the internal substrate reverse biased. Pin 3 connects to the dc power supply, which should be regulated. The zener diode cathode, pin 1, connects into the circuit in the ordinary manner for groundpreferenced zeners. Circuits such as Fig. 7-4 are often used with the LM-199.

Another type of zener device that can be used as an ordinary zener, but with greater stability, is the band-gap regulator. These are made by several manufacturers, one of which is the *Ferranti Semiconductor Division* (87 Modular Avenue, Commack NY 1725). They offer versions in either 2.45 or 1.26 volts. The construction of these diodes is shown in Fig. 7-6. The internal circuitry is basically a current-boosted operational amplifier with a band-gap reference diode at the noninverting input. These Ferranti devices are two-terminal affairs that can be used as if they are ordinary zener diodes.

The Ferranti ZN404 and ZN458A/B are 2.45-volt regulators.

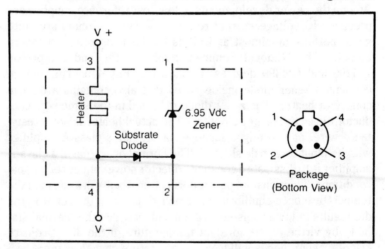

Fig. 7-5. LM-199 heated zener.

116

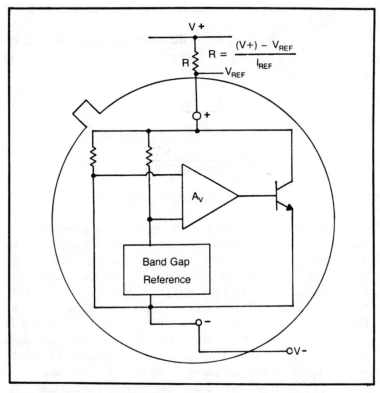

Fig. 7-6. Band-gap reference IC.

They differ as to initial calibration tolerance and thermal drift. All of them perform better than ordinary zener diodes. All three Ferranti devices will sink up to 120 milliamperes, but will operate with as little as 2 milliamperes.

The long-term stability of the Ferranti regulators can approach 10 ppm per 1000 hours of operation. The temperature coefficient is rated at 0.003 percent.

A current limiting resistor, just as in ordinary zener operation, is needed for the Ferranti band-gap devices. The value of this resistance is found from Equation 7-7.

$$R = \frac{(V+) - V_{ref}}{I_{ref}} \qquad \textbf{7-7}$$

R is the series resistance in ohms, $V+$ is the supply voltage in volts, V_{ref} is the nominal rated voltage of the regulator in volts either

(1.26 or 2.45 volts), and I_{ref} is the zener current in amperes (0.002 to 0.120 amperes).

Example. Find the series resistance needed in a ZN458 (2.45-volt) regulator if the supply voltage is +5 volts dc. Assume a 4-mA reference current.

$$R = \frac{(V+) - V_{ref}}{I_{ref}}$$

$$= \frac{(5\ V) - (2.45\ V)}{(0.004)}$$

$$= (2.55)/(0.004) = 637.5\ ohms$$

There is some tolerance in the value of the series resistor, especially if you do not use a reference current value that is exactly at the limits (2 and 120 mA). In most cases, you could use the nearest standard value and then rework the example to make sure that the reference current remains in the tolerable region. In the previous example, 680 ohms is a standard value. If you substitute 680 for R and then solve for I_{ref}, you find I_{ref} = 2.25 V/680 = 3.75 mA. This current is well within the normal range and is quite close to the initially selected reference value. In most cases, it would be wise to use a precision resistor, or at least a wirewound power resistor, for R. This is not actually called for by the manufacturer, but it eliminates one possible source of drift. The idea is not so much to guarantee a specific resistance as it is to obtain the low temperature coefficient of these resistors. At the very least, a low-temperature coefficient film resistor should be selected.

Another example of a band-gap reference source is *Intersil, Inc.'s* (1071 - Tantau Avenue, Cupertino, CA 95014) type ICL8069

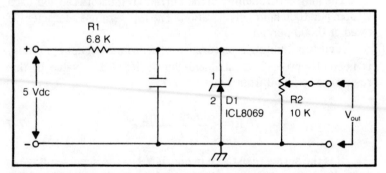

Fig. 7-7. Reference supply based on Intersil ICL-8069.

Table 7-1. Specifications for Various Grades of ICL-8069.

MAX. TEMPERATURE COEFFICIENT OF V_{REF}	TEMP RANGE	ORDER PART #
.001%/°C	0°C to +70°C	ICL8069ACQ
.0025 %/°C	0°C to +70°C	ICL8069BCQ
.005 %/°C	−55°C to +125°C	ICL8069CMQ
.005 %/°C	0°C to +70°C	ICL8069CCQ
.01 %/°C	−55°C to +125°C	ICL8069DMQ
.01 %/°C	0°C to +70°C	ICL8069DCQ

(see Fig. 7-7). This device is a 1.2-volt temperature compensated reference source that will operate with very low noise down to zener currents of 50 microamperes. Intersil makes various versions of this device. The suffix (see Table 7-1) appended to the type number indicates both the temperature coefficient and the operating temperature range. Both commercial (0° to 70°C) and military (−55° to +125°C) temperature ranges are available. The temperature coefficients available can be any of several between 0.001%/°C and 0.01%/°C. The ICL8069 devices are available in the two-lead TO-52 (Q-package) casing, as shown in Fig. 7-8.

Two precision applications of the ICL8069 are shown in Figs. 7-9 and 7-10. The circuit in Fig. 7-9 is a precision reference source based on the ICL8069. The zener is used in the feedback loop of an LM108 premium operational amplifier. A feedback resistor network is used to produce the gain. One of the resistors in the network is a potentiometer, whose resistance is less than 10 percent of the total. If this resistor is a trimmer potentiometer with low temperature coefficient and at least 10 turns, it can be used to precisely set the output potential to +10.00 volts. This 10-volt reference supply is buffered and can be used as a general reference source in data converter applications and in general calibration work.

Fig. 7-8. Intersil ICL-8069.

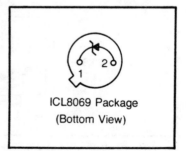

ICL8069 Package
(Bottom View)

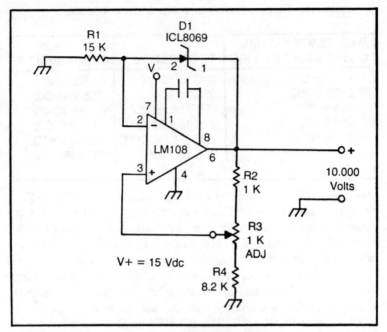

Fig. 7-9. Reference power supply based on ICL-8069.

Figure 7-10 shows the use of the ICL8096 as a reference source for an ADC integrated circuit. In this particular case, the ADC is an Intersil ICL7107 one-chip digital panel voltmeter system (DVMs are A/D converters!). Again, a potentiometer is used for precise setting. This diode will make a small voltage reference source that is more than capable to handle the reference needs of

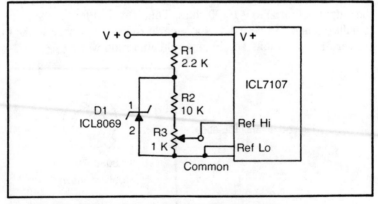

Fig. 7-10. ICL-8069 used as a reference for the ICL-7107.

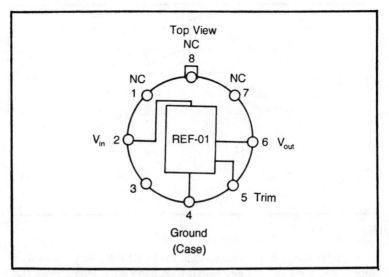

Fig. 7-11. REF-01 by Precision Monolithics, Inc.

most ADCs. The operating current range is 50 μA to 10 mA.

Precision Monolithics, Inc. makes two precision voltage reference integrated circuits especially designed for use with data converters in the 8-bit to 10-bit word length. The REF-01 is a 10.00-volt device, and the REF-02 is a 5.00 volt device. The untrimmed output of the REF-01 (with pin 5—see Fig. 7-11) is 9.9 to 10.1 volts. With trimming, it can be set to within ± 300 mV, or 3 percent. In most cases in my experience, the device can be trimmed to within a few millivolts of 10.00 volts. The trimmed temperature coefficient is 0.7 ppm/°C, or 0.00007%/°C.

The REF-01 can supply up to 20 mA to the external load and will operate from unipolar dc power supplies in the +12 to +40-volt range. A large V_{in}-V_{out} differential in any regulator, however, is undesirable because of heating caused by the extra power dissipation.

The REF-02 device is a 5.00-volt reference (see Fig. 7-12). The untrimmed output voltage will be 4.975 to 5.025 volts dc, and it can be trimmed to within ±150 millivolts (3 percent). The input voltage range is 7 to 40 volts, but once again, try to avoid high voltage differentials for the same reason of power dissipation.

One difference between the REF-01 and the REF-02, other than the obvious voltage output differences, is that the REF-02 has a temperature output terminal. Semiconductor pn junctions have a voltage characteristic that can be used for temperature measure-

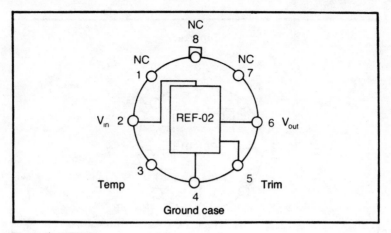

Fig. 7-12. REF-02.

ment under the right circumstances. In the REF-02, pin 3 shows an output voltage that is approximately 2.1 mV/°C. This allows the REF-02 to be used as a temperature sensor. The PMI applications notes on this device give details for this type of operation.

The PMI REF-01/02 devices and similar devices from Motorola, Inc. are some of the easiest to apply voltage references in DAC/ADC applications. Because of this, some of the REF-01/02 circuits offered by PMI will be covered. Figure 7-13 shows the basic connection scheme for both REF-01 and REF-02 devices. The

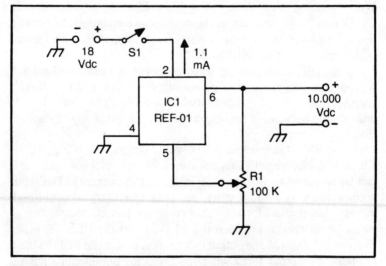

Fig. 7-13. REF-01 (and REF-02) trimmable reference supply.

supply voltage is applied between pins 2 and 4 (pin 2 is positive with respect to pin 4). The ground is pin 4. Output is taken from pin 6, which can supply up to 20 mA. We can trim the output voltage ±3 percent by connecting the wiper of a trimpot to pin 5. The 100 K potentiometer should be a precision trimpot, with at least 10 turns operation. The output voltage can easily be set to within a few millivolts of 10.000 volts. In a DAC that I built, it was possible to see 10.000 volts, with last digit bobble, on a precision digital voltmeter.

The circuit of Fig. 7-13 is the most common application of the REF-01/02 devices. This is the circuit one would select in most DAC and ADC applications up to 10-bit operation. There is some justification for also allowing the use of this device to 12-bit operation.

The REF-01 and REF-02 devices are capable of delivering up to 20 milliamperes of current. This is more than sufficient for most ADC and DAC applications, so no current output boost is needed. In the occasional application where a higher output current is needed, you may use a circuit such as Fig. 7-14. In this case, transistor Q1 is used to pass the higher current demanded by the load. If the β of the transistor is nominally greater than 75, up to 1 ampere of current can be passed at the rate output of 10.000 volts. A similar circuit will also work with the REF-02 at 5 volts.

PRECISION CURRENT REFERENCES

In many DAC and ADC circuits, a reference current rather than a reference voltage, is needed. If the load resistance remains constant (often a near impossibility), we can generate a precision reference current by applying a precision voltage to a known precision resistance. Usually, though, load resistances will vary, often unpredictably. In those cases, a dynamic regulator must be used to track those changes and compensate for them.

One of the simplest current regulators is the simple JFET circuit of Fig. 7-14A. In this circuit, the source and gate terminals of a junction field-effect transistor are shorted together. A voltage V_{DS}, sufficient to drive the current I_{DS} into its saturation region, must be applied. At potentials greater than this point, the current through the JFET (I_{DS}) will not increase, but remain constant. Some semiconductor manufacturers make constant-current diodes that are merely JFETs connected in the manner of Fig. 7-14A. They are given the name diode, because there are only two terminals from the package. They are really diode-connected, three-terminal

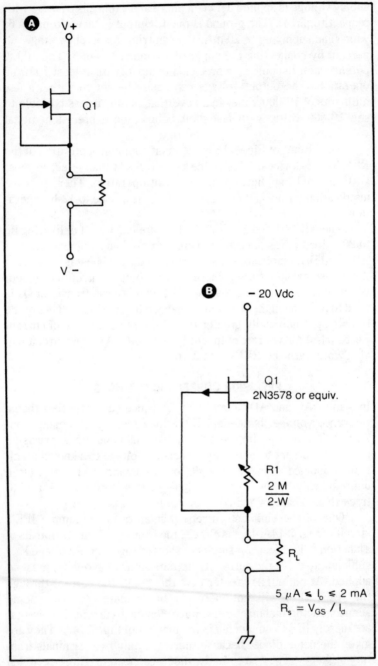

Fig. 7-14. JFET constant current source (A) and adjustable JFET CCS (B).

124

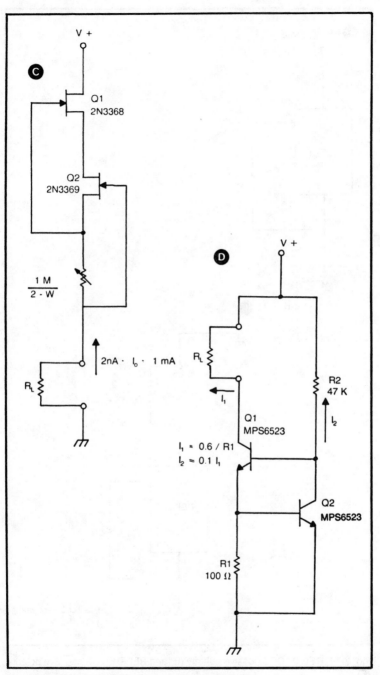

Fig. 7-14. Two-JFET CCS (C), and bipolar CCS (D).

125

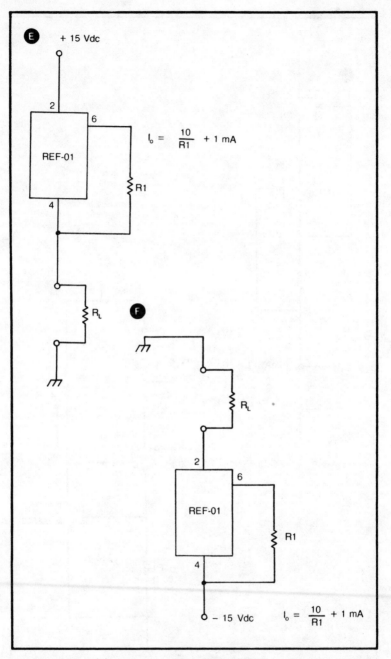

Fig. 7-14. REF-01 CCS positive polarity (E) and REF-01 CCS negative polarity (F).

126

JFETs. The only problem with the simple circuit of Fig. 7-14A is that it is not adjustable. The output current is fixed by the JFET characteristics. The choice of which JFET is the only control you have over the output current.

A modification of this same idea is the JFET circuit shown in Fig. 7-14B. This circuit allows adjustment of the constant current over the range 5 microamperes to 2 milliamperes. A series resistor, R_s, is used to make the adjustment. Once set, however, the current will remain constant enough for the circuit to be used as a DAC/ADC reference source.

Still another modification of the basic theme is shown in Fig. 7-14C. In this case, two JFETs are used in cascade. The circuit is adjustable, using the same technique as shown in Fig. 7-14B, over the range 2 microamperes to 1 milliamperes. All three of these circuits are useful for DAC/ADC applications.

Figure 7-14D shows the use of a pair of bipolar transistors in a classic constant-current source circuit. This circuit was originally designed around the Motorola MPS-6523 transistor, but thermal tracking is improved through the use of a dual transistor such as the PMI MAT-01. These devices build both transistors on the same semiconductor die, so they share a common thermal environment and have similar properties. The output current, I_1, is approximately $0.6/R1$. Current I_2 is variable, but it is set to approximately 10 percent of output current I_1.

Figures 7-14E and 7-14F are current generators using the PMI REF-01 or REF-02 voltage regulators. The circuit in Fig. 7-14E is a constant current source. The circuit in Fig. 7-14F is a constant current sink; i.e., it will absorb a constant current. Both circuits are essentially the same, except for polarity. The level of the output current can be found with the appropriate equation.

$$I_{out} = \frac{10.0}{R} + 1 \text{ mA} \quad \text{for REF-01}$$

$$I_{out} = \frac{5.00}{R} + 1 \text{ mA} \quad \text{for REF-02}$$

These circuits have a high voltage compliance. The REF-01 current source has a compliance of -25 to $+3$ volts, while the current sink has a compliance of -3 to $+25$ volts.

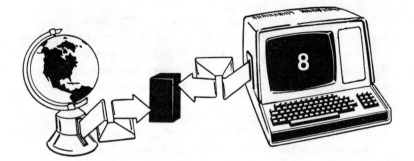

Sample-and-Hold Circuits

T he *sample-and-hold* circuit, also called the S/H, is used in the microcomputer analog subsystem to take a *snapshot* of an analog input signal. Most often, S/H circuits are found at the inputs of A/D converters. The S/H freezes the input signal so that it can remain at one value during the A/D conversion process. There are different reasons why this is a good thing. A/D converters, for example, do not work well on varying input signals (the successive approximation is typical). In other cases, the same A/D will serve various inputs. If the input signals are to represent simultaneous phenomena, then it is necessary to freeze the values in time while the A/D successively does the conversion job.

The basis for the S/H is a capacitor to store the value and a field effect transistor (FET) electronic switch.

Figures 8-1 and 8-2 show the basic circuit topology of an FET switch. The example in Fig. 8-1 is a JFET switch, and that of Fig. 8-2 is an enhancement MOSFET switch. In the JFET example, a resistor to the input side of the switch is used to facilitate the on-state of the JFET. When the driver switch (shown here as an SPST toggle switch) is open, the JFET will conduct, so the input signal will appear across the output load resistor, R_L. When the switch is closed, however, the gauge of the JFET is connected to a V-source that is sufficient to force the transistor deep into pinch-off. The channel resistance will then increase to many megohms, and the current flow will cease. The input waveform will not appear

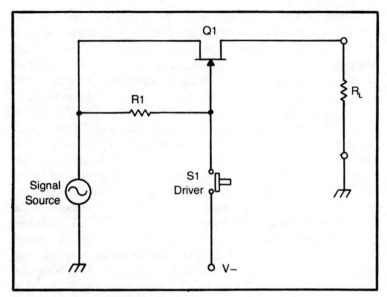

Fig. 8-1. JFET electronic switch.

across the load. The switch is off.

The MOSFET example of Fig. 8-2 operates in a similar manner. When the driver switch is open, no voltage is applied to the gate of the enhancement MOSFET switch element. By the rules of

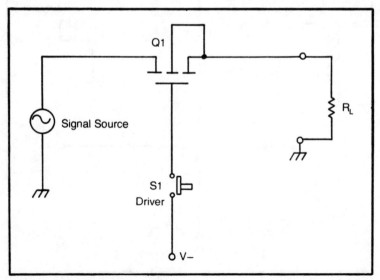

Fig. 8-2. MOSFET switch.

the enhancement MOSFET, then, the device is turned off; the channel resistance will be very high. But when the driver switch is closed, the gate is connected to a V-source that is sufficient to turn the channel on. Note that if an n-channel enhancement MOSFET were used, the polarity of the voltage source used to turn the switch on would be reversed; i.e., a positive voltage would be used.

A sample driver switch is shown in Fig. 8-3. Transistor Q1 is the switch element, as in the previous two examples. Transistor Q2 is the driver transistor. When the base potential is zero (i.e., the base is at ground potential), this npn bipolar transistor is then turned off. The switch turn-on V-source is not connected to the JFET. When the base voltage applied to Q2 is positive, though, the transistor is turned on, allowing the V-supply to be connected to the JFET base. Similar circuits are used for the MOSFET switches. Figure 8-4 shows the waveforms in this circuit. The input waveform is applied to the switch all the time, but the output waveform can exist only when the base potential applied to Q2 is low. Note that the waveform diagram for the MOSFET switch of Fig. 6-11 will be

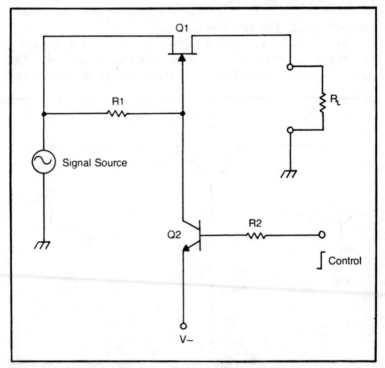

Fig. 8-3. JFET electronic switch with bipolar electronic switch.

130

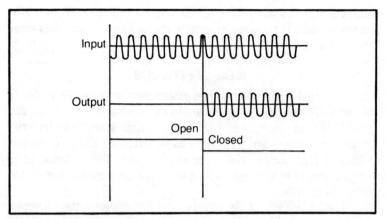

Fig. 8-4. Switch operation.

exactly the opposite: The output waveform exists when the Q2 base is high.

Figure 8-5 shows several of the circuit symbols sometimes used for FET analog switches. Both A and B are positive-enable types. In these switches, the on-stage occurs when the control line

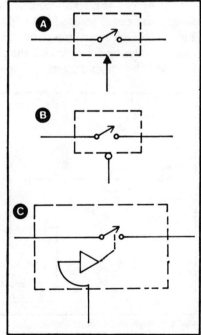

Fig. 8-5. Electronic switch symbols.

(the Q2 base) is high. The version shown in Fig. 8-5C is a low-enable switch. In this type of switch, the switch element is on when the control is low.

IDEAL S/H CIRCUITS

One principal application of analog switches is in sample-and-hold circuits. These circuits will sample the analog input voltage and then hold it at the output. ADCs will contain substantial linearity errors if the input changes as little as 10 hertz for a 12-bit converter. Changes for shorter ADCs are even lower. The solution is to sample and hold the signal, so that it remains constant over the conversion period.

Figure 8-6 shows the basic circuit for an elementary sample-and-hold circuit. The major components of this minimum system are the analog switch, a holding capacitor (C_H), and an output buffer amplifier. When switch S1 closes, the charge in the capacitor will reflect the input signal. The output amplifier buffers the capacitor against the load resistance of the circuits to follow. Amplifier A1 is used in the unity gain configuration, and it must be selected to have a very high input impedance. Low-cost devices, such as the 741 or 1458, are not suitable for sample-and-hold service. The amplifier should have a JFET, MOSFET, or superbeta (Darlington) input stage. The requirement for a high impedance is actually twofold. First, the high input impedance of the amplifier reduces the discharge of the capacitor during the period when the switch is open. Second, the high-impedance operational amplifier has a very

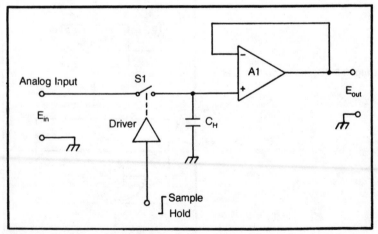

Fig. 8-6. Sample-and-hold circuit.

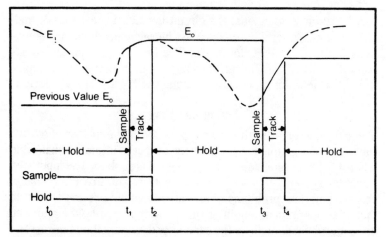

Fig. 8-7. S&H transfer function.

small input bias current. Some MOSFET input devices, for example, will have an input bias current in the nanoampere, or picoampere, range. An excessive input bias current would tend to either charge or discharge the capacitor, depending upon the polarity of the current.

An example of the operation of the sample-and-hold circuit is shown in Fig. 8-7. The dotted waveform is the analog input signal, F_i, while the heavy line is the amplifier output waveform, E_o. From time t_0 to t_1, the output of the amplifier will be at whatever level existed on a previous sampling interval. But at time t_i, the same line goes high, so switch S1 in the sample-and-hold circuit closes, and this applies the analog signal to the capacitor. During the interval (t_1 to t_2) in which the sample line is high, the capacitor and output voltages will track the analog input signal.

When the sample pulse drops low again (at time t_2) the output voltage will retain the last value that existed before the pulse dropped low. The analog signal may vary higher and/or lower, but E_o will remain at the value existing at time t_2. This value remains until time t_3, at which point a sampling pulse is received, which once again turns on switch S1. The capacitor voltage will then assume the value of the analog input voltage existing at that time. Once again, E_o will track the analog input signal, E , during the interval in which the sample pulse is high.

SAMPLING ERRORS

This description of the sample-and-hold circuit assumes something

133

that is patently ridiculous; the circuit is ideal. In real sample-and-hold circuits, several problems must be recognized that are deviations from the ideal performance. The error can be classified according to when they occur: during sampling, during the sample-to-hold period, during hold, and during the hold-to-sample period.

During Sampling

The principal error in the sampling period is the matter of *settling time*. This is the time required for the output to attain its final value when a full-scale step function input signal is applied. The input step might be 0 to $+E_{fs}$, 0 to $-E_{fs}$, or $-E_{fs}$ to $+E_{fs}$. This error is similar to the settling time problems of operational amplifiers and DACs. In fact, the operational amplifier of the sample-and-hold circuit can contribute substantially to the sample-and-hold settling time error.

Settling time is shown graphically in Fig. 8-8. The input step function rises instantaneously to its full-scale value. The output does not track the input instantly, however; there is a slight delay. The actual of E_o (the output) will overshoot the correct value before it settles back to the normal value. There is always a small band of correct output values called a normal error band; the same phenomenon was seen on the DAC settling time problem discussed earlier. A definition of settling time is the period t_0 to t_1 required for the output voltage to enter the normal error band permanently, following a full-scale step-function input signal.

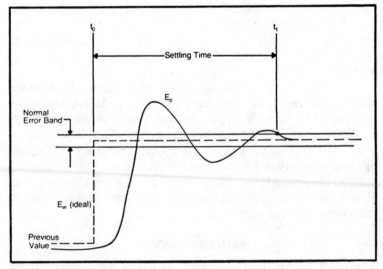

Fig. 8-8. Settling time.

134

Sample-to-Hold

There are four basic errors in this class: aperture time, switching transients, settling time, and sample-to-hold offset.

Aperture time is the time elapsed between the command-to-hold and the actual opening of the hold switch. There are two basic contributions to aperture time: time delay of the switch and jitter. The time delay is a function of the circuit used to drive the actual switch and the time required for the switch state to settle. This is usually a constant for any given switch, so it can be compensated for in the design of the sample-and-hold circuit. The uncertainty caused by the aperture time affects the maximum resolution possible for any given input slew rate. Consider the situation when you want to resolve a signal to 0.5 percent, and the full scale is 10 volts and the slew rate is 2 volts/microsecond ($2V/\mu s$):

$$t_a = \frac{E_{fs} \times r}{[\ S_r}$$

8-1

t_a is the minimum aperture time, in seconds, required for resolution r, E_{fs} is the full-scale input voltage, r is the resolution expressed as a decimal (i.e., 1 percent is 0.01, and 0.1 percent is 0.001), and S_r is the slew rate of the input signal in volts per second (V/s).

$$T_a = \frac{(10\ V)\ (0.005)}{2\ V/\mu s}$$

$$= \frac{\mu S}{2\ V} \times \frac{1\ s}{10^6 \mu S} \times (10V)\ (0.005)$$

$$= (5 \times 10^{-7}s)\ (10\ V)\ (0.005)$$

$$= 2.5 \times 10^{-8}s = 25\ nanoseconds$$

It requires an aperture time of less than 25 nanoseconds to resolve the $2\ V/\mu s$.,'10 V input signal to a level of 0.5 percent. Figure 8-9 shows aperture time graphically.

Switching transients exist at the instant the sample-and-hold switch opens. The transient is due to the circuits possibly not being in equilibrium. Amplifier delay error becomes especially important on fast changing input signals.

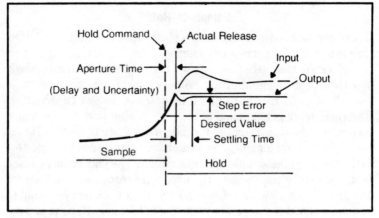

Fig. 8-9. Aperture time.

Settling time in this context is a little different from the full-scale settling time discussed previously. In this case, it is the settling to a specified percentage of full scale, following the opening of the switch.

The *sample-to-hold offset* is a step error that occurs at the instant the hold mode is commanded. This error is due to the stray capacitances and the FET gate-to-drain capacitances. These capacitances will store a charge, which is dumped into the main storage capacitor at the instant the sampling switch is opened. There is also a capacitance across the open switch, and this will feed some of the input signal into the charge capacitor at a time when none is supposed to be present. The units for the offset are coulombs/farad (or, alternatively, picocoulombs per picofarad), in which the capacitance is the value of the hold capacitor, C_H.

During Hold

There are three basic errors found during the hold period: droop, feedthrough, and dielectric absorption. The phenomenon of *droop* is shown in Fig. 8-10. Ideally, when the sample command pulse goes high, capacitor C_H will charge to the value of E_i and track. At the instant when the command goes low again, the capacitor voltage is E_1 (see Fig. 8-10). Ideally, the capacitor voltage will remain at E_1, but this does not occur in real amplifiers. A leakage current will always be present, and this current will tend to discharge capacitor C_H. There are three sources to the leakage current: amplifier input bias currents, leakage back to the source through the switch element (and to the switch element driver circuitry), and leakage

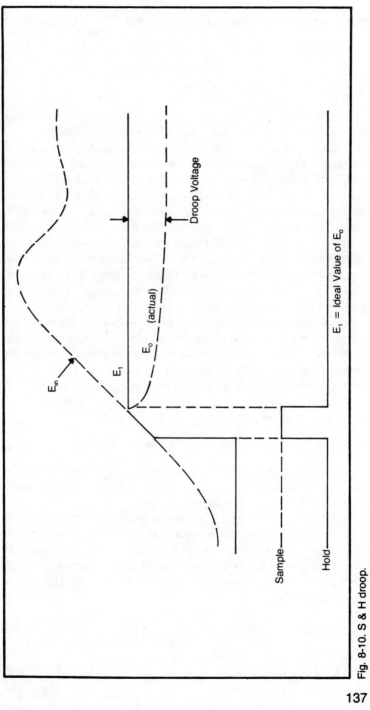

Fig. 8-10. S & H droop.

137

across the series resistance of the capacitor. The amount of droop is:

$$\frac{dE_o}{dt} = \frac{I}{C_H} \qquad \qquad \textbf{8-2}$$

E_o is the output voltage, I is the total leakage current from all sources, and C_H is the capacitance of the holding capacitor.

There are several approaches to limiting the droop factor, although it cannot be eliminated. One is to use an output amplifier with only a few picoamperes of bias current. A MOSFET-input operational amplifier will usually meet this specification. Another method is to select only quality capacitors for C_H. Most paper, mylar, and ceramic capacitors tend to have too low a leakage resistance. Polyethylene and polycarbonate capacitors are sealed against moisture absorption, so they retain their initially high series resistance. In general, these types of capacitors are preferred for C_H. The last thing that can be done is to specify electronic switches for S1 that have an extremely high off-impedance.

Feedthrough is leakage across the switch. It is caused by both the series off-resistance of the switch and the capacitance of the open switch. In most cases, however, the capacitance causes the trouble. The switch capacitance will form a series voltage divider with the holding capacitor, so the feedthrough signal will be:

$$E_f = \frac{E_i X_{CH}}{X_{CS} - X_{CH}} \qquad \qquad \textbf{8-3}$$

E_f is the feedthrough voltage across C_H, X_{CH} is the reactance of the holding capacitor C_H, X_{CS} is the reactance of the switch capacitance, and E_i is the input signal voltage.

It is general practice to specify a certain frequency, say 10 kHz, at which the feedthrough is measured and then apply a full-scale ac sine wave signal at that frequency. It is then possible to measure the output voltage for the 10-kHz component. In some cases, the feedthrough is expressed as an attenuation in decibels (dB). The voltage ratio is given by Equation 8-4.

$$dB = 20 \, \text{Log}_{10} \frac{E_f}{E_{10}} \qquad \qquad \textbf{8-4}$$

E_f is the feedthrough signal voltage, as measured at the E_o

output terminal, and E_{10} is the output signal, E_o, present when the sample switch is closed.

Dielectric absorption is a phenomenon of capacitors that is often overlooked in electronics textbooks. The electrostatic field deforms the orbital paths of the electrons in the atoms of the dielectric. When the capacitor is discharged, these orbits return to their uncharged state. Not all will return at the same time, however, and a few will be redistributed later. This becomes dangerous when working on high-voltage devices such as CRT second-anode circuits, medical defibrillators, and high-power radio or tv transmitters. Operators who think they have safely discharged the high voltage capacitors in these devices are often rudely—sometimes fatally—taught about dielectric absorption. In sample-and-hold amplifiers, the results are not quite so spectacular, but there is still a possibility of some output error due to the phenomenon.

Dielectric absorption is most pronounced on fast-changing signals. In polystyrene and Teflon (polytetrafluoroethylene) dielectric capacitors, the dielectric absorption could be as low as 0.01 percent or less. Certain other capacitors, notably ceramic, oil-filled, and mylar, however, can have dielectric absorption figures of up to 10 percent. This factor is another good reason to select polystyrene, Teflon, or polycarbonate capacitors for C_H.

Hold-to-Sample

There are two principal errors in this period: acquisition time and hold-to-sample transients. These are shown in Fig. 8-11. The *acquisition time* is the time required for the output to arrive at the desired level of accuracy. This factor is essentially the same as

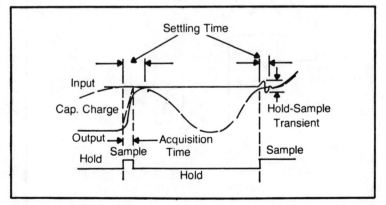

Fig. 8-11. Settling time.

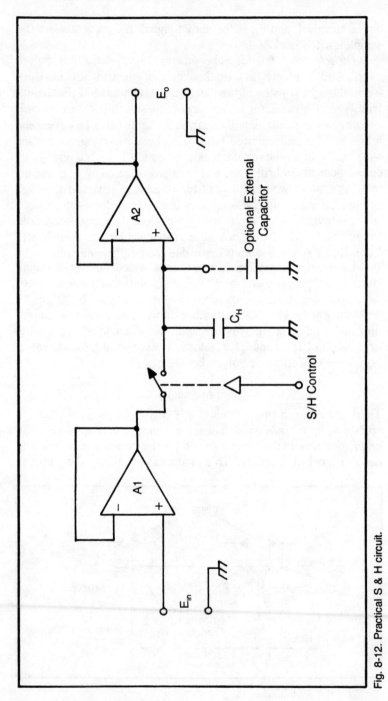

Fig. 8-12. Practical S & H circuit.

settling time but is applied to feedback sample-and-hold amplifiers.

Although it is possible to design sample-and-hold amplifiers, it is often more economical to simply buy a ready-built version. Several manufacturers offer sample-and-hold amplifiers and monolithic IC hybrid, or discrete function module form.

There are three basic types of sample-and-hold amplifiers in commercial production: buffered input, integrator output, and floating switch. The integrator output and floating switch are feedback sample-and-hold amplifiers because they are normally connected with some negative feedback between E_o and the input stage.

Figure 8-12 shows a circuit for a buffered input sample-and-hold amplifier. This circuit is available in integrated circuit form and is merely a modified version of the circuit given previously. The addition is in the form of a unity gain, noninverting follower between the analog input signal, E_i, and the switch. This provides a degree of isolation and protection. The amplifier is selected to have a low output impedance so that the time constant, $R_o C_H$, does not seriously limit the slew rate of the circuit.

This method also insures that the output impedance of driving sources does not affect the operation of the sample-and-hold amplifier. Some of these (and other types) of sample-and-hold circuits will have internal capacitors for C_H. It is mostly the hybrid and function module versions that have an internal C_H. Most of the others, notably the IC versions, will have a terminal to the outside world that allows the user to select a value for C_H between $0.001\ \mu\text{F}$ and $0.01\ \mu\text{F}$.

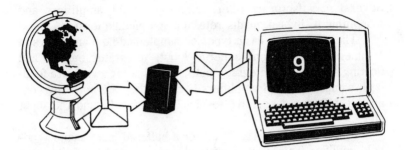

Number Systems and Binary Codes for Data Acquisition

Digital computers and other binary circuits are called *binary* because they only respond to two states, high and low, which are represented by the two permissible digits of the base-2 number systems. The binary number system must, therefore, be understood by anyone wishing to understand computers. In addition to binary numbers used to represent *quantities*, we must also learn the use of the n-bit binary numbers to represent characters.

NUMBER SYSTEMS

One of the first complaints heard from new students of digital electronics is over the matter of learning the binary (base 2) number system. Learning this system is necessary, and it is also essential that you become at least familiar with the octal (base 8) and hexadecimal (base 16) number systems. The two latter systems are frequently used in computer work as a shorthand for the binary numbers actually used by the computer. For example, binary 01001110_2 can also be equivalently represented as hexadecimal $4E_{16}$ or octal 116_8.

We all grew up using the decimal, or base 10, number system, so it is seemingly simpler to us. But it is, in reality, no easier than base 2, base 8, or base 16, or even base 99, for that matter. The same basic concepts used in decimal numbers are also found in binary, octal, and hexadecimal. Only the specific digits change between the number systems; the concepts and ideas remain the same. A comedian/mathematician from an early '60s television show used to claim that "base 8 is exactly like base 10 if you're missing two fingers!" While that statement was designed to raise laughs from parents of children struggling with "new math," it is nonetheless true. Similar statements could easily be made of the other bases. Of course, with hexadecimal, you would need extra fingers or use some of your toes..

Because several base number systems are used in this text, we will adopt a special notation. The base will be given as a subscript. Therefore, 101_2 means 101 in the binary (base 2) system, while 101_8 means 101 in the octal (base 8) number system, 101_{10} is 101 in the decimal (base 10) system, and 101_{16} is 101 in hexadecimal (base 16).

Decimal Numbers

Before tackling number systems in other bases, let us first review the basic concepts of all number systems, using the familiar base 10, or decimal, number system as an example. If you passed third grade, then you learned this system. And even if you did not get past the third grade, but are able to figure out if the clerk who sold you this book gave the correct change, then you still learned the decimal number system. After relearning the basics, you will tackle the binary, octal, and hexadecimal number systems.

All four number systems that we have mentioned (binary, octal, decimal, and hexadecimal) are examples of weighted number systems. The actual value of a number is dependent upon the digits used, such as 0, 1, 2 . . . , and their respective position with respect to each other.

The decimal, or base 10, number system has 10 digits: 0, 1, 2, 3, 4, 5, 6, 7, 8, and 9. These digits each represent different quantities, or values that are familiar to you already.

With only 10 digits, however, we can represent only 10 different quantities. But instead of creating a different digit—a digit is merely a symbol—to represent each possible quantity from zero to infinity, *positional notation* is used. This means that a digit's position relative to other digits confers added value. For example, the decimal number 682_{10} can be broken down in the following manner:

$$682_{10} = (6 \times 10^2) + (8 \times 10^1) + (2 \times 10^0)$$
$$682_{10} = (600) + (80) + (2)$$

The base of the number system (10, in this case) is called the *radix*. In general, all weighted number systems use a digit multiplied by a radix raised to some power at each position. The general form for all weighted number systems is as follows:

$$D_n R^n + \ldots + D_3 R^3 + D_2 R^2 + D_1 R^1 + D_0 R^0$$

The D terms are the digits (0 through 9 in base 10), and the R terms are the radix (10 in base 10). When we place 682_{10} in the general form, it looks like this:

$$(0 \times 10^n) + \ldots + (0 \times 10^3) + (6 \times 10^2) + (8 \times 10^1) + (2 \times 10^0)$$

Any number raised to the zero power, such as 10^0, is equal to 1. So $10^0 = 2^0 = 8^0 = 16^0 = N^0 = 1$.

We can use the general form equation to represent either whole or partial quantities. A partial quantity is a fraction. A decimal point must be used to separate the two.

$$+ \ldots + D_3 R^3 + D_2 R^2 + D_1 R^1 + D_0 R^0$$

$$. \, D_{-1} R^{-1} + D_{-2} R^{-2} + D_{-3} R^{-3} + \ldots +$$

The digits to the left of the decimal point represent whole quantities, while those to the right represent fractional quantities. For example, 18.23 is represented in the following manner:

$$18.23_{10} = (1 \times 10^1) + (8 \times 10^0). + (2 \times 10^{-1}) + (3 \times 10^{-2}),$$
$$18.23_{10} = (10) + (8) \, . \, (2 \times 0.1) + (3 \times 0.01)$$
$$18.23_{10} = 10 + 8. + 0.2 + 0.03 = 18.23_{10}$$

Binary Numbers

The binary number system is just like the decimal number system if you're missing eight fingers. Such a situation would leave you two fingers, or two digits, which could be used for counting. These digits are 0 and 1. In the notation of the general forms equation, then, a weighted binary number system would be described this way:

$$D_n 2^n + \ldots + D_3 2^3 + D_2 2^2 + D_1 2^1 + D_0 2^0$$

The D terms are the binary digits (0 and 1). For example, the binary number 01011_2 is the shorthand way of writing:

$$(0 \times 2^4) + (1 \times 2^3) + (0 \times 2^2) + (1 \times 2^1) + (1 \times 2^0) =$$
$$(0) + (8_{10}) + (2_{10}) + (1_{10}) = 11_{10}$$

At this point, we'll illustrate why the subscript notation must be used to let you know which system is being used. The digits 10 do not represent the same quantity in binary and decimal systems.

$$10_2 = (1 \times 2^1) + (0 \times 2^0) = 2_{10}$$
$$10_{10} = (1 \times 10^1) + (0 \times 10^0) = 10_{10}$$

Obviously, then 10_2 does not equal 10_{10}.

The term *bit* used in digital electronics means binary digit and is the smallest unit of data possible. A bit can be either of the binary digits, 0 or 1. A byte is an array of eight bits arranged in a positional number representation from 00000000 to 11111111.

Example. Find the decimal values of the following binary numbers. Use the notation of $D_n 2^n + \ldots + D_4 2^4 + D_3 2^3 + D_2 2^2 + D_1 2^1 + D_0 2^0$.

$$101_2 = (1 \times 2^2) + (0 \times 2^1) + (1 \times 2^0)$$
$$101_2 = 2^2 + 0 + 2^0 = 4 + 0 + 1 = 5_{10}$$

a.	101101	i.	0010
b.	110	j.	0011
c.	111111	k.	0100
d.	0010111	l.	0101
e.	100110	m.	0110
f.	1001111	n.	0111
g.	0000	o.	1000
h.	0001	p.	1001

Octal Numbers

The octal number system is just like the decimal number system. This time, though, you're missing two fingers. The octal number system uses the digits 0, 1, 2, 3, 4, 5, 6, and 7. Using the notation of the general form equation, a weighted octal number would look like:

$$D_n 8^n + \ldots + D_3 8^3 + D_2 8^2 + D_1 8^1 + D_0 8^0$$

The D terms are any of the digits 0 through 7. In the notation of this equation, then, 362 would be:

$$(3 \times 8^2) + (6 \times 8^1) + (2 \times 8^0) =$$
$$(3 \times 64) + (6 \times 8) + (2 \times 1) =$$
$$(192) + (48) + (2) = 242_{10}$$

Example. Using the notation of this previous equation, find the decimal value of the octal numbers given below.

a.	321_8	i.	72_8
b.	377_8	j.	544355_8
c.	201_8	k.	011110_8
d.	110_8	l.	324_8
e.	35421_8	m.	327_8
f.	672_8	n.	666_8
g.	5012_8	o.	721_8
h.	51754_8	p.	345_8

Hexadecimal Numbers

The hexadecimal number system could be just as simple as the decimal number system if you could grow five extra fingers. The hexadecimal system—nicknamed hex—uses the 16 digits 0-15. Because all digits greater than 9 are double digits (10, 11, 12, 13, 14, and 15) and a single symbol is wanted to represent each digit, the letters A through F are used to represent the digits 10 through 15. The digits of the hexadecimal number system are: 0, 1, 2, 3, 4, 5, 6, 7, 8, 9, A, B, C, D, E, and F, where A=10, B=11, C=12, D=13, E=14, and F=15.

Then a hexadecimal number would look like this.

$$D_n 16^n + \ldots + D_3 16^3 + D_2 16^2 + D_1 16^1 + D_0 16^0$$

The hex number $7F6D_{16}$, then, is equal to 32621_{10}.

$$7F6D_{16} = (7 \times 16^3) + (F \times 16^2) + (6 \times 16^1) + (D \times 16^0)$$
$$7F6D_{16} = (7 \times 4096) + (15 \times 256) + (6 \times 16) + (13 \times 1)$$
$$7F6D_{16} = 28,672 + 3840 + 96 + 13 = 32621_{10}$$

Example. Find the decimal value of the following hexadecimal numbers. Use the equation, $D_n 16^n = \ldots + D_3 16^3 + D_2 16^2 + D_1 16^1 + D_0 16^0$.

a.	FF_{16}	i.	$1B_{16}$
b.	$ABCDEF_{16}$	j.	$2C_{16}$
c.	$7F2_{16}$	k.	$4BB_{16}$
d.	$3A1_{16}$	l.	BBC_{16}
e.	$3A7B_{16}$	m.	377_{16}
f.	$4E_{16}$	n.	$A7F_{16}$
g.	$6F_{16}$	o.	$A6_{16}$
h.	$9C_{16}$	p.	$B2_{16}$

CONVERSION BETWEEN SYSTEMS

It sometimes becomes necessary to convert from one number system to another. This is often done by service technicians because they must correlate numbers given in the documentation for a piece of equipment. A manual for a computer, for example, might tell you to examine the eight-digit binary number stored in "memory location 372_8." But when you look at the front panel of the machine, it becomes immediately apparent that binary switches are the only means for calling up the specified address. A specialized pocket calculator made by Texas Instruments, called the programmer, will convert the numbers for you.

When conversion tables or calculators are not available, use the following procedures. This procedure converts all numbers to decimal form.

1. Write down the number being converted.
2. Multiply the most significant digit (the left-most) by the radix of the number.
3. Add the result of step 2 to the next most significant digit (MSD).
4. Multiply the result obtained in step 3 by the radix.
5. Repeat steps 3 and 4 until all digits are exhausted. The final result is the answer.

Example. Convert 1101101_2 to decimal form.

1101101	Multiply MSD by radix	$1 \times 2 = 2$
1101101	Add result to next digit	$2 + 1 = 3$
	Multiply result by radix	$3 \times 2 = 6$
1101101	Add result to next digit	$6 + 0 = 6$
	Multiply result by radix	$6 \times 2 = 12$

1101101	Add result to next digit	$12 + 1 = 13$
	Multiply result by radix	$13 \times 2 = 26$
1101101	Add result to next digit	$26 + 1 = 27$
	Multiply result by radix	$27 \times 2 = 54$
1101101	Add result to next digit	$54 + 0 = 54$
	Multiply result by radix	$54 \times 2 = 108$
1101101	Add result to next digit	$108 + 1 = 109_{10}$

Example. Find the decimal equivalent of 234_8.

234_8	Multiply the MSD by radix	$2 \times 8 = 16$
234_8	Add result to next digit	$16 + 3 = 19$
	Multiply result by radix	$19 \times 8 = 152$
234_8	Add result to next digit	$152 + 4 = 156_{10}$

Example. Find the decimal equivalent of $7F3A_{16}$.

$7F3A_{16}$	Multiply the MSD by the radix	$7 \times 16 = 112$
$7F3A_{16}$	Add result to next digit	$112 + 15 = 127$
	Multiply result by radix	$127 \times 16 = 2032$
$7F3A_{16}$	Add result to next digit	$2032 + 3 = 2035$
	Multiply result by radix	$2035 \times 6 = 32560$
$7F3A_{16}$	Add result to next digit	$32560 + 10 = 32570_{10}$

This procedure converts any number in any base, R, to the equivalent number in decimal notation. The next procedure does just the opposite and converts a decimal number to an equivalent number in base R.

1. Divide the decimal number by the radix of the new number system.
2. The remainder from this step becomes the least significant digit (LSD) of the equivalent number in base R.
3. Divide the quotient from step No. 1 by the radix.
4. The remainder from this operation becomes the next digit of the new number system.
5. Continue this process until the digits are exhausted.

Example. Find the binary equivalent of 109_{10}.

Operation	Remainder
$2\overline{)109}$	

Operation	Remainder
2$\overline{)54}$	1 LSD
2$\overline{)27}$	0
2$\overline{)13}$	1
2$\overline{)6}$	1
2$\overline{)3}$	0
2$\overline{)1}$	1
0	1 MSD

This result agrees with the previous binary conversion.

$$109_{10} = 1101101_2$$

Example. Convert 156_{10} to octal.

Operation	Remainder
8$\overline{)156}$	4 LSD
8$\overline{)19}$	3
8$\overline{)2}$	2 MSD
0	

This result agrees with the previous octal example.

$$156_{10} = 234_8$$

Example. Find the hexadecimal equivalent to $32,570_{10}$.

Operation	Remainder	
	Dec.	Hex.
16$\overline{)32570}$	10	A LSA
16$\overline{)2035}$	3	3
16$\overline{)127}$	15	F
16$\overline{)7}$	7	7 MSD
0		

This result agrees with the previous hex example.

$$32570_{10} = 7F3A_{16}.$$

These procedures allow you to convert into decimal form from radix R, or from decimal into radix R. It is usually less trouble to use both procedures when converting from radix R1 to radix R2, when neither R1 nor R2 are decimal. For example, when converting from hex to octal, it may be better to convert from hex to decimal and then decimal to octal.

Example. Find the hex equivalent to 377_8.

1. First find the decimal equivalent of 377_8.

377_8	Multiply MSD by radix	$3 \times 8 = 24$
377_8	Add result to next digit	$24 + 7 = 31$
	Multiply result by radix	$31 \times 8 = 248$
377_8	Add next result to next digit	$248 + 7 = 255_{10}$

The decimal equivalent of octal 377_8 is 255_{10}.

2. Now, find the hexadecimal equivalent to 255_{10}.

$$\begin{array}{r} 16\overline{)255} \\ 16\overline{)15} \quad \text{15 LSD} \\ \overline{0} \quad \text{15 MSD} \end{array}$$

The hexadecimal notation for the digit 15_{10} is F, so the answer is FF_{16}. We now know that the hexadecimal equivalent of 377_8 is FF_{16}.

$$377_8 = 255_{10} = FF_{16}$$

BINARY ARITHMETIC

Binary arithmetic is used in computers and is also very handy to use when trying to figure out almost any complex digital instrument. With more and more instruments on the market employing the microprocessor chip, the understanding of binary arithmetic techniques is even more critical.

Addition

The rules governing binary addition are simple; some people believe that they are simpler than decimal arithmetic! The rules are as follows:

$$0 + 0 = 0$$
$$1 + 0 = 1$$
$$0 + 1 = 1$$
$$1 + 1 = 0 \text{ plus carry } 1$$

Example. Add the binary numbers 01001_2 and 01110_2.

$$
\begin{array}{cccccc}
 & 1 & & & & \\
 & C & 1 & 0 & 0 & 1 \\
+ & 0 & 1 & 1 & 1 & 0 \\
\hline
 & 1 & 0 & 1 & 1 & 0 \\
\end{array}
$$

Example. Add the binary numbers 00001_2 and 01001_2.

$$
\begin{array}{cccccc}
 & & & & 1 & \\
 & 0 & 1 & 0 & 0 & 1 \\
+ & 0 & 0 & 0 & 0 & 1 \\
\hline
 & 0 & 1 & 0 & 1 & 0 \\
\end{array}
$$

Subtraction

Note, however, that it is difficult to build a digital electronic circuit that performs straight binary subtraction operations. It is, however relatively trivial to build binary adder circuits. In most digital devices that are required to subtract, therefore, it is simpler to use two's complement arithmetic to fool the circuit into thinking that it is adding.

Before discussing subtraction by two's complement, let's find out what *two's complement* is. We begin by telling you about the one's complement of a binary number. The complement of any binary number is its inverse; i.e., the complement of 1 is 0, and the complement of 0 is 1. To form the one's complement of any binary number, therefore, we change all of the 1s to 0s and change all of the 0s to 1s.

Digit	Complement
0	1
1	0

For example, the complement of 1 0 1 1 0 0 1 1 is 0 1 0 0 1 1 0 0. Note that all ones became zeros and all zeros become ones.

Example. Find the complement of 1011001_2.

number	1011001
complement	0100110

The two's complement of any binary number is found by adding 1 to the one's complement of that number.

Example. Find the two's complement of 1011001_2.

Number	1	0	1	1	0	0	1
One's complement	0	1	0	0	1	1	0
Add one						+	1
	0	1	0	0	1	1	1

0100111_2 is the two's complement of 1011001_2.

Two's Complement Subtraction

Keep in mind that subtraction can be viewed as adding a negative number, and that two's complement notation is a form of representation for negative binary numbers. The following are several examples of two's complement arithmetic, given several different types of situations that could arise.

Before studying the examples, however, a standard convention concerning the use of "+" and "−" signs is important. An extra digit will be added, separated from the number by a comma(,), to denote the sign of the number. A 0 will represent positive (+) numbers, while a 1 will represent negative (−) numbers.

Example. Perform subtraction when minuend and subtrahend are both positive, and the minuend is larger than the subtrahend.

Subtract $0,0100_2$ (4_{10}) from $0,0111_2$ (7_{10}).

Minuend	0,0111	+7
Subtrahend	−0,0100	−(+4)
	?	?

1. Complement the		0,0100	
subtrahend		1,1011	+7
2. Add 1		+1	−4
		0,1100	?

3. Add two's complement			
of subtrahend to the		0,0111	+7
minuend		+1,1100	−4
1		0,0011	3

(carry 1 discarded)

The problem is worked correctly because $0,0011_2 = +3_{10}$. Notice that the carry one is generated, but in this case it is discarded or ignored.

Example. Perform subtraction of a negative subtrahend from a positive minuend when the minuend is larger than the subtrahend.

Subtract $1,0100_2$ (i.e., -4_{10}) from $0,0111_2$ (+7).

$$
\begin{array}{rr}
0,0111 & +7 \\
-1,0100 & -(-4) \\
\hline
? & ?
\end{array}
$$

Note in the decimal version that we are subtracting a minus quantity, so the problem is the same as adding their respective values:

$$
\begin{array}{rr}
0,0111 & +7 \\
+0,0100 & +4 \\
\hline
0,1011 & +11
\end{array}
$$

We know the problem is correctly worked because $0,1011_2 = +11_{10}$.

Example. Perform subtraction of a positive subtrahend from a larger, negative minuend.

Subtract $0,0100_2$ ($+4_{10}$) from $1,1001_2$ (-9_{10}).

$$
\begin{array}{rr}
1,1001 & -9 \\
-0,0100 & -(+4) \\
\hline
? & ?
\end{array}
$$

Complement the minuend because it is a negative number.

$$
\begin{array}{rr}
& 1,1001 \\
& \text{becomes} \\
& 0,0110 \\
\text{Add 1} \quad & +1 \\
\hline
& 0,0111
\end{array}
$$

This is the two's complement of the minuend.

Add the two's complement of the minuend to the subtrahend.

$$
\begin{array}{rr}
0,0111 & -9 \\
+0,0100 & +4 \\
\hline
0,1011 & -5
\end{array}
$$

Recomplement the answer.

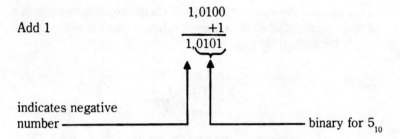

Add 1

$$
\begin{array}{r}
1{,}0100 \\
+1 \\
\hline
1{,}0101
\end{array}
$$

indicates negative
number ———————————————— binary for 5_{10}

The problem is correctly worked because $1{,}0101_2 = -5_{10}$.

Multiplication

Binary multiplication can be done using the same method as decimal multiplication, or by repetitive addition. The usual method by pencil and paper is shown in the next Example.

Example. Multiply 1101_2 (D_{16} or 13_{10}) by 0100_2 (4_{16} and 4_{10}).

$$
\begin{array}{r}
1101_2 \\
\times\ 0100_2 \\
\hline
0000
\end{array}
\qquad
\begin{array}{r}
D \\
\times\ 4_{16} \\
\hline
34_{16}
\end{array}
\qquad
\begin{array}{r}
13_{10} \\
\times\ 4_{10} \\
\hline
52_{10}
\end{array}
$$

$$
\begin{array}{r}
0000 \\
1101 \\
0000 \\
\hline
0110100_2
\end{array}
$$

Multiplication is nothing more than addition performed over and over again. For example, 4×5 is 20_{10}.

$$
4 \times 5 = 4 + 4 + 4 + 4 + 4 = 20_{10}
$$
5 repetitions of $+4$

The same thing can be done with binary numbers; the technique is called repetitive addition or the shift left method.

1. Set the answer initially to zero; i.e., 00000000_2.

2. Write down the multiplication so that the least significant digit of the accumulated answer is aligned with the LSD of multiplicand.

3. Inspect, the multiplier beginning with the LSD. If it is a 1, then add the multiplicand to the answer. But if it is a 0, then add 0 to the answer.

4. Repeat steps 2 and 3 until finished.

154

Examine the process by performing the same problem as in the previous Example to see if we get the same answer.

Example. Use repetitive addition to solve Example 9-14.

$$\begin{array}{r} 1101_2 \text{ Multiplicand} \\ \times\ 0100_2 \text{ Multiplier} \\ \hline ? \end{array}$$

1. Tentative answer   00000000000
   Multiplicand   1101

2. Test LSD of multiplier
   for I/O. It is
   0, so answer remains
   unchanged.

3. Tentative answer   00000000000
   Multiplicand shifted   1101
   1 bit to the left

4. Test (LSD+1) of multiplier
   for I/O. It is 0, so
   answer is unchanged

   $$\overset{0100}{\underset{\text{LSD+1 is 0}}{}}$$

5. Tentative answer   00000000000
   Multiplicand again   1101
   shifted 1 bit to the
   left.

6. Test (LSD+2) of multiplier
   for I/O. It is
   1, so add multiplicand
   to tentative answer.

   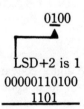

7. New Tentative answer   00000110100
   Multiplicand shifted   1101
   1 bit to the left.

8. Test multiplier
   for I/O. It is
   0, so answer
   remains the same

9. There are no further digits in this binary number, so the answer is the same as in step 7: 00000110100.

Because the zeros to the left of the most significant 1 are merely leading zeroes, drop them to shorten the answer to 110100.

The repetitive addition method seems a little cumbersome. On pencil and paper this is true, but in digital electronics circuits, adding and left-shifting are very easy to accomplish. In fact, it is difficult to do other operations.

LOGICAL OPERATIONS

Digital circuits perform logic operations called NOT, OR, AND, and exclusive-OR (XOR). The OR and AND functions also have inverted versions called NOR and NAND. In each case, two (or more) bits are compared, and the logical outcome is determined by which of these basic functions is being used.

Again consider some matters of notation. The NOT function is an inverting function. In the NOT function, a 1 will become 0, and a 0 will become 1. We represent the NOT function as a symbol with a bar overhead; $\overline{A}$ means the same as NOT A. This means that if A = 1, then the $\overline{A}$ value is 0. If A=0, then $\overline{A}$=1. The NOT symbol is also used in conjunction with other functions, as is the idea represented. A NOT gate connected with an OR gate produces a NOR gate. Similarly, a NOT gate connected with an AND gate produces a NAND gate.

Multiplication (×) and addition (+) symbols are used to represent the AND and OR functions, respectively. A circled addition symbol is used to represent the exclusive-OR(XOR) function. The NAND and NOR functions are represented by the equivalent AND and OR expressions with a NOT bar overhead.

DIGITAL CODES

A digital code is a binary representation of data. Nothing is mysterious about codes; they are merely methods for presenting data in formats that digital machines can easily use. A code may represent numerical, alphabetic, alphanumeric, control signals, etc. Most computer or teletypewriter keyboard codes, for example, contain numbers, alphabetic characters (upper and lower case), and control codes, such as carriage return.

One property of any useful machine code is its binary nature so that on-off switching circuits can be used in the machine. It turns out that binary circuits are easiest to use in such cases.

Binary numbers are a form of code used to represent numerical quantities, but ordinarily, a binary code does not correspond to the binary number with the same bit structure. For example, in the ASCII code to be discussed shortly, the numerical character 7 is 00110111, while the binary number 7 (when expressed with the same number of bits) is 00000111. It is important to remember the difference between a symbol and a number. A computer may perform an arithmetic operation in which the result is the number seven (representing a quantity), but the output display device, which could be a printer or CRT video terminal, may require ASCII coding. If the programmer does not first convert the binary number 00000111 to 00110111, an incorrect result will be displayed to the outside world.

In this particular example, it just happens that 00000111 in ASCII is the BEL symbol, so the signal bell of the printer would ring instead of character 7 being printed. It would be a rare situation, indeed, if the binary representation for a quantity were the same as the code for the character (s) that represents that quantity.

Hexadecimal Code

A binary code of four bits could be represented by a hexadecimal (base 16) code. This would greatly simplify entering data or instructions into a digital machine. Entering 7F, for example, is a lot easier than entering all eight binary digits, or 011111111, needed in the binary representation. Using hexadecimal notation permits four bits to be entered at a time. Let us say that we have an eight-bit binary number:

$$1\ 0\ 1\ 1\ 1\ 1\ 0\ 1$$

To enter this number on a bit-by-tedious-bit basis would mean using eight keystrokes: 1-0-1-1-1-1-0-1. But we can break the number 10111101 into four-bit groups.

$$1\ 0\ 1\ 1 \qquad\qquad 1\ 1\ 0\ 1$$

Because 1011 is hexadecimal number B_{16} and 1101 is hex D_{16}, the hexadecimal number BD_{16} represents the binary pattern 10111101.

The hexadecimal system can also represent binary words that have bit lengths not divisible by four, provided that we assume the leading digits to be zeros. For example, assume a 10-bit number.

$$1\ 0\ 0\ 0\ 1\ 0\ 1\ 0\ 1\ 1$$

We can represent this with three hexadecimal digits

$$0\ 0\ 1\ 0 \qquad 0\ 0\ 1\ 0 \qquad 1\ 0\ 1\ 1$$

Fill in the extra position with zeroes. Because 0010 is hexadecimal 2_{16} and 1011 is hexadecimal B_{16}, hexadecimal $22B_{16}$ represents the same quantity as binary 1000101011 (no extra zeroes this time).

Split-Octal

We can also represent binary data in the split-octal system by grouping the binary bits in groups of not more than three each. For example, the binary code 10111101_2 was represented by hexadecimal BD_{16} in the previous section. This same binary number can be divided up into octal groups:

$$0\ 1\ 0 \qquad 1\ 1\ 1 \qquad 1\ 0\ 1$$

Fill in any leading zeroes that are needed. Because binary 010 is octal 2_8, binary 111 is octal 7_8, and binary 101 is octal 5_8, octal 275 produces the same binary bit pattern as binary number 10111101. In this case, however, only three keystrokes (2-7-5) are needed instead of eight (1-0-1-1-1-1-0-1). Both octal and hexadecimal notation can represent the numerical, alphabetic, and control codes of code systems that are commonly used on keyboards, printers, teletypewriters, etc.

Binary-Coded Decimal

The binary-coded decimal (BCD) is used to represent the 10 digits of the decimal number system in a four-bit format.

BCD is merely another form of decimal notation that is compatible with computers and other digital circuits. BCD words are therefore grouped exactly the same as regular decimal digits. The actual value of a BCD word is determined by its position relative to the other words, in a power of 10 system. The BCD number system is difficult to use in making calculations, but it is not impossible. Its main use is in systems requiring a numerical output display, such as a frequency counter, digital panel meter, clock, scientific instrument, a toy, etc.

Several BCD decoder chips will convert a BCD input to an output capable of driving the principal display devices, which could be Nixie tubes, seven-segment LED readouts, and so on. These are discussed in a later chapter.

Excess-3 Code

The excess-3 code is formed by adding three to the BCD numbers. $(3_{10} = 011_2)$. Excess-3 code is used to make digital subtraction in BCD a little easier. Recall that complement arithmetic is often used with binary digits. This cannot be done in BCD, however, because it would occasionally result in a disallowable bit pattern that is not recognizable as any of the 10 BCD numbers.

Gray Code

Shaft encoders and certain applications work best if the binary code generated changes only one bit at a time for each change of state. An example of such a code is the Gray code. The Gray code is used most often where a transducer on a mechanical device is directly generating digital data, such as shaft position.

Alphanumeric Codes

Actually, several different codes each represent alphabetic or numeric characters. Remember the distinction between characters and numbers—both represent quantities, but in different ways. We will discuss the obsolete but still found Baudot code, the popular ASCII code, and the IBM EBCDIC code.

Alphanumeric codes are used in cases where there is an output display device, such as a CRT video terminal, teletypewriter, or computer printer. Standardization, at least to a few different codes, allows connection of devices by different manufacturers.

Baudot Code. One of the earliest machine codes in general use was the Baudot code. Used in most of the earlier models of teletypewriter machines, Baudot has been largely replaced by another, more modern code (ASCII). Many Baudot machines are still in daily use; in fact, as this paragraph is being written, I can hear an old Model 27 Teletype in the office across the hall! Amateur radio computer operators who favor radio teletype (RTTY) operation and amateur computer buffs on the lookout for a reliable, low-cost, hard-copy printer have kept the prices of these older machines high, even though it is a surplus market.

Note that most teletypewriters will have a keyhole with a shift key just like a regular typewriter. In most cases, the capital letters are on the shifted keyboard and the lower case letters are on the unshifted keyboard. But some teletypewriters are just the opposite.

The Baudot code uses five bits, so it's capable of representing only 2^5, or 32, different characters or control signals. A shift control, much like that found on a regular typewriter, allows another 32 characters, for a total of 64. Note that not all 64 characters are used on all Baudot-encoded teletypewriters.

ASCII Code. The American Standard Code for Information Interchange (ASCII) is the code most often used on computer and video terminal keyboards. It is especially common among hobby computers. The ASCII code is a seven-bit code and can represent up to 2^7, or 128, different characters or control signals. Recall that this is twice the capacity of the five-bit Baudot machines.

An eight-bit format is often used in ASCII machines, especially those used with eight-bit microcomputers. The eighth-bit is used as a parity indicator in some cases and as a strobe bit in others. A strobe bit, incidentally, tells the computer or other digital machine that the data on the seven data lines is valid and stable. Most machines are designed to ignore activity on the ASCII input line until a strobe bit is present.

EBCDIC. EBCDIC representation of numbers places a hexadecimal F_{16} in the most significant position, so the four most significant binary digits will be 1111_2. Those positions are used when representing alphabetic characters and indicate which third of the alphabet the letter falls in. There are 26 letters in our alphabet, so the alphabet can be divided roughly into thirds.

Two punches are required to represent a letter on a Hollerith card. A zone punch tells us which third of the alphabet in which the letter appears, and the numeric punch tells us the letter number, letters in the first third of the alphabet have a row-12 zone punch, those in the second third of the alphabet have a row-11 zone punch, while those in the third third of the alphabet have a row-0 zone punch.

Consider, for example, the letter D. It is the fourth letter in the first third of the alphabet. It will be represented by a row-12 zone punch and a row-4 numeric punch, both in the same column. The letter N, on the other hand, is the fifth letter in the second third of the alphabet. It is, therefore, represented by a row-11 zone punch and a row-5 numeric punch. A slight departure from the system is noted in the last third of the alphabet. There is no row-1 punch. The first letter in this group is S and it is represented by a row-0 zone punch and a row-2 numeric punch.

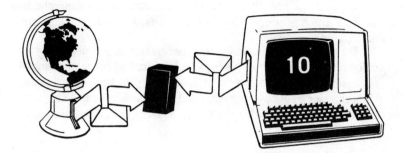

Data Conversion

The interface between the digital world of the computer and the analog world is the *data converter*. There are two basic types of data converter: D/A and A/D. The D/A (digital-to-analog) converter produces an analog voltage or current output that is proportional to an analog reference (another voltage or current) and a binary word applied to the digital inputs. The A/D (analog-to-digital) is just the opposite: it converts an analog voltage or current to a proportional binary word at the digital output. There are several chapters in this book that deal with basic data converter circuits. There are some circuits that contain sufficient information for you to duplicate or modify the converter to your own uses. In this chapter, we will discuss a little philosophy regarding data conversion. While I know that most readers are not too fond of philosophizing in a practical book, it is unfortunately necessary if you are to get the most out of your system.

First, let's put to rest a common myth. Many people (perhaps most) hold computers in absolute awe. It takes a certain amount of knowledge before one realizes just how dumb these machines really are! Unfortunately, awe of the computer results in a belief that the computer is almighty, and can never make a mistake. While certain people might debate the use of the word mistake, it is quite likely that the computer will contain errors in its output. Both analog and digital electronics have their own forms of error. In general, the computer error is smaller (if designed correctly) and more consistent. In many cases, we are able to tolerate error, so long as the error is consistent from operation to operation. Analog circuits might operate differently at different temperatures, for example, so the data they produce may become suspect under some circumstances.

On the other hand, however, there are some times when an analog circuit is needed. This is especially true where a lot of signal processing is required and no memory or cycle time is available. While the merits of co-processors and other niceties can be argued, one must not overlook the possibility of using an analog solution to the problem.

TYPES OF SIGNAL

Before going further, let's consider the types of signals that we will be dealing with in this book. Figure 10-1 shows several forms of the

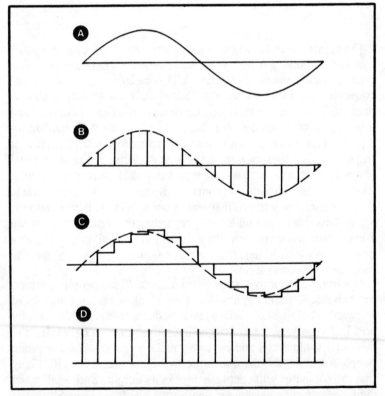

Fig. 10-1. Examples of signals A) analog, B) sampled, C) sampled-and-held, D) sampling clock signal.

162

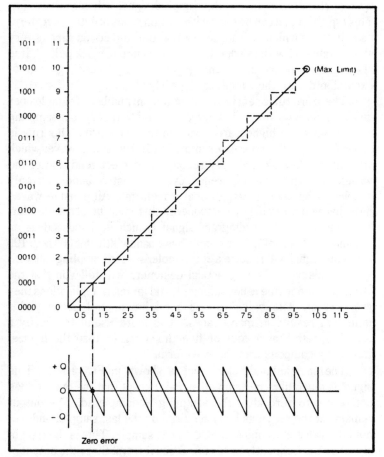

Fig. 10-2. Quantization error.

same basic signal. Figure 10-2A is a straight analog signal, Fig. 10-1B is a sampled signal, Fig. 10-1C is a sampled-and-held signal, and Fig. 10-1D is a clock signal used here as a reference.

The straight analog signal (Fig. 10-1A) is represented here as a sine wave for the sake of simplicity, even though it could be any waveform. Note that the analog signal is continuous in both range and domain—which is a fancy way of saying that it can take on any voltage value (range) and any time value (domain) within the limits. No value is excluded—the function is continuous.

The sampled signal is allowed to take on any value in its range (i.e., voltage), but can exist only at certain discrete times, as determined by the clock pulses (Fig. 10-1D). At times other than

163

when a clock pulse exists, the sampled signal will cease to exist. This type of signal can be used with certain types of data converters, namely those which operate so fast that the conversion time is very short compared with the duration of the sampling clock pulses. It is also used where the signal changes too slowly to undergo a great excursion during the sampling.

There are rules regarding the minimum number of samples per unit of time. The very minimum according to theory is a sampling rate of twice the highest frequency in the waveform. This rule is called *Nyquist's theorem*. An example is a 100 hertz sinewave, which will require 200 samples per second for correct rendition of the waveform. When we say frequency, we must consider not only sinewaves but also non-sinusoidal waveforms. All nonsine waves have harmonic frequency components that must be accounted for. The human electrocardiogram signal (which is discussed as an example in this book), for example has a bandwidth of 0.05 Hz to 100 Hz. This signal will require a 200 sample/second sampling rate or it will be distorted. Most practical designers will tell you that the twice frequency rule is not sufficient, and for many applications they are correct. The twice rule is a minimum, and hence yields minimum results in many cases. It is more useful to specify a sampling rate that is four or five times higher than the highest frequency component in the waveform.

The sampled-and-held signal is shown in Fig. 10-1C. This signal is much like the sampled signal, except that the output does not return to zero after the sampling is completed. The output remains at the previous level acquired by the last sample, and will hold the value until updated by the next sample. This is the type of signal that is frequently used in A/D converters. Since the output of the sample-and-hold circuit remains at the same value during the entire interpulse period, the A/D converter has the time to make its conversion. Otherwise, a much faster (and much more costly!) converter is required. The sampled-and-held signal is like the sampled signal in that it can take on any value within the range (voltage) but can change value only at discrete times.

The digital signal is allowed to exist only in discrete values (range) and at discrete times. The digital signal is really nothing more than a tabulation of values represented by binary numbers. The smallest discrete step permissible is the voltage or current change that is represented by a change in the least significant bit (LSB) of the binary word. This value is sometimes called the *1-LSB value*. It will always be $\frac{1}{2}^n$ of full-scale, where n is the number of bits in the binary word. An eight-bit binary word, then has a 1-LSB value of $\frac{1}{2}^8$, or 1/256 of full-scale. If, for example, an eight-bit A/D converter as a full-scale of 10-volts, the 1-LSB voltage, the voltage change in the input signal that will cause a minimum change in the binary output number is 10-V/256, or about 9 millivolts. Similarly, on an 8-bit D/A converter with a 10-volt maximum output voltage, a 1-LSB change in the binary input word will produce a 39 mV change in the output voltage.

Since a digital signal can exist only in certain discrete values in its range, we have a *quantization error* in digital circuits (see Fig. 10-2). Here we have graphed a 0 to 10 volt signal. The vertical axis has two scales: one is the analog voltage value, while the other is the equivalent in a four-bit binary representation (to simplify the illustration!). Along the horizontal axis are the so-called *decision points*, i.e., those voltages at which the A/D converter will change to the next state. We find, therefore, that the binary output will be 0000 for all analog voltages from 0 to the decision point, 0.5 volts. At all voltages from 0.5 volts to 1.0 volts, the output will be 0001. Thus, there will be an error at all voltages except those input voltages that are half-way between decision points.

In the example of Fig. 10-2, the binary output says 0001 volt as soon as the input voltage is greater than 0.5 volt, so there is a great error. The input voltage has to rise to 1.0 volt before it agrees with the binary output. The quantization error(Q) is graphed below the main graph, and shows how the error varies from $-Q$ to $+Q$, and is zero only at input voltages that are halfway between decision points. The dotted line in the main graph also illustrates the error because it represents the "sampled-and-held" nature of the output; error is zero only when the dotted and solid lines coincide.

The trick in eliminating the dire effects of quantization error is to use a bit-length data converter that is sufficient for the application at hand. This requirement means that you will have to analyze the circuit and application to determine how much error is tolerable.

Let's consider a pressure meter as an example. Suppose you wanted to measure 0 to 100 torr (note: 1 torr = 1 mmHg) to the nearest torr. If we used a 4-bit data converter, our resolution will be $100-T/2^4$, or 100/16, which is 6.25 torr. Thus, our quantization error is intolerable. A 6-bit converter produces $100/2^6$, or 100/64, which is 1.56 torr: almost, but not good enough. A 7-bit converter yields $100-T/2^7$, or 100-T/128, which is 0.78 torr. This is good enough for our purposes. Since 8-bit converters are both common

n	2^n	2^{-n}	dB
0	1	1	0
1	2	.5	−6
2	4	.25	−12
3	8	125	−18.1
4	16	.0625	−24.1
5	32	.03125	−30.1
6	64	.015625	−36.1
7	128	.0078125	−42.1
8	256	.00390625	−48.2
9	512	.001953125	−54.2
10	1024	.0009765625	−60.2
11	2048	.00048828125	−66.2
12	4096	.000244140625	−72.2
13	8192	.0001220703125	−78.3
14	16384	.00006103515625	−84.3
15	32768	.000030517578125	−90.3
16	65536	.0000152587890625	−96.3

Fig. 10-3. Resolution for different bit lengths.

and cheap, we would probably use one of them and achieve a resolution of 100/256 or, 0.39 torr. Figure 10-3 shows the resolutions expected from various bit lengths from 0 to 16; also shown is the equivalent resolution in decibels.

CONVERSION TIME

The conversion time (t_c) is the specification that tells us how much time is required to make an analog-to-digital conversion. In some cases, the conversion time is specified in units of time, e.g., 10 milliseconds. This method of specification is usually used when the clock frequency of the A/D converter is fixed. In other cases, the conversion time is specified as a number of clock cycles.

For example, the successive approximation form of A/D converter is usually specified to have a conversion time of n+1 clock periods, where n is the bit-length of the digital output binary word. On an 8-bit SA A/D converter therefore, a total of 9 (i.e., 8+1) clock periods are needed. In the case of a 1 MHz clock rate, the period of each cycle is 1/1,000,000 second, or 1 microsecond (1 μs). Thus, the conversion time of this form of converter would be 1 μs × 9 cycles, or 9 μs.

Another form of A/D converter specifies the conversion time as 2^n clock cycles, where again n is the bit-length. The 8-bit converter in that case would need up to 2^8, or 256 clock pulses to make

166

the conversion. This means a total of 256 μs for the 1μs clock used previously.

The significance of the conversion time is that it impacts the maximum number of samples or conversions per unit of time. If we take the second as the unit of time (the usual case!), then we can determine the absolute maximum number of samples per second by taking the reciprocal of the conversion time, i.e., $1/t_c$.

APERTURE TIME

The measure of how well a signal can be represented in a data acquisition system is the number of samples per second. In part, this is limited by the conversion time of the converter (see previous section), but there are also other time losses in the system. The measure of the overall phenomenon is called *aperture time*. This measure can represent both time and voltage uncertainties. Figure 10-4 shows the effect of aperture time on the measurement. Notice that the signal voltage, V, can change its actual value and amount, V, over the time required to make the measurement. If dV/dt represents this small change, and t_a is the aperture time, then Equation 10-1 describes the voltage.

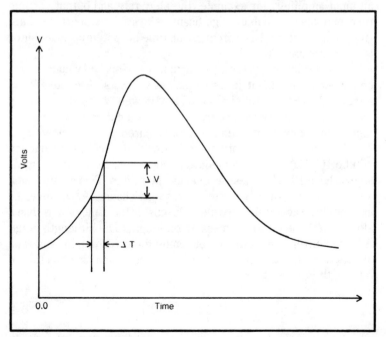

Fig. 10-4. Acquisition time error.

$$V = (t_a) (dV(t))/dt \qquad \textbf{10-1}$$

This equation, in slightly different form, can be used to compute the maximum allowable aperture time to make any given data conversion. The input signal is considered a Fourier series, and the highest frequency component in the series is used as the point of examination. First, specify the percentage of resolution (r) required of the data converter, which is given by $r = (V/V)$.

$$t_a = V/(V \times 2 \times F)$$
$$t_a = r/(2 \times F)$$

where   V/V is the resolution, r
                 r is (V/V), the resolution
                 F is the highest frequency
                     in the Fourier series for
                     a given waveform.

The conversion time is a big percentage of the aperture time in many A/D converters, but it is not the only contributer. If there is an input amplifier, for example, the slew rate and output settling time may also contribute significant delays to the aperture time. Any component that has a propagation time is a potential contributor to aperture time.

Conversion speed is one of the most over-speced values in data converters. This habit leads to excessive costs. A quote that is attributed to Soviet Admiral Gorshkov is well worthwhile for any engineer: "Better is the enemy of good enough." Why buy a super high-speed converter when the data requirements are slow?

In most instrumentation applications, the highest frequency will be 100 Hz or less. In medical applications, for example, most signals have 100 Hz or less frequency spectrums. This means that a 1 μs conversion time is wasted on a single channel A/D converter and should be acquired only where the cost is the same or less than a slower A/D converter of the same bit length. The bit length of the A/D converter is a factor in determining the resolution, and thus affects the required aperture time. The resolution as a function of bit length is given by:

$$r = (100\%) / (2^n) \qquad \textbf{10-2}$$

In this equation, r is the resolution and n is the bit length. A

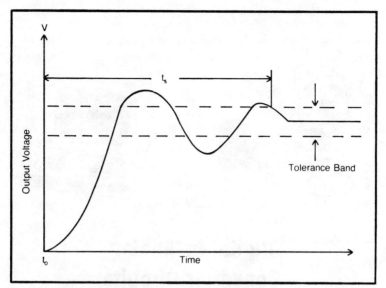
Fig. 10-5. DAC settling time.

more complete treatment of this subject is given in my book *Microcomputer Interfacing: A/D & D/A* (TAB Book No. 1271).

SETTLING TIME

The *settling time* of a digital-to-analog converter (DAC) is defined as the time required for a step-function input to result in an intolerance output voltage. Figure 10-5 shows this concept. The setting time, t_s, is defined as the time for the output voltage to permanently settle inside of the tolerance band following a step function input. For an analog circuit, such as an operational amplifier, the settling time is measured with a very fast rise-time input step function voltage (such as a squarewave or pulse), while in a DAC it might be represented by a transition of the input binary word from either OOH to FFH, or, from FFH to OOH.

In most cases, the DAC settling time is a function of the output amplifier used in the circuit. The resistor ladder (most often an R-2R ladder) has a very fast response time, so it contributes little to the overall settling time. The operational amplifier used on the output, however, may have a considerable settling time, often 100 times the settling time of the resistor ladder.

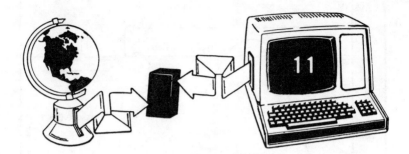

Digital-to-Analog
Converter Circuits

There are two fundamental types of data converter in the analog system. As we learned in Chapter 10, the A/D converter provides a binary (i.e., digital) output that is proportional to an applied analog voltage or current *input*. The D/A converter, or DAC, is the inverse: it provides an analog voltage or current *output* that is proportional to an applied binary word. Thus, the DAC can be used to drive readout devices such as analog or digital voltmeters, oscilloscopes, strip-chart paper recorders and X-Y paper recorders. The DAC can also be used to drive analog amplifiers in servo systems and other such uses.

FUNDAMENTALS

An digital-to-analog converter (DAC) is a circuit that produces an analog current or voltage output that is proportional to both an analog reference (voltage or current) and an n-bit binary word. In general, the DAC will produce an output that can be defined by Equation 11-1.

$$X = k \times A \times B \qquad \text{11-1}$$

X is the output voltage or current, k is a constant (which is often 1), A is the analog reference voltage or current, and B is the applied binary word.

Figure 11-1 shows a block diagram of the principal components

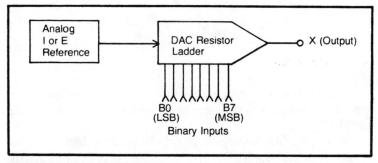

Fig. 11-1. DAC block diagram.

of the DAC system. The analog reference source will be a precision dc reference power supply that will produce a voltage or current output. Some DACs have the reference supply inside the package, while others are found external to the DAC package. Those DACs in which the reference source is external are called multiplying DACs. In actuality, all DACs multiply, by virtue of the previous equation. But the designation, multiplying DAC, always refers to a model in which the user can apply an external reference. In many models, incidentally, the internal reference source is brought outside and must be connected to the reference input. Some of these models are considered in a later chapter. Those models seem to offer the best of both multiplying and nonmultiplying DACs.

There are two different types of DAC circiuts, and both are based on current output resistor ladders: binary weighted and R-2R ladders. Figure 11-2 shows the basic binary weighted resistor ladder circuit. It consists of a series of resistors that can be connected to either the reference voltage, V_{ref}, if the digit is 1 or ground if the digit is 0. In this example, the resistors are connected to 1 and 0 levels wth ordinary switches, although in actual DACs it will be electronic switches doing the job.

The operation of this circuit becomes more apparent when we note that the resistor values are power of 2 multiples of each other. The value of R1 is taken to be R, so R2 is 2R, R3 is 4R, and so forth, until we see that R_n has a value of $2^{(n-1)}R$. When these resistors are connected to ground, the current associated with the particular resistor will be zero. But if the resistor is connected to V_{ref}, a current will flow equal to the quotient of the reference voltage to the resistance of that resistor (E/R). The currents from each branch are summed in a summation junction, so the output current, I_o, is the sum of the branch currents. Equation 11-2 expresses this idea mathematically.

$$I_o = \sum_{i=1} V_{ref} \frac{a_i}{2^{(i-1)}R} \qquad \textbf{11-2}$$

I_o is the output current in amperes, a_i is the binary digit for that input (1 or 0), and R is the value of the first resistor in the ladder, i.e., R1.

Example. Find the output current of a binary weighted resistor ladder of six bits length if R = 1000 ohms, $V_{ref} = 10$ volts dc, and the applied binary word is 110011.

$$I_o = V_{ref} \sum_{i=1}^{6} \frac{a_i}{2^{(i-1)}R}$$

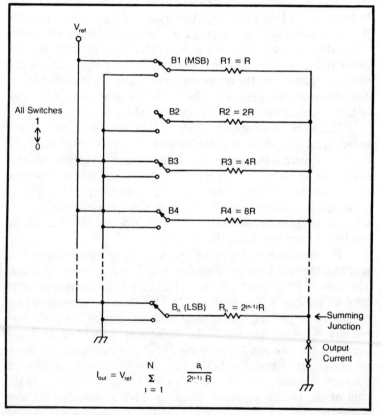

Fig. 11-2. Binary weighted resistor ladder DAC.

$$= 10\,V\left(\frac{1}{R} + \frac{1}{2R} + \frac{0}{4R} + \frac{0}{8R} + \frac{1}{16R} + \frac{1}{32R}\right)$$

$$= \left(\frac{10\,V}{1000}\;\frac{1}{1} + \frac{1}{2} + \frac{0}{4} + \frac{0}{8} + \frac{1}{16} + \frac{1}{32}\right)$$

$$= (0.01)\,(1 + 0.5 + 0 + 0 + 0\,.0625 + .03125)\ \text{amperes}$$

$$= (0.01)\,(1.59375) = 0.0159375\ \text{amperes}$$

$$= 17.59375\ \text{milliamperes}$$

The circuit shown in Fig. 11-2 is merely an example. Most DACs will use electronic switching to connect the various resistors to the summation node. Figure 11-3 shows electronic switching used in a four-bit DAC. A series of transistors are used as the switches. The binary inputs are isolated from the transistors from the transistors by diodes, and the transistors are biased by a current source. When the bit is low, then the diode for that bit is forward biased, and the emitter of the pnp transistor is grounded. But when the bit is high, the diode is reversed biased, and the emitter of the pnp transistor is biased by the reference source main supply, $+V_s$. In this case, the current source can bias that transistor and adds its current to the total applied to the input of the operational amplifier. The purpose of the amplifier is to provide a voltage output, E_o, which is equal to the product of the ladder output current, I, and the feedback resistor.

The binary weighted resistor ladder has problems if the bit length is longer than about 8-bits. The resistor values at the ends of the ladders become out of line. For example, if R is set to 10 K, bit 8 will be $2^{(8-1)}$ (10 K), or 1.28 megohms. Consider what happens when the reference voltage is +10.00 volts. Current I_8 will be 10.00/1.28 megohms, or 7.8 microamperes. Finding operational amplifiers that will respond to input currents of this level become a little difficult, unless cost is no object. Only premium devices will amplify such a current. In lower cost devices, the LSB current of the circuit will be down in the noise and will not produce an output.

Similarily, if you try to extend the range by making R very small, you run into exactly the opposite problem. For those circuits, the current may be too large. If r is set to 100 ohms, then for $V_{ref} =$ 10.00 V, current I_1 will be 100 mA. This is more than most operational amplifiers want to see. Reducing the value of R to 10 ohms produces a current of 100 mA (1 ampere).

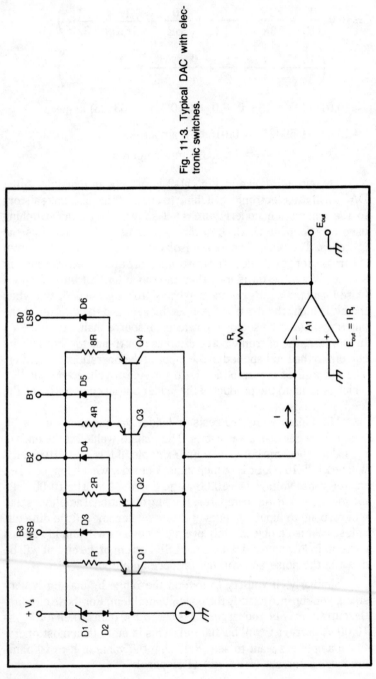

Fig. 11-3. Typical DAC with electronic switches.

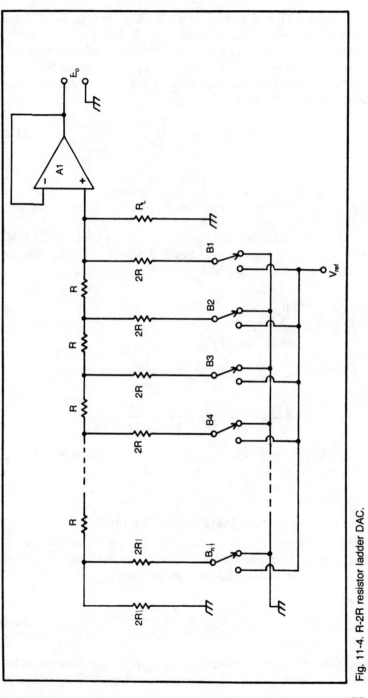

Fig. 11-4. R-2R resistor ladder DAC.

A solution to this problem is the R-2R ladder (Fig. 11-4). All of the resistors have a value of either R or 2R. If you assume that the output load (R1) has a resistance that is so much higher than 2R that its contribution to dropping the ladder output voltage can be considered negligible, then we may claim the following relationship (the amplifier has unity gain):

$$E_o = V_{ref} \sum_{i=1}^{n} \frac{a_i}{2^i} \qquad \text{11-3}$$

E_o is the output voltage, V_{ref}, is the reference voltage, and a_i is the value of the ith bit (1 or 0). This equation assumes that the load resistor is much larger than R or 2R.

Example. Calculate the output voltage of a six-bit R-2R DAC with a unity gain output amplifier if the value of the reference potential is +5.5 volts. The input word is 101101.

$$
\begin{aligned}
E_o &= V_{ref} \sum_{i=1}^{6} \frac{a_i}{2^i} \\
&= 5.5 \text{ V} \left(\frac{1}{2^1} + \frac{0}{2^2} + \frac{1}{2^3} + \frac{1}{2^4} + \frac{0}{2^5} + \frac{1}{2^6} \right) \\
&= 5.5 \text{ V} \left(\frac{1}{2} + \frac{0}{4} + \frac{1}{8} + \frac{1}{16} + \frac{0}{32} + \frac{1}{64} \right) \\
&= (5.5 \text{ V}) (0.5 + 0 + 0.125 + 0.0625 + 0 + 0.015625) \\
&= (5.5 \text{ V}) (0.703125) = 3.867 \text{ volts}
\end{aligned}
$$

FULL-SCALE OUTPUT VOLTAGE

Most commercial DACs are made using the R-2R resistor ladder technique. The maximum, or full-scale, output voltage depends upon the reference voltage and the bit length.

$$E_{o(fs)} = \frac{V_{ref}(2^n - 1)}{2^n} \qquad \text{11-4}$$

$E_{o(fs)}$ is the full-scale output potential, V_{ref} is the reference potential, and n is the bit length.

Example. Calculate the full-scale output potential of a 10-bit DAC (using the R-2R resistor ladder technique) if the reference voltage is +10.00 volts.

$$E_{o(fs)} = \frac{V_{ref}(2^n - 1)}{2^n}$$

$$= \frac{(10.00 \text{ V}) (2^{10} - 1)}{2^{10}}$$

$$= \frac{(10.00 \text{ V}) (1023)}{(1024)} = 9.99 \text{ volts}$$

The output potential or current of a DAC can exist only in certain discrete states because one of the inputs is binary word. Each successive binary number changes by 1-LSB. The smallest increment of voltage output allowed at the output of a DAC is that produced by a 1-LSB change of the binary word. This voltage is expressed mathematically in Equation 11-5.

$$\Delta E_o = \frac{V_{ref}}{2^n} \qquad \textbf{11-5}$$

Example. Calculate the output change caused by a 1-LSB change in the binary word applied to the input of an eight-bit DAC if the reference voltage is +2.56 volts dc

$$\Delta E_o = \frac{V_{ref}}{2^n}$$

$$= (2.56 \text{V})/2^8$$
$$= (2.56)/(256) = 0.01 \text{ volts} = 10 \text{ millivolts}$$

AMPLIFIER SETTLING TIME

One of the principal limiting factors in any commerical DAC is the settling time of the output amplifier. Figure 11-5 shows an R-2R ladder DAC with an amplifier output. Any change in the input state will not be reflected as an output state change immediately. There is always some sort of lag between the two events. This lag, incidentally, determines the maximum operating frequency of the DAC.

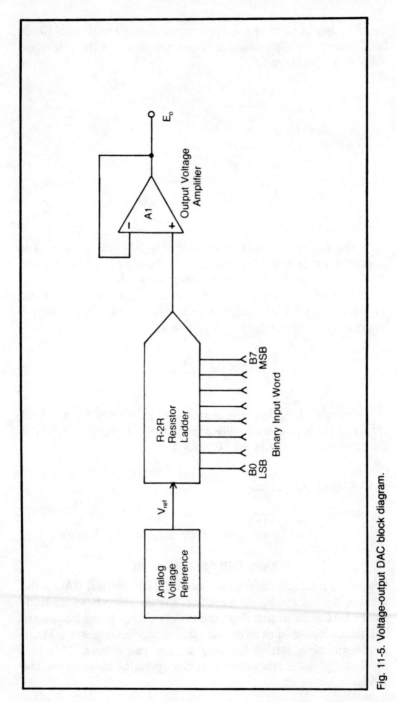

Fig. 11-5. Voltage-output DAC block diagram.

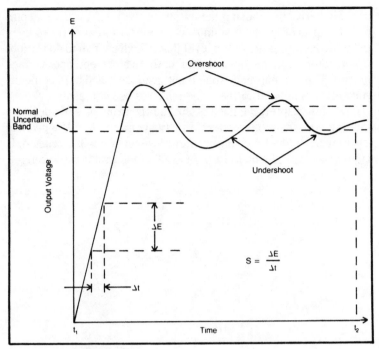

Fig. 11-6. DAC characteristic.

Assume in Fig. 11-6 that an input bit change occurs at time t_1. The output voltage increases rapidly to the correct value but is limited by the slow rate of the amplifier(s). The voltage will overshoot the mark in most cases and will then settle down to the correct value. The correct value, incidentally, will actually be a small voltage band clustered around the desired output potential. This is due to normal circuit errors. The settling time of the amplifier is the time difference between the onset of the input change at time t_1, and the point, t_2, at which the output voltage finally settles into the normal uncertainty band. The settling time is $t_2 - t_1$.

Since electronic switching is already pretty fast, it is best to concentrate on the settling time of the amplifier when trying to achieve faster speeds. In many cases, the DAC manufacturer will produce a current output DAC in order to keep the operating speed high. When trying to operate near the rated operating speed of the DAC (very often in the megahertz range if it is a current output type), it is necessary to keep the settling time of the output amplifier used external to the DAC less than $1/f$, where F is the operating frequency of the DAC.

179

Similarly, when using the output of the DAC to drive a comparator, as is often the case in A/D converter circuits, try to keep the total operating speed at a level that is high enough to do the job. Comparators can be operated in both the current and voltage modes. The current mode (one input grounded, and both comparison currents applied to the same input) is usually faster.

In this chapter, we have discussed the principles of operation for digital-to-analog converters. Practical examples will be given in Chapter 13. In the following chapter however, we will discuss A/D circuits—some of which use DACs as an integral component.

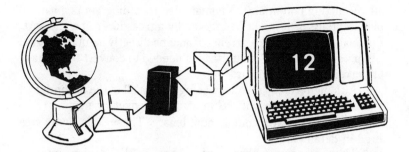

Analog-to-Digital Converter Circuits

The Analog-to-Digital Converter (A/D or ADC) is used to convert an analog voltage or current to a proportional binary word. Thus, the ADC is used to interface a computer with an analog instrument or transducer. For practical projects, therefore, the ADC is absolutely essential.

At one time, A/D converters were terribly expensive. Prices of $1000 and more were once commonplace. So was large size. A typical 1960 ADC used vacuum tubes and was housed in an 8-inch high × 19-inch wide "relay rack" cabinet. Today, you can still spend close to $1000 for extreme precision in 16-bit, 24-bit or 32-bit word lengths. Size, or course, is vastly reduced since the modern high-cost DAC is a printed circuit board mountable hybrid. On the low end of the price scale, where we can sacrifice either word length (i.e., 8-bit through 12-bit instead of 24-bit or more) of precision, costs are very low. In fact, it is almost true that cost is so low that each channel of a multi-channel system can have its own ADC, instead of sharing with other channels.

To reiterate, analog-to-digital converters (ADCs) are circuits or devices that will examine an analog input—in other words, a current or a voltage-and then convert it to an equivalent binary word. The ADC will have an encoded output in which each change of 1-LSB in the output word represents some given increment of the input voltage or current.

ADCs are used to interface digital instruments and computers to devices in the analog world. In a typical instrumentation system, some form of amplifier output must be applied to the computer. The amplifier output may represent the amplified version of some naturally occurring potential (the human electrocardiogram is a natural biopotential), or it might be created by a transducer of some sort. But analog voltages and currents cannot be directly input to a digital computer. Some form of interface is needed to convert the voltage or current to a binary word.

Although ADCs are known using almost all of the major digital codes, most of them will be in straight (offset or symmetrical) binary, BCD, or twos' complement binary. These codes were covered in detail earlier.

There are several basic approaches to ADC design: integrating, servo (ramp), successive approximation, parallel, and voltage-to-frequency conversion. This chapter covers the popular integration, parallel, binary ramp, and successive approximation (SA) converters. In Chapter 14 you will be introduced to some of the commercially available ADC devices on the market, and some circuits that perform the analog-to-digital (A/D) function using ordinary IC devices.

INTEGRATION

Integration ADC circuits use an analog (operational amplifier) integrator to create a ramp voltage from the input voltage being measured. Three basic types are known: single-slope, dual-slope, and multiple-slope. Multiple-slope is composed of two different categories, triple-slope and quad-slope.

Figure 12-1 shows the basic operational amplifier integrator

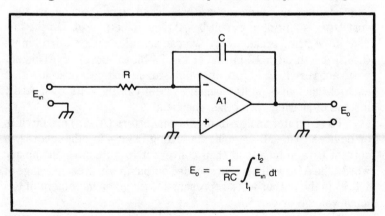

$$E_o = \frac{1}{RC} \int_{t_1}^{t_2} E_{in} \, dt$$

Fig. 12-1. Operational amplifier integrator.

circuit. The op amp is a perfect—well, nearly so—amplifier that was discussed in Chapter 4 in greater detail. A resistor (R) is connected in series with the input, and a capacitor (C) is connected in the feedback loop between the output and input. By the rules of the operational amplifier, currents I_1 and I_2 are equal to each other.

$$I_1 = I_2$$

$$I_1 = \frac{E_{in}}{R}$$

$$I_2 = C\frac{dE_o}{dt}$$

By substituting the last two equations into the first, we get Equation 12-1.

$$\frac{E_{in}}{R} = \frac{CdE_o}{dt} \qquad \textbf{12-1}$$

By integrating both sides of this equation, the transfer function for the operational amplifier integrator circuit is obtained.

$$\frac{CdE_o}{dt}dt = \int \frac{E_{in}\,dt}{R} \qquad \textbf{12-2}$$

$$CE_o = \int \frac{E_{in}\,dt}{R}$$

$$E_o = \frac{1}{RC}\int_0^T E_{in}\,dt$$

Because this integral is over time, the output is said to be proportional to the time average of the input signal. The proportionality factor will be the term 1/RC, which also describes the gain of the circuit. Note that very low values of capacitance (C) will charge more rapidly with any given resistor, so the maximum value is reached rapidly. The gain of an integrator can become very high, very quickly, as the RC time constant is reduced.

Single-Slope

The simplest form of integrating ADC circuit is the single-slope integrator of Fig. 12-2. The principal components of this circuit are an integrator, a voltage comparator, a gate, a clock, and the gate generator. The gate generator keeps the timing of the circuit straight.

The integrator circuit is the operational amplifier circuit just discussed and will have an output voltage that obeys the last equation. Switch S1 is used to initially discharge the capacitor, so the integrator output begins the conversion cycle at zero. This switch is usually an electronic field-effect transistor switch that is turned on by ordinary digital logic level signals. When S1 is closed, capacitor C is shorted out, and its charge goes to zero. But when S1 is open, capacitor C can function normally, and the circuit will integrate the input voltage.

A comparator is a device that will compare two analog voltages and issue an output that indicates whether the voltages are equal to each other, or which of the two is the higher. Figure 12-3 shows the operation of a voltage comparator. This is a graph of the output voltage-versus-input voltage. The comparator is basically a differential input operational amplifier with too much gain. In fact, an op amp can easily be used as a comparator if no negative feedback is supplied. When $E_1 = E_x$, the differential input voltage seen by the amplifier is zero, so the output E_o is zero. When E_1 is greater than E_x, however, the output of the comparator is a constant negative voltage. When E_1 is less than E_x at the input, the output of the comparator is a high positive voltage. In most bipolar comparators, the absolute values of $+E$ and $-E$ are equal. In comparators usually used for ADC work, the output is monopolar; i.e., only the $E_1 = E_x$ and $E_1 < E_x$ conditions are needed.

The gate and clock sections of the single-slope integrator circuit are the same as in any digital electronic circuits; a three-input gate is specified here. The counter is an ordinary binary counter, although it might be in BCD in some applications, such as digital voltage measurement.

The operation of this circuit can be seen by examining the timing diagram in Fig. 12-4. The gate generator circuit issues a start conversion pulse that will reset the integrator output to zero by turning on S1 for a brief instant. It will also insure that the counter is in the zero state by issuing a reset pulse to the counter circuit.

Immediately after the reset pulse is received, the output of the

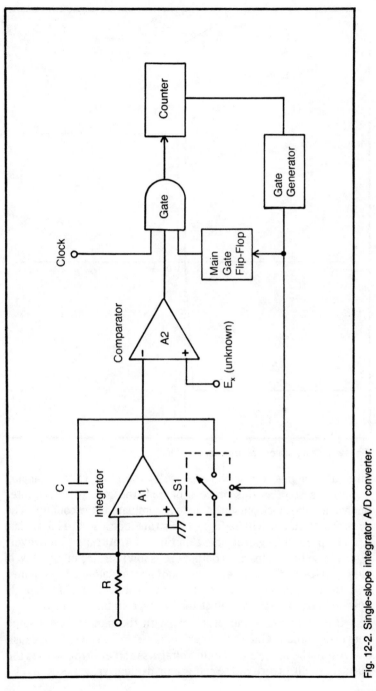

Fig. 12-2. Single-slope integrator A/D converter.

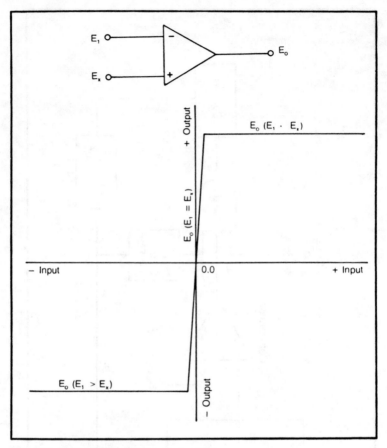

Fig. 12-3. Comparator and transfer function.

integrator begins to rise in response to the input voltage (analog signal). As soon as this process begins, the gate to the counter opens, and the clock pulses begin to accumulate in the counter. The comparator output will be high at this time because E_1 is less than E_x. The process began at time t_1 in Fig. 12-4. At time t_2, however, $E_1 = E_x$, so the comparator output drops low; turning off the flow of clock pulses to the counter. The count accumulated in the counter will then be proportional to the input voltage, and if properly decoded, will correctly reflect that voltage in binary form.

But there are some problems with the simple single-slope converter circuit. One is that certain noise impulses tend to cause an error in the integrator output voltage. Another error class is the normal circuit errors in the integrator design: values of R and C, bias currents, etc. It is also necessary that the clock frequency be accurate and stable over the conversion period.

The advantages of the single-slope converter are that it is simple and low-cost. In fact, some of the lowest cost digital voltmeters use the single-slope ADC circuit. If you use the single-slope ADC, however, be prepared to put up with the errors inherent in the design. Because of these problems, the single-slope ADC has been eclipsed (although there has been some recent comeback) by the dual-slope ADC.

Dual-Slope

Figure 12-5 shows a block diagram for the basic dual-slope integrator ADC circuit. The principal parts are an integrator, a comparator, a main gate, a counter, a control logic section, a reference voltage or current, and an input switch that is controlled by the logic section. Some of the components parts of the dual-slope circuit are the same as those of the single-slope circuit, so their description will not be repeated here.

The reference section is a precision analog voltage or current

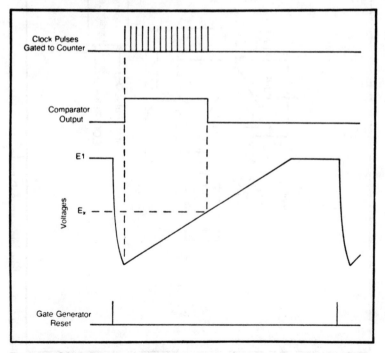

Fig. 12-4. SSI A/D converter timing.

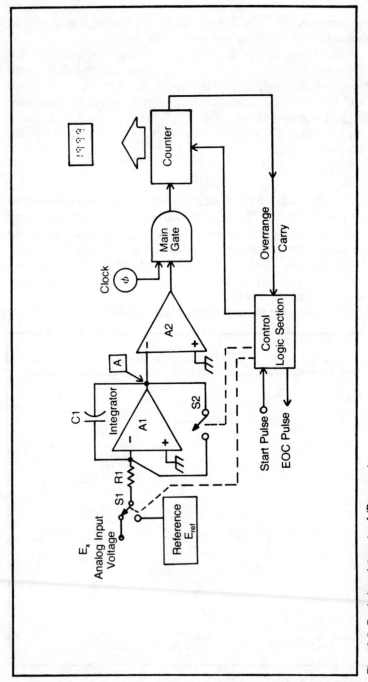

Fig. 12-5. Dual-slope integrator A/D converter.

to which the unknown input signal is compared. First, the unknown signal is integrated, much in the manner of the earlier single-slope circuit. However, this signal is then compared with the precision reference by integrating the reference in the same manner.

When a start pulse is received by the control logic section, several things occur. One is that switch S1 connects to the input signal, switch S2 momentarily closes to reset the integrator output to zero, and a reset pulse is applied to the counter to insure that its starting state is zero.

The analog input signal is applied to the input of the integrator, so the voltage at point A begins to rise. The comparator is ground referenced in this case, so its output will snap high as soon as the integrator output is more than a few millivolts (the comparator will have a small hysteresis, so it will not respond until E_A is more than a few millivolts). The instant the comparator output is high, clock pulses will begin to flow into the counter.

The counter is allowed to overflow, and the carry signal is applied to the control logic. When the overflow occurs, the output of the integrator is proportional to the input signal (see Fig. 12-6). At this time, the control logic section will switch the integrator input to the precision reference source. The polarity of this source is selected such that it will discharge the integrator capacitor that has

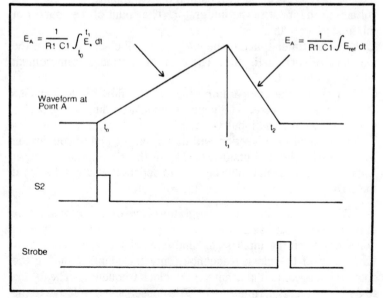

Fig. 12-6. DSI A/D converter timing.

been charged by the unknown signal. Because the reference has a constant level, though, the slope of the discharge will be constant, yet proportional to the analog input signal.

The counter state at the instant the switching of the input occurs will be 0000 (overflow plus one count is zero). The counter will continue to increment all during the period when the integrator is discharging and will stop only when the integrator output returns to zero, causing the comparator output to snap low and turn off the gate.

Let's review the operation of this circuit (refer to Fig. 12-6) again.

☐ At time t_o, switch S2 is closed momentarily to dump any residual charge in the integrator capacitor, the counter is reset, and switch S1 is set to the analog input.

☐ The integrator begins to charge due to current $E_{in}/R1$, so E_A begins rising from zero.

☐ As soon as E_A is greater than zero, plus a small hysteresis, the comparator output goes high, which enables the main gate to pass clock pulses into the counter.

☐ The counter increments until it overflows at time t_1. The overflow pulse generated by the counter causes switch S1 to switch to the analog reference source (position B). This applies the reference voltage to the input of the integrator. The count of the counter at this instant is 0000.

☐ Between times t_1 and t_2 the integrator will discharge under the influence of current $-E_{ref}/R1$. The counter continues to increment during this period.

☐ At time t_2, the comparator shuts off the flow of clock pulses through the main gate. The count accumulated during the period $t_2 - t_1$ represents the input voltage.

☐ The control logic section will now issue an end of conversion (EOC) pulse to let the outside world know that the data at the output is valid. This pulse may also be used to update the output display if the ADC is being used as a digital voltmeter.

Although the dual-slope integrator is one of the slowest forms of ADC circuits, it has certain advantages: relative immunity from noise errors on the input signal and immunity to error caused by inaccuracy of the clock frequency (only the stability during the conversion cycle is important viz the clock frequency). The 10-ms to 50-ms conversion times are of little consequence, relative to the advantages, in many applications.

Triple-Slope

The triple-slope integrator is basically the same as the dual-slope integrator, except that one additional slope is added. As in the case of the dual-slope integrator, the triple slope integrator (Fig. 12-7) converts the analog input voltage to a time interval, as measured by a digital pulse counter. The first ramp, V_A/RC, is of fixed time duration (the same as in dual-slope converter). But there are two reference ramps: coarse $(-V_{ref}/RC)$ and fine $(-V_{ref}/2^k RC)$. The coarse ramp has a much steeper slope than the fine ramp. The coarse ramp, then, rapidly integrates the first portion of the signal until it is in the ball park. When the coarse ramp drops to a level of approximately V_t, the fine ramp is switched in to provide greater resolution.

The high resolution is not needed in the coarse ramp, so the circuit goes for speed instead. The triple-slope integrator is capable of providing the advantages of integration A/D conversion, as outlined in the section on dual-slope circuits, yet reduces the speed from the normal 10-ms to 50-ms speed to 1-ms to 10-ms. Some triple-slope designs are capable of operating as fast as successive approximation converters.

Analog Devices, Inc. offers integrating ADCs of all types. One of them is a refinement of the multiple-slope idea called a *quadslope* ADC.

PARALLEL

Very few ADC circuits are as fast as the parallel converter. This converter operates at such blazing speeds that it is sometimes called the flash ADC. Figure 12-8 shows a parallel ADC circuit. It consists of a stack of voltage comparators. One input of each converter in the stack is connected to the analog input signal. The other inputs are biased by a dc reference source. Each comparator is biased 1-LSB higher than the next one down in the chain. A simple precision resistor network is used to accomplish the biasing scheme.

Why have any other converter circuit if the flash converter is so rapid? After all, speed is a critical parameter, isn't it? There are actually a couple of disadvantages to the parallel converter. One of them is that the cover is limited as to the number of bits of resolution that can be accommodated. Normal problems with real voltage comparators limit the value of the LSB and this, of course, limits the total bit length.

The second problem is that the output is not encoded in any of

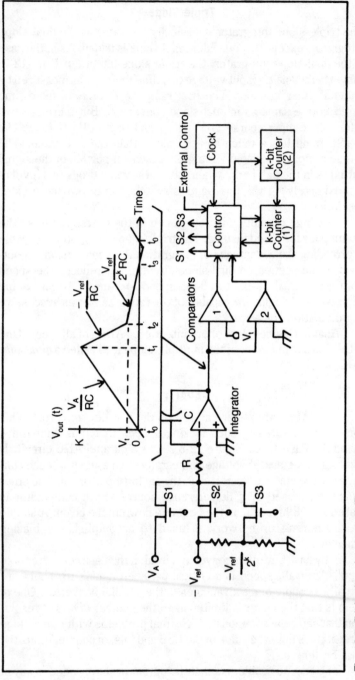

Fig. 12-7. Triple-slope integrator A/D converter.

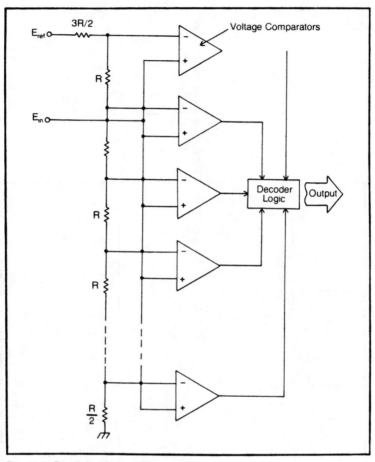

Fig. 12-8. Parallel or flash A/D converter.

the standard binary codes. A decoder logic circuit at the output of the comparator is needed in order to make the unit compatible with the outside world. Of course, if you have a computer, and the parallel ADC is sending data to the computer, the decoding can be done in software. But software decoding merely increases the program overhead of the CPU, and thus might prove more costly in the long run. Only a few companies are making parallel converters. TRW, for example, offers some video ADC circuits that depend upon the speed of the parallel circuit in order to broaden bandwidth.

BINARY RAMP

The binary ramp, or servo, ADC circuit is part of a class called

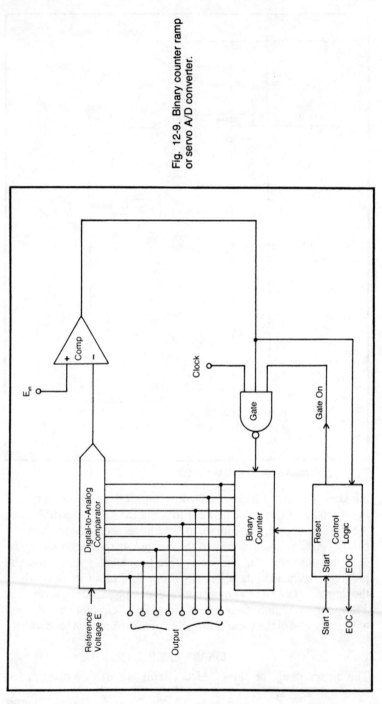

Fig. 12-9. Binary counter ramp or servo A/D converter.

feedback ADC circuits. Most of the members of this class use a digital-to-analog converter in the feedback loop to make the comparison. DACs were discussed in the last chapter.

The circuit for a basic servo ADC circuit is shown in Fig. 12-9. The major components are the DAC, comparator, main gate, binary counter, reference source, and control logic section.

The DAC used could be either a binary weighted resistance ladder, or an R-2R ladder design. Both current-output and voltage-output models are used in ADC circuits. The example shown in Fig. 12-9 is a voltage output design. Designs that use current output DACs usually have both the DAC output current and the analog input current (or the voltage converted to a current by passing it through a resistor) applied to the same comparator input. The other comparator input will be either grounded or connected to a small current source to compensate for any error in the circuit. Current operation of the DAC and the comparator is generally faster than voltage operation.

When a start pulse is received by the control logic section, the binary counter is reset, and a gate-on signal is applied to the main gate. The binary outputs of the counter are connected to the digital inputs of the DAC, so when the main gate is opened, pulses that increment the counter have the effect of causing the DAC output to ramp upwards from zero toward E_{in}. When DAC output E_o is equal to analog input voltage E_{in}, the output of the comparator will drop low, turning off the main gate. This will stop the flow of clock pulses into the counter. The count will remain at the level existing when the counter dropped low. This count is proportional to the value of the analog input voltage. When this occurs, the control logic section will issue an end of conversion (EOC) pulse (see Fig. 12-10). To reiterate, the operation of the ramp ADC circuit is as follows:

☐ When a start pulse is received, the control logic section will reset the counter to zero, and place a high on one input of the main gate.

☐ The clock pulses now through the open main gate to begin incrementing the binary counter.

☐ The DAC output voltage begins to ramp upward because the digital inputs of the DAC are connected to the counter output.

☐ When DAC output E_o is equal to the analog input voltage E_{in}, the comparator output drops low, causing the gate to close.

☐ The counter output remains in its present state, which is proportional to the analog input signal.

195

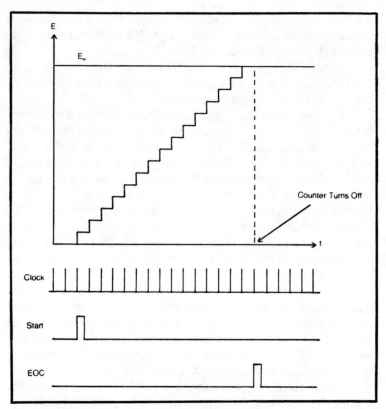

Fig. 12-10. Ramp/servo A/D converter timing diagram.

☐ The control logic section issues an end-of-conversion pulse to let the outside world know that the data on the outputs is valid.

The EOC pulse is also sometimes used to strobe the data into an output latch. The computer that is receiving the ADC data always sees this latched data, so all data appearing at the output of the converter is valid. Without the latch, the incrementing counter data would appear at the output and would thus be nonvalid.

The converter circuits shown thus far require a separate start and EOC pulse to operate properly. These lines can be tied together, however, if we want to make a continuous operation ADC. The EOC pulse from one conversion becomes the start pulse for the next conversion. Note that some designers will use a set-reset flip-flop, or a pulse delay (one shot) between the EOC output and the start input to give one clock pulse to the external device (that is using the data) to either latch the output or input the data.

196

The binary ramp ADC is faster than most integration methods. The time required to make a conversion depends upon the input voltage. The closer the voltage is to full scale, the longer the conversion time (of course, zero volts requires zero time). The time required for a full-scale conversion is the benchmark against which we often measure ADC performance. For the servo type, this time is 2^n clock pulses, where n is the bit length.

Example. Find the conversion time for a 10-bit binary ramp (servo) ADC if the clock speed is 2 MHz.

$$t_c = 2^{10} \text{ pulses} \times \frac{1 \text{ second}}{2 \times 10^6 \text{ pulses}}$$

$$= 0.000512 \text{ seconds} = 512 \text{ ms}$$

Binary ramp, servo, ADC circuits are very easy to implement. Consequently, they have become very popular. Modern IC and hybrid DACs are capable of operating to clock speeds of at least 200 kHz, with many capable of operation to 4 MHz. These clock counters allow very rapid conversions. The principal operating limitation seems to be comparator settling time, which is similar to amplifier settling time. Of course, this is assuming that no output amplifier problem exists with the DAC itself.

Despite the speed of the DAC, there are still limitations that must be of concern to some users. For longer bit lengths, 2^n clock pulses can be a problem. The successive approximation ADC of the next section solves some of the speed problems because it will make a complete conversion in n+1 clock pulses.

SUCCESSIVE APPROXIMATION

The successive approximation (SA) analog-to-digital converter makes use of a technique that more nearly resembles the way we measure most physical quantities: i.e., trial and error. The SA ADC will make a trial conversion, test the results, and then modify the output according to the results of the test. It will continue to make trials until the available bits are exhausted or it scores a finished conversion.

Figure 12-11 shows the SA technique in analogy form. Here we have an ordinary platform balance. The unknown weight is placed on one pan, while different trial weights are placed on the other pan. When the trial weights match the unknown weight, the scale is in balance. The pointer will be exactly in the center of its scale. The technique for making a measurement is simple. The trial weights are calibrated such that they are related by powers of two; i.e., W/2, W/4, W/8, W/16, etc. Begin the measurement by placing the heaviest trial weight (W/2) on the lefthand pan and the unknown on the righthand pan.

If W_x is greater than W/2, the scale pointer tilts to the right. But if the trial weight is less than the unknown, the scale tilts to the left. This is the test we must make, and its result determines whether we increase the trial weight or make another trial with the next lower weight. In the SA ADC circuit, the trial is made with a voltage comparator and the result will be to either set or reset a bit in a register.

The trial process continues until the scale is in balance. At each trial, a weight is placed on the scale and the test performed. If the test shows that W_x is still higher, the operator will add additional weights. If W_x is less, however, the trial weight must be reduced.

Figure 12-12 shows the clock diagram of a successive approximation ADC circuit. The main components are voltage comparator, DAC, control logic, shift register, and output latches. The last three of these are usually part of a successive approximation register (SAR) integrated or hybrid circuit. The output latches are needed so that the bit affected can be set or reset according to the

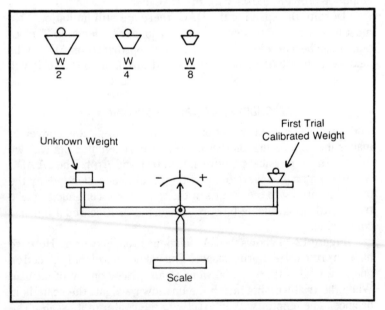

Fig. 12-11. Representation of successive approximation A/D converter.

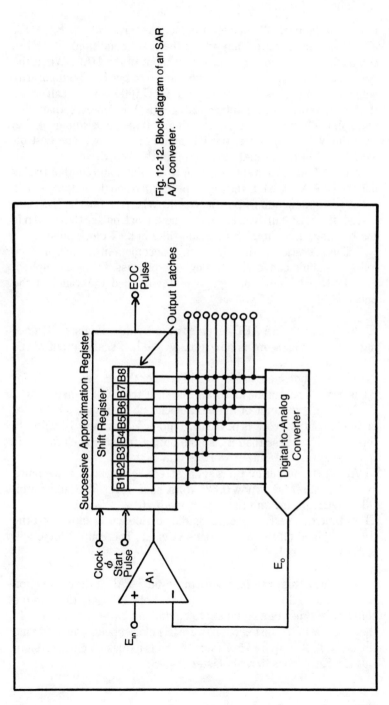

Fig. 12-12. Block diagram of an SAR A/D converter.

199

results of the trial. When a start pulse is received by the SA ADC, all bits are set to zero (they are in the reset condition). Bit B1 is connected to the most significant bit input of the DAC. When the first clock pulse after the start pulse arrives, but B1 is temporarily set high. This makes the output to the DAC 10000000, or half scale. If the unknown analog input voltage (E_{in}) is greater than this voltage, the output latch is set to 1 (high). If the input voltage is less than this value, however, the B1 latch is reset low. The first bit would be 1 in the former case and 0 in the latter.

The SA ADC then shifts one bit to the right, and another trial is undertaken. At each bit, the test is performed and the output latch is set or reset, depending upon the result. When the final bit has been tested, the SAR will overflow on the next clock pulse. Hence, if n is the bit length, the total conversion time is n+1 clock pulses.

The operation of this circuit may become a little clearer if we follow a sample conversion through the process. In the example of Fig. 12-13, the full-scale range is 1 volt, and the value of the unknown E_{in} is 0.625 volts.

☐ At time t_1, the SA ADC receives a start pulse. Register B1 goes high. The output word is now 100, so the half-scale output of the DAC is 0.5 volts.

☐ The test indicates that E_{in} is still greater than E_o, so the latch for B1 is high. The output following the first trial will remain 100.

☐ At time t_2 (receipt of the next clock pulse), register B2 is set high. The output word is now 110. Voltage E_o is now 0.75 volts. In this case, E_{in} is less than E_o, so the output register latch for B2 is reset to zero. The output word is now 100.

☐ At time t_3, output bit B3 is set high, so the output word becomes 101. The value of E_o is now 0.625 volts, so $E_o = E_{in}$. The latch for bit B3 is set high, making the output word 101.

☐ At time t_4, overflow occurs, so the outside world knows that the data contained on the output lines is valid. The control logic will issue an EOC pulse.

Because this example used a three-bit SA ADC, the conversion time would be 3+1, or 4, clock pulses. Let's compare the relative conversion times of a 10-bit servo circuit and a 10-bit SA circuit. In the example of the last section, a 2-MHz clock speed was used, and the servo ADC required 512 microseconds to make the conversion. But the SA is considerably faster.

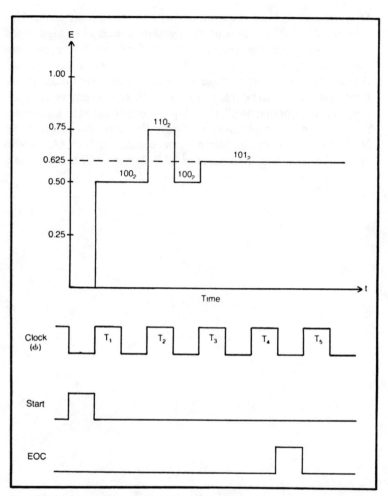

Fig. 12-13. Typical operation of SAR A/D converter.

$$t = \frac{1 \text{ second}}{2 \times 10^6 \text{ pulses}} \times (n+1) \text{ pulses}$$

$$= 4 \text{ seconds}/2 \times 10^6 = 0.000002 \text{ s} = 2 \text{ } \mu s$$

The SA ADC is 512/2, or 256, times faster than the servo ADC for the 10-bit word length. The SA ADC becomes even more favorable as word length increases.

In the past, development of SA ADC circuits was limited by the large amount of logic required to make the SA circuit work. This required a lot of TTL devices, so it was only used when high speed was necessary and the coding problems of the parallel circuit were too much trouble. Today though, ADC designers can implement the SA design a lot easier because semiconductor makers offer appropriate DACs, comparators, and best of all, IC successive approximation registers that do all of the logic once relegated to a huge pile of TTL ICs. *Motorola Semiconductor Products, Inc.* makes the MC14459, and Advanced Micro Devices makes an 8-bit (AM-2500) and 12-bit SAR ICs. Examples of SAR designs will be given in a later chapter.

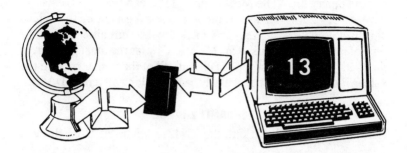

Microcomputer-Compatible
DAC Circuits

I n recent years, digital-to-analog converters (DAC's) have become available in several easy to use forms, including monolithic integrated circuits and hybrids. Some of these devices are merely adapted and/or adopted into microcomputers and are of older design. Others are specifically designed for microcomputer application. While it can sometimes be argued that the latter are the more optimal for computerniks, both classes are called *"microcomputer-compatible."*

What are the generalized criteria for microcomputer compatibility? The DAC must have TTL-compatible in/out leads because most microcomputers on sale today use TTL voltage and current levels (note: in TTL, the low state is 0 to + 0.8 volts, and the high state is +2.4 volts to +5 volts. One TTL input will source a current of 1.8 mA). In this chapter, we will discuss practical examples. Due to the rapidly changing technology, however, you are advised to check the latest manufacturer's catalogs for possible alternate selections. In an earlier chapter the basic theory for the two main types of digital-to-analog converters was discussed. These devices will output an analog voltage or current (depending upon type) that is proportional to the product of the analog reference voltage or current and a binary word applied to the digital inputs. The output will be a fraction of the reference level, with that fraction being $A/2^n$, in which A is the applied binary word and n is the bit length of the converter.

Two different types of DACs are available. The binary-weighted version uses a resistor ladder to sum currents weighted per the binary bits. The MSB resistor is R, and the other resistors have $2^{n-1}R$ values. These are limited to some extent by the values permissible for these resistors in real-world circuits. The other type of resistor ladder used in DACs, and by far the most popular, is the R-2R ladder. In that type of circuit, all of the resistors have the values R or 2R. This is particularly handy for long bit length DACs.

FERRANTI ZN425E

Ferranti of England markets the ZN425E eight-bit DAC through

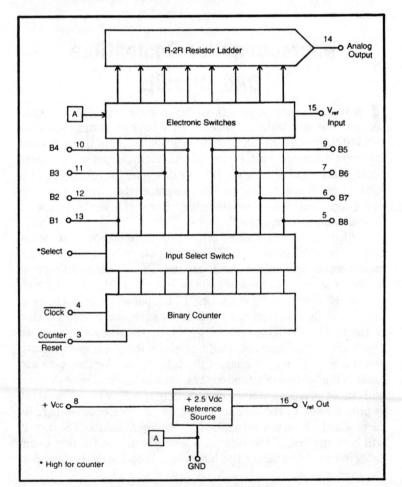

Fig. 13-1. Block diagram of the Ferranti ZN-425 DAC.

204

Ferranti Semiconductors, Ltd. of New York, NY. This digital-to-analog converter is shown in Fig. 13-1. It uses R-2R ladder and an internal +2.5-volt reference source. This reference is derived internally. This reference is output through pin 16. The reference input to the R-2R ladder is via pin 15. If you desire to use the internal reference, then you need to short these two terminals together. If you want to use an external reference source, then apply it directly to pin 15.

This particular DAC has one feature that makes it desirable for many different applications: An internal binary counter (eight-bit) can be connected to the DAC digital inputs through some electronic switches. When the select input is low, the switches disconnect the counter, and the digital inputs control the DAC output. But when the select inputs is high, the counter output is connected to the DAC inputs, and the counter controls the DAC. When this occurs, the counter output state appears on the DAC package terminals (B1 through B8). In this case, B1 is the most significant bit, and B8 is the least significant bit.

The internal counter can be used for several different applications. One is the analog-to-digital converter discussed in a later chapter. Another is to make a binary ramp generator. If a clock is applied to the input of the counter, the select input high is set, and then the analog output is monitored, a ramp voltage that is determined by the reference and the binary counter will be seen. The frequency of the output sawtooth is determined by the clock rate, while its amplitude will be the full-scale output of the DAC.

The accuracy of the ZN425E is 0.2 percent full-scale voltage per the reference (FSR) at room temperature, with a ½-LSB linearity. The E suffix device operates over the commercial temperature range of 0 to 70 C, while the J suffix device is mil-speced over −55 to +125 C. The power supply is a monopolar +5-volt (TTL) supply. Settling time for this DAC is typically 1 microsecond.

Figure 13-2 shows a typical circuit using the ZN425E. The internal reference is used, and the output voltage is applied to the noninverting follower operational amplifier. Zero and full-scale output adjustments are provided. The calibration procedure is as follows:

1. Set all input bits low.
2. Adjust potentiometer R2 (Fig. 13-2) until the output voltage is zero.
3. Set all input bits high.
4. Adjust R1 until the output voltage is FSR-1LSB.

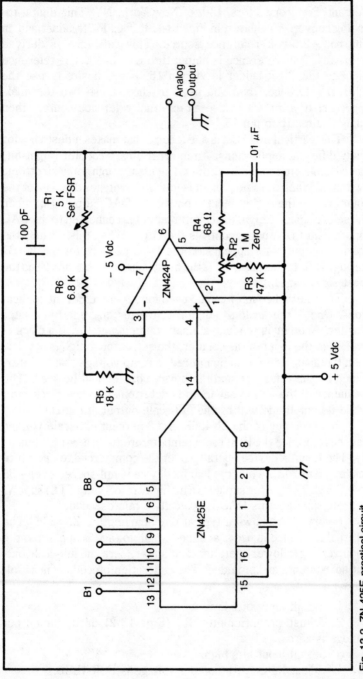

Fig. 13-2. ZN-425E practical circuit.

In this case, the FSR is 3.840 volts, so the 1-LSB is 3.840/256, or 0.015 volts, or 15 millivolts. The maximum output voltage at which this adjustment is made, then, will be $3.84 - 0.015$ volts, or 3.825 volts.

DAC-08

The DAC-08 is an eight-bit current-output digital-to-analog converter originally manufactured by Precision Monolithics, Inc. and second-sourced by Advanced Micro Devices (AMD) and others. The DAC-08 requires an external reference source, so it is a multiplying DAC. It contains the R-2R ladder, the electronic switching and current sources, and reference amplifier. The multiplication feature of this DAC makes it useful in a number of applications in which the nonmultiplying DAC could not operate.

The block diagram to the DAC-08 is shown in Fig. 13-3, and the pinouts are shown in Fig. 13-4. Most of the pins are self-explanatory, but several require a little explanation. There are two current output terminals, and these are complements of each other. The I_o output will rise from zero to full scale as the input increments from 00000000 to 11111111. The I_o output will drop from full scale to zero as the digital inputs increment over the same range: 00000000 to 11111111.

The DAC-08 offers very fast settling time, on the order of 85 nanoseconds (current-output DACs typically have fast settling times), and will operate 1 MHz. The output currents are matched to within ±½-LSB and are low drift ±10 ppm/ C). The dc power supplies required are typically around 12 to 15 volts, but the DAC-08 can operate over the range ±4.5 volts to ±18 volts. At ±5 volts, the device power dissipation is a low 33 milliwatts.

The output current will be determined by the expression:

$$I_o = I_{ref} (A/2^n) \qquad \textbf{13-1}$$

I_o is the current output in milliamperes, I_{ref} is the reference current in milliamperes, A is the binary word applied to the digital inputs expressed as a decimal, and n is the bit length (i.e., 8 bits, n=8).

Example. Calculate the output current when 10010111 is applied to the input of a DAC-08 when the reference current is 4 milliamperes.

$$I_o = I_{ref} (A/2^n)$$

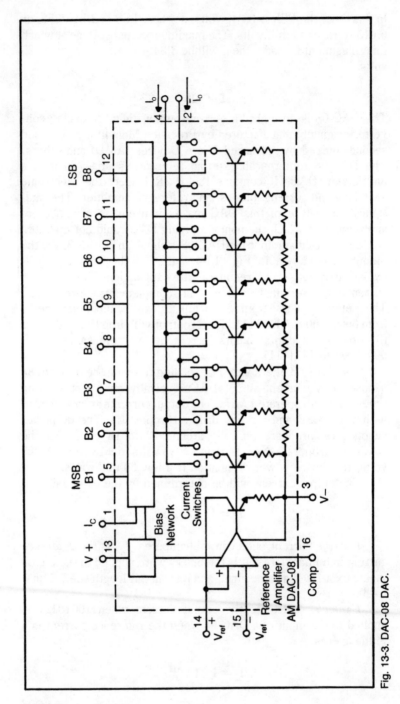

Fig. 13-3. DAC-08 DAC.

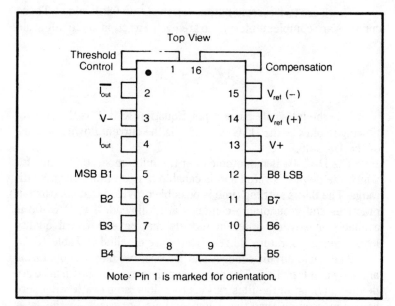

Fig. 13-4. DAC-08 pin-outs.

$(A = 10^0 1^0 111_2$ converted to decimal form, so $A = 151$)

$$I_o = (4 \text{ mA}) (151/2^8)$$
$$= (4 \text{ mA}) (151/256)$$
$$= (4 \text{ mA}) (0.589) = 2.359 \text{ mA}$$

The full-scale output current is given by Equation 13-2.

$$I_o = I_{ref} \times \frac{2^n - 1}{2^n} \qquad \textbf{13-2}$$

Because n=8, this can be expressed in the form given by Equation 13-3.

$$I_o = (I_{ref}) (255/256) \qquad \textbf{13-3}$$

Example. Find the full-scale output current of a DAC-08 when the input reference current is 4.0 mA.

$$I_{fs} = (I_{ref} (255/256)$$
$$= (4 \text{ mA}) (0.996)$$
$$I_o = 3.984 \text{ mA}$$

There are two current outputs on the DAC-08: I_o and $\overline{I}_o$. These currents are complementary, and are each a fraction of the full-scale current.

$$I_{fs} = I_o + \overline{I}_o$$

I_{fs} is the full-scale current per Equation 13-3. I_o is the current flowing in pin 4 of the DAC-08, and I_o is the current flowing in pin 2 of the DAC-08.

The DAC-08 is monotonic over the full temperature range for which the device is rated and is capable of operation over a 32 dB range. The 85-ns settling time is possible provided that good layout practices and grounding techniques are followed. The DAC-08 is available in several different models that have different quality levels and temperature ranges. These are detailed in Table 13-1.

The basic circuit connections for positive unipolar operation are shown in Fig. 13-5. The power-supply connects shown here are deleted in most of the illustrations to follow, so pay attention here and then assume that these connections are made in the later circuits. The V− and V+ terminals are connected to the negative and positive dc power supplies, respectively. Each dc power supply terminal is bypassed to ground through a 0.1-μF disc capacitor, and these should be mounted close to the body of the DAC-08. The fast settling time of this DAC makes such layout practices somewhat more important than in slower devices. The compensation input is used to mold the ac frequency response properties of the circuit. In most TTL applications, this input is bypassed to the V-power supply through a 0.01-μF capacitor.

The reference inputs go to the inverting (−) and noninverting (+) inputs of an internal operational amplifier. In the positive quandrant operation shown, the reference current is applied to the noninverting input, and the inverting input is grounded through

Table 13-1. DAC-08 Models.

Model	Linearity (%)	Temp. Range (°C)
DAC-08AQ	± .1	− 55 to + 125
DAC-08Q	± .19	− 55 to + 125
DAC-08NQ	± .1	0 to + 70
DAC-08EQ	± .19	0 to + 70
DAC-08CQ	± .39	0 to + 70

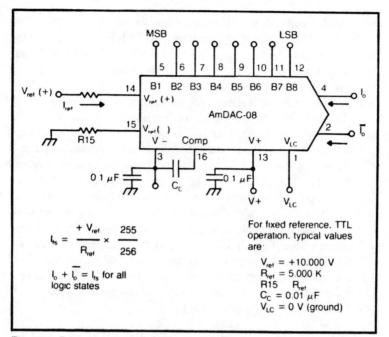

Fig. 13-5. Basic pin connections for the DAC-08.

resistor R15. In most cases, it is specified that R15 be made equal to R14, and that the value of R14 be used to set the level of the reference current:

$$I_{ref} = V_{ref}/R14$$

Resistor R14 is sometimes called R_{ref}. For TTL compatibility, set R14 and R15 to 5 K, C_c is 0.01 μF, and the reference voltage is 10.000 volts. This potential is usually derived from an REF-01 PMI reference IC.

One feature of this DAC makes it compatible with almost any logic protocols, regardless of whether it is standard (TTL, CMOS, etc.) or one of your own concoction. The threshold voltage terminal (V_{LC}) controls the voltage levels that will be recognized as high and low by the digital input terminals. When the power-supply voltages are maximum, the logic levels that will be recognized will be between −10 and +18 volts dc. The logic levels for different digital circuits are quite different. The TTL device, for example, wants to see a potential of less than 800 millivolts (the closer the zero, the better for low, and a potential greater than a certain threshold (1.4

211

volts to 2.4 volts, depending upon the spec sheet) for high. Similarly, the CMOS devices can operate with TTL levels, at which the low is zero and the high is greater than 2.5 volts. But CMOS can operate with negative voltages to −15 for low and positive potentials to +15 for high. Popular are ±7 and ±12 volts for the logic levels. The transition between the two states will be $(V_{DD}−V_{SS})/2$.

The DAC-08 can also be interfaced to some of the older, now obsolete logic levels. DTL and RTL used zero for low and 5.6 and 3.6 volts, respectively, for high. Some older instruments that predate IC technology are still in daily operation, especially in school laboratories. These devices might easily have home brew logic levels that are unique to one manufacturer. Common was −9 or −12 volts for low and +5 or +12 volts for high. Most commercial DAC ICs would not be capable of interfacing these instruments, as they are designed for TTL or CMOS (or, at best, limited to TTL and CMOS). But the V_{LC} terminals permit you to adjust the threshold value of the transition from high/low. The threshold voltage is controlled by the voltage applied to the V_{LC} terminal of the DAC-08, and is described by Equation 13-4.

$$V_{th} = V_{LC} + 1.4 \text{ volts} \qquad \textbf{13-4}$$

The threshold voltage is also expressed by

$$V_{th} = (V-) + 2.5 + (I_{ref} \times 1000 \text{ ohms}) \qquad \textbf{13-5}$$

For both equations, V_{LC} is the potential applied to pin 1 of the DAC-08, V_{th} is the logic threshold voltage, $V-$ is the negative power-supply potential, and I_{ref} is the reference current expressed in amperes.

Example. Calculate the threshold voltage for a 4-mA reference current and a −15-volt power-supply potential.

$$
\begin{aligned}
V_{th} &= (V-) + 2.5 + (I_{ref} \times 1000 \text{ ohms}) \\
&= (-15 \text{ V}) + 2.5 + (0.004 \text{ A} \times 1000 \text{ ohms}) \\
&= (-15 \text{ V}) + 2.5 + (4) \\
&= -8.5 \text{ volts}
\end{aligned}
$$

In this example, the logic transition point between high and low occurs at −8.5 volts. Next, let us calculate the voltage needed at pin 1 (V_{LC}) in order to realize this operation.

Example. Calculate the value of V_{LC} needed for the previous example in which

$$V_{th} = -8.5 \text{ volts}$$
$$V_{LC} = V_{th} - 1.4 \text{ volts}$$
$$= (-8.5 \text{ V}) - 1.4 \text{ volts} = -9.9 \text{ volts}$$

If this same example is worked for TTL, the 1.4-volt transition point of TTL requires you to make V_{LC} zero. In that case, ground pin 1. This same arrangement will work for the obsolete DTL circuitry.

The reference current input can be anything between 0.2 milliamperes and 4.0 milliamperes, but the manufacturer recommends 2 mA for TTL/DTL operation and 1 mA for compatibility with the high-speed ECL logic family. The inputs of the DAC-08 require only 2 μA of current, and will therefore load the digital outputs of the driving device very little.

The circuit shown in Fig. 13-5 was for positive operation. Negative reference operation can be accomplished with a negative voltage supply and reversal of the roles of the two inputs. In negative reference operation, connect R_{ref} to ground and R15 to the $-V_{ref}$ power supply.

The resistors used in the reference input should be low temperature coefficient precision types. Otherwise, large errors are likely to result due to ordinary temperature drift phenomenon.

We can trim the output current of the DAC-08 by varying the reference current. This is done by the balancing circuit of Fig. 13-6. A low-temperature coefficient, 4500-ohm resistor is connected between the noninverting reference input and the 10.00-volt power supply. The inverting input, however, is connected to a potentiometer wiper. The ends of the potentiometer are connected to the

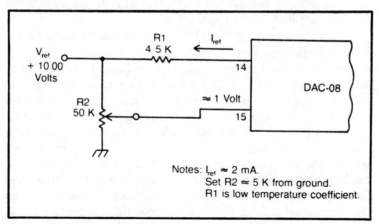

Fig. 13-6. Variable zero control.

10.000-volt supply and ground, respectively. The correct adjustment point will be when the resistance to ground seen by the inverting input of the DAC-08 is approximately 5000 ohms. This circuit can be used as a full-scale output adjustment.

Although not always strictly necessary, the manufacturer recommends that a slightly modified reference resistor circuit be adopted when there might be a noise problem. In those cases, split the total reference resistance into two portions and connect the two half-value resistors in series between the 10.00-volt supply and the DAC-08 input. A 0.1 μF bypass capacitor is then connected between the junction of the resistors and ground. Of course, both of the resistors should be low-temperature coefficient types of equal value.

It is necessary to keep the reference current as precise as possible. The output current is directly proportional to this current, so changes in the reference current will be directly reflected as output errors. The need for precision, low-temperature coefficient resistors in the reference circuit has already been mentioned. It is also necessary to mention that the reference voltage power supply is also subject to some specifications. Use only a reference-type power source for this voltage—never use the V− or V+ power-supply voltages. This last rule must be observed even when the V− and V+ voltages are regulated. The ordinary transients present on these lines from normal operation cannot be allowed into the reference current input of the DAC-08. Always use one of the precision sources shown earlier for the reference voltage used to create the current I_{ref}. The manufacturer of the DAC-08 also makes two different reference voltage ICs. Use the REF-01 for 10.000-volt supplies and REF-02 for 5.000 volts.

It is usually not sufficient to use a simple zener diode for the reference. Besides thermal drift, these diodes also exhibit large untrimmable errors in the actual output voltage. In addition, they can also produce an excessive noise component in the output. In fact, rf engineers sometimes use zener diodes in noise generator circuits of certain types of receiver and amplifier test equipment.

Thus far, only the primary mode of operation has been considered: current output. But many applications require voltage output operation. Thanks to Ohm's law, however, that operation can be provided with the DAC-08. The simplest method is to cause the output currents to flow through a resistance and use the voltage drop across the resistor as the output potential. Figure 13-7 shows the connections for unipolar negative operation. A 2-milliampere

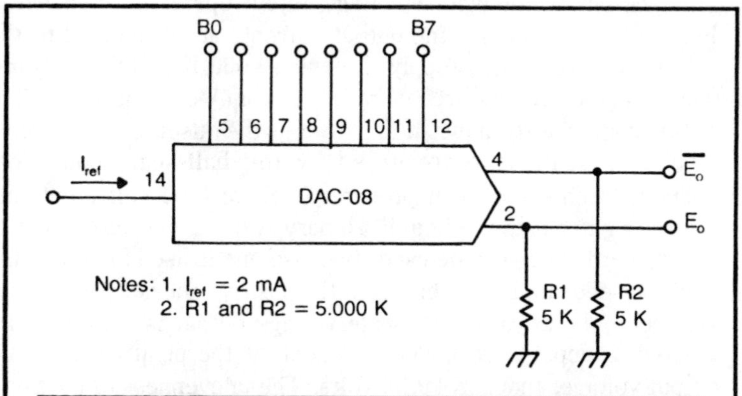

Fig. 13-7. High impedance voltage output for DAC-08.

	B1	B2	B3	B4	B5	B6	B7	B8	I_O mA	$\overline{I}_O$ mA	E_O	$\overline{E}_O$
FULL SCALE	1	1	1	1	1	1	1	1	1.992	.000	−9.960	.000
FULL SCALE −LSB	1	1	1	1	1	1	1	0	1.984	.008	−9.920	−.040
HALF SCALE +LSB	1	0	0	0	0	0	0	1	1.008	.984	−5.040	−4.920
HALF SCALE	1	0	0	0	0	0	0	0	1.000	.992	−5.000	−4.960
HALF SCALE −LSB	0	1	1	1	1	1	1	1	.992	1.000	−4.960	−5.000
ZERO SCALE +LSB	0	0	0	0	0	0	0	1	.008	1.984	−.040	−9.920
ZERO SCALE	0	0	0	0	0	0	0	0	.000	1.992	.000	−9.960

reference current is applied to the noninverting input of the DAC-08. This current can be generated with a 10.00 volt REF-01 and a 5000-ohm, precision, low-temperature coefficient resistor.

Both output currents are passed through pulldown resistors to ground. Both resistors have a 5000-ohm value. The full-scale output current will be 2 mA, and the output voltages can be calculated with Ohm's law.

$$E_o = I_o \times R$$
$$= (0.002)\,(5000)$$
$$= 10.000 \text{ volts}$$

The two output voltages are complementary to each other. This does not mean that one is positive while the other is negative; it means that both are negative. The difference is that one will be at full scale (−9.96 volts) when the other is zero, and vice versa. A chart of the output coding is shown in Fig. 13-7. This is the regular binary coding in which the zero condition ($E_o = 0$) is designated by 00000000. The full output is the maximum full-scale reference current less 1−LSB; i.e., −9.96 volts. For the 8-bit, 10-volt operation, the 1-LSB voltage is 40 mV, so the output is 10.000 − 0.040, or 9.96.

The circuit for bipolar voltage-output operation is shown in Fig. 13-8. In this case, the output currents are connected to the +10.00-volt reference supply through 10.000 K pullup resistors. The DAC-08 outputs are operating as 2-mA current sinks. The output coding, also shown in Fig. 13-8, is the offset binary scheme. The zero scale is represented by the half-scale condition, 10000000. This code will produce an E_o of 0.00 volts, but this creates a glitch in the coding. In a binary system, an even number of binary word states can be used. Because one is used for zero, this leaves an odd number to represent the positive and negative output voltages. The negative full-scale voltage output is −10.00 volts created by input code 00000000. Look at the positive full-scale output voltage, though: +9.92 volts. The unevenness of the positive and negative output voltages is a reflection of the decision to use one state to represent zero.

Note one other aspect to this code; the 1−LSB quanta are twice as high as in the unipolar case. The range is now twice as large for the same number of binary code states, so each increment must represent a voltage jump twice that in the unipolar circuit. Range is gained for resolution.

The decision as to the input code and output range is a matter of design in the system. If it is more important to correctly specify the

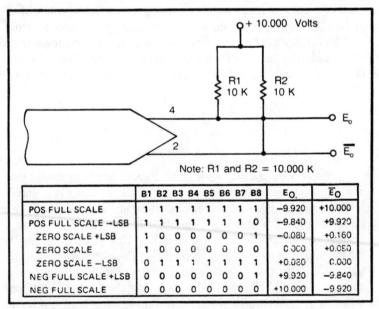

	B1	B2	B3	B4	B5	B6	B7	B8	E_O	$\overline{E}_O$
POS FULL SCALE	1	1	1	1	1	1	1	1	−9.920	+10.000
POS FULL SCALE −LSB	1	1	1	1	1	1	1	0	−9.840	+9.920
ZERO SCALE +LSB	1	0	0	0	0	0	0	1	−0.080	+0.160
ZERO SCALE	1	0	0	0	0	0	0	0	0.000	+0.080
ZERO SCALE −LSB	0	1	1	1	1	1	1	1	+0.080	0.000
NEG FULL SCALE +LSB	0	0	0	0	0	0	0	1	+9.920	−9.840
NEG FULL SCALE	0	0	0	0	0	0	0	0	+10.000	−9.920

Fig. 13-8. Offset zero voltage output.

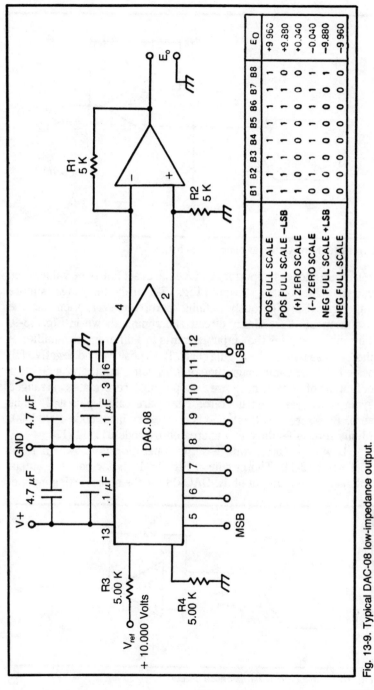

Fig. 13-9. Typical DAC-08 low-impedance output.

	B1 B2 B3 B4	B5 B6 B7 B8	E_O
POS FULL SCALE	1 1 1 1	1 1 1 1	+9.960
POS FULL SCALE −LSB	1 1 1 1	1 1 1 0	+9.880
(+) ZERO SCALE	1 0 0 0	0 0 0 0	+0.040
(−) ZERO SCALE	0 1 1 1	1 1 1 1	−0.040
NEG FULL SCALE +LSB	0 0 0 0	0 0 0 1	−9.880
NEG FULL SCALE	0 0 0 0	0 0 0 0	−9.960

217

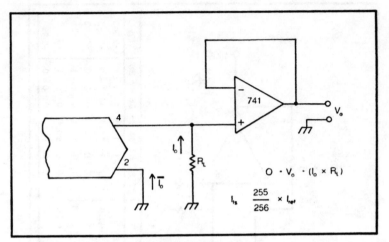

Fig. 13-10. Noninverting low-impedance output.

zero state and less important to have the exact full-scale value, then use the offset binary shown in Fig. 13-8. If the full range is more important than rigorously defining zero, however, then use the symmetrical offset binary circuit and coding shown in Fig. 13-9. This circuit applies the output currents to a differential amplifier of the 741 class. Note the coding chart. Both positive and negative full scale have the same magnitude of 9.96 volts, but there is no clear definition of zero. There are two possible zero states, arranged symmetrically about true zero. These are called plus and minus zero. Plus zero is +40mV and is created by input code 10000000. Minus zero is −40mV and is created by code 01111111.

Low-impedance voltage-output operation is shown in Figs. 13-10 and 13-11. The circuit in Fig. 13-10 is for positive output voltages. The I_o output of the DAC-08 and the noninverting input of

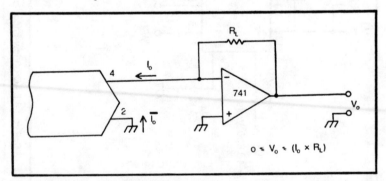

Fig. 13-11. Inverting low-impedance output.

218

the amplifier are grounded. The I_o output of the DAC-08 is connected directly to the inverting input of the DAC-08. Feedback resistor R_L provides any needed voltage gain. The maximum output voltage is given by Equation 13-6.

$$E_o = \frac{255 I_{ref} R_L}{256} \qquad \textbf{13-6}$$

Example. Calculate the maximum allowable output voltage from the circuit of Fig. 13-10 if the reference current is 2 mA and R_L is 10 K.

$$
\begin{aligned}
E_o &= (255 I_{ref} R_L / 256 \\
&= (\,(255)\,(0.002)\,(10,000)\,)\, /\, (256) \\
&= 5100/256 = 19.92 \text{ volts}
\end{aligned}
$$

The negative output operation of the DAC-08 is shown in Fig. 13-11. This circuit develops the output voltage by applying the current to a precision resistor. The voltage drop across this resistor is applied to the noninverting input of the unity gain 741 op amp follower. The 741, in this case, is used mostly for the impedance transformation available in the noninverting circuit.

Operation with pulsed and alternating current reference inputs is shown in Figs. 13-12 and 13-13, respectively. These circuits find use in cases where we want to control the amplitude of the output

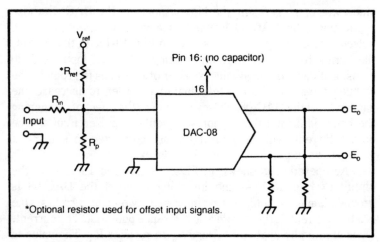

Fig. 13-12. Pulse operation.

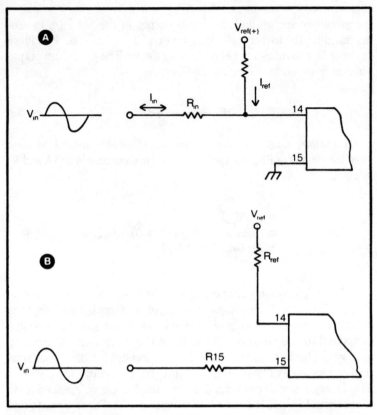

Fig. 13-13. Ac operation.

sine wave or pulse using the binary inputs of the DAC. In those applications the DAC-08 is used as a variable attenuator. The pulsed-reference operation is shown in Fig. 13-12. In this circuit, the series resistor to the noninverting reference input is 5000 ohms, and there is a low-value resistor of 200 ohms to ground. The compensation capacitor is eliminated in order to increase the bandwidth of the DAC-08. The capacitor has the effect of dampening the bandwidth, and that is not acceptable in pulse circuits. The output currents will be pulsed and are converted to equivalent voltages when passed through resistances.

Ac operation is shown in Figs. 13-13A and 13-13B. In the circuit of Fig. 13-13A, the inverting input of the DAC-08 is grounded, and the noninverting input sees two input currents. One is a bias current derived from a dc reference potential. The current, I_{in}, is created by applying voltage V_{in} to resistor R_{in}. The value of

R_{ref} (ohms)	Cc (pF)
1000	15
2500	37
5000	75
10,000	150

reference current I_{ref} must be greater than or at least equal to the greatest negative swing of I_{in}. The idea is to use I_{ref} to bias the DAC-08 input to some midpoint and then allow the actual DAC input current to vary around this quiescent value as the ac signal causes $\pm I_{in}$ to vary the total current into that junction.

The circuit in Fig. 13-13A suffers from low input impedance. The input impedance of the circuit can be increased by using the configuration of Fig. 13-13B. The same basic rules apply here, but refer to the voltage levels, $+V_{ref}$ must be greater than or at least equal to the greatest positive swing of V_{in}.

The slew rate of the DAC-08 must be considered when dealing with ac or pulse signals. We improve the situation in pulse circuits by deleting the compensation capacitor. Some proper combinations of reference resistor and compensation capacitor are listed in Table 13-2.

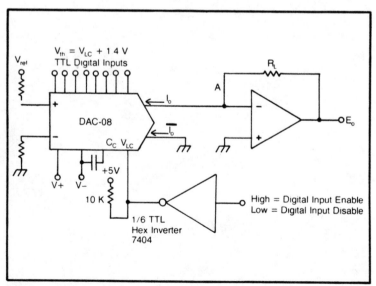

Fig. 13-14. Digital enable control.

221

The use of the 1000 ohm, 15 pF combination will give a maximum slew rate of approximately 16 mA/μs. The pulse circuit of the previous example, with no compensation, can handle rise times on the order of 500 nanoseconds.

The DAC-08 can also be strobed on and off under control of some external digital circuit. Just use the V_{LC} terminal (pin 1) of the DAC-08 and a 7404 TTL inverter circuit. A pullup resistor is tied between the inverter output and +5 volts. When the input to the inverter is high, the output is low, and this causes the DAC-08 input to be grounded. Under the normal rules for using the DAC-09 in TTL circuits, this will turn on the device. When the inverter is low, the V_{LC} terminal of the DAC-08 is high. This places V_{LC} at 5 volts, so no TTL pulse will become high enough to turn on the DAC-08 (see Fig. 13-14).

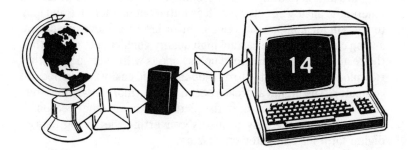

Microcomputer Compatible ADC Circuits

The analog-to-digital converter (ADC) produces an n-bit binary word that is proportional to an applied voltage or current. Although there are several coding schemes, a useful example is obtained by examining the so-called *straight binary*, unipolar case. The input range could be, say, 0 to +10 volts (actually +9.96 volts). For an 8-bit ADC, permissible codes are 00000000_2 (00H) to 11111111_2 (FFH). Thus, we can configure our ADC to represent 0 volts with 00H, and +9.96 volts with FFH.

In this chapter, we are going to examine several popular ADC circuits that are specifically designed or adopted to microcomputer applications. Be aware that this field moves so rapidly that the reader is advised to check current manufacturer catalogs when actually making a selection. These devices will work nicely, but may not be best suited to your application at the time.

APPLICATION

The analog-to-digital converter is used to reduce analog data, such as voltage and current levels, to binary words that represent the value of the analog signal. The binary word can then be used in the computer to process the information provided by the analog instrumentation in a manner much simpler to handle. In general, it is usually preferable to handle data reduction chores in software rather than in analog circuits. The analog circuitry tends to have sufficient cummulative errors that overshadow the inherent quantizing errors of the digital format. Temperature drift, for example, can be terrible in many analog circuits.

In addition to temperature problems, there are other problems inherent in analog circuitry, such as initial out of tolerance and long term drift of component values. In order to achieve precision, analog circuits require certain high quality components. Even then the results are not guaranteed unless one is willing to spend rather ridiculous sums of money to do a job that could easily be handled in a computer. The digital approach becomes even more appealing when there is a digital computer in the picture for some other reason. It then becomes very easy to justify converting the analog data to digital form for computer processing.

Another side of the coin, not valid only a few years ago, is that microprocessor chips are becoming so inexpensive that it is almost worthwhile to begin the project with digital circuitry in mind. In medical/physiological instrumentation, for example, analog circuits were once the only method available. Now even relatively mundane instruments are turning up microprocessor-based for no other reason than economics: It's cheaper to do the job in software. Other instruments have become either more useful, or possible for the first time because of the microprocessor.

Bit Length

The correct application of an ADC depends a lot upon knowing the problem that has to be solved. Although this sounds trivial, it is very common to find ADCs overspeced or underspeced. If the ADC is overspeced, then the price of the unit outruns any possible advantage, while if it is underspeced the product will not work well or at all. You cannot become too enamoured of bit length. Bit length costs money. It is easy to obtain low-cost 8-bit, and even 10-bit, ADCs. Soon, it may be a lot less costly to obtain precision 12-bit devices.

But does that extra bit length pay off relative to its cost? The answer can be seen by analogy to the handheld digital calculator. My Sharp calculator packs 12 digits of answer into a thinline case that fits behind my checkbook. But do I need 12 digits? If I calculate an answer to 12 digits, is it precise? No, of course not. Suppose I divide 10 volts by 3 amperes. The answer, according to my calculator is 3.33333333333 ohms. But is this correct? I only know the voltage to ±5 percent, and the current to ±10 percent. Using any more than 3.3, or even 3+, is ridiculous, because the data that went into the calculation was not precise.

In all of instrumentation, we must concern ourselves with the matter of significant figures. Adding bit length does not do anything to add precision if the analog signal applied to the ADC is not well defined. Assume that the transducer used to acquire the data is accurate to 5 percent (0.05). The data converter needs to be better than the accuracy of the transducer by one order of magnitude, but any more ADC precision is wasted. You would then try to locate an ADC with a bit length that provides 0.005 percent accuracy. This is 50 ppm. An 8-bit data converter would provide 0.4 percent (0.004) and would be sufficient and less costly than the 10-bit or 12-bit versions.

But there is another side of the resolution coin. You must have sufficient resolution for the job. If an application requires more than the level of accuracy than can be obtained with a given bit length, then an ADC with a greater bit length is needed. An 8-bit ADC simply cannot do the job of a 10-bit or 13-bit device.

ADC Speed

Another area where ADCs tend to be overspeced is in the matter of conversion speed. It is awfully appealing to look at a data sheet and then specify a 1-μs ADC. Slower ADCs don't seem quite so decent. But consider the nature of the application. In many cases, the data interval may be in terms of dozens of milliseconds, seconds, or even days. In this respect, you must be cognizant of these factors.

Consider, for example, the data conversion rates required in a certain medical research problem. The investigator was measuring arterial blood pressure, ECG (from which heart rate is derived), respiration rate, and the rectal temperature of a dog undergoing anesthesia for surgery. The natures of these signals are quite different. The arterial blood pressure waveform, for example, contains components up to 30 Hz, and the ECG of up to 100 Hz. The respiration is a slow semisinusoid occurring at rates between 10 and 100 times per minute. The frequency components, then, are on the order of 0.1 minutes. In addition, the accuracy of the temperature must only be to 0.1° C (36.8° C).

Clearly, these signals can be processed with higher order ADCs, but in most cases, the speed would be wasted. A 40-millisecond dual-slope integrator would not seriously affect the accuracy of the respiration or temperature signals. But measuring the arterial blood pressure would require a total conversion time of (60 conversions per second, following the twice-frequency rule) less than 17 milliseconds. When you try to accurately score an ECG waveform, the frequency spectrum is 0.05 to 100 Hz, so you must sample at 200 times per second, requiring a data conversion speed of less than 5 milliseconds.

There are two aspects to the speed problem that must be considered. One is the actual conversion speed; i.e., the time required to make a conversion. This is expressed in the T_c figure in some cases, but it might also be part of the aperture time. This leads us to the second aspect of the problem: inter-sample time. We may want to sample a fast-changing signal only intermittently. In that case, the aperture time of the ADC becomes important. You would not want the ADC to see a signal at its input that changed too much during the measurement. This is dealt with by using a very fast conversion time or holding the analog input signal sample in a sample-and-hold circuit.

Once you have selected the factors which are important to your application, then you are ready to select an ADC for your task. The rest of this chapter is dedicated to our practical examples, of which, several are provided.

8-BIT BINARY ADC

The circuit for a complete 8-bit binary ramp (servo) ADC is shown in Fig. 14-1, and a typical conversion timing diagram is shown in Fig. 14-2. This circuit is based upon the Ferranti Semiconductor ZN425E digital-to-analog converter integrated circuit.

The Ferranti ZN425E is almost unique among DAC ICs in that it contains a complete binary counter along with the voltage-output R-2R DAC circuitry. Pin 2 on the ZN425 device is the counter select. If this pin is held high, the counter is connected to the input switches to the R-2R ladder. The state of the counter is output on the DAC input lines. But if pin 2 is low, the digital word applied to the eight input lines will drive the R-2R ladder, and the counter outputs are disconnected. In Fig. 14-1, pin 2 is permanently tied high through a 1 K pullup resistor, so the counter is connected to the B1 and B8 pinouts and the DAC input lines.

The ZN425E contains its own built-in +2.5-volt precision reference voltage source, which is brought outside of the package via pin 16. The V_{ref} input (pin 15) is also brought outside of the package and can be connected either to the internal reference or to some external reference source. In the circuit shown, the internal reference is being used, so these two pins are shorted together. A 0.22 μF reference capacitor (C1) is connected between the reference and ground.

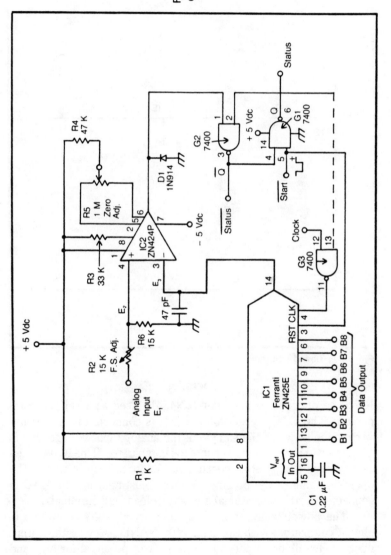

Fig. 14-1. ZN-425E A/D converter.

227

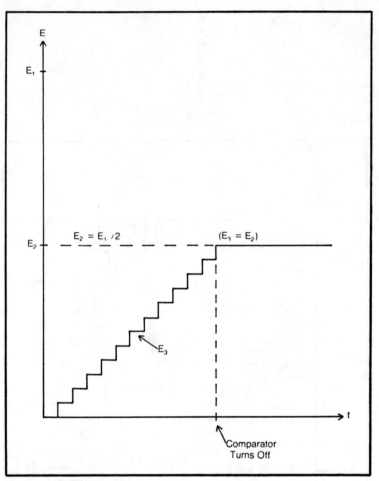

Fig. 14-2. Timing diagram.

Operation

IC2 is an operational amplifier (ZN424P) used as a voltage comparator. The DAC output voltage (E_3 is connected to the noninverting input, while the sample of the analog input voltage (E_2) is connected to the inverting input of the comparator. This IC operates as a voltage comparator, because no feedback loop is around the open-loop gain of the op amp. A zero adjustment for the DAC is connected to the operational amplifier offset null terminals.

The power source for the op amp is ±5 volts dc, which is almost compatible with the TTL 7400 NAND gate and the output drives. This device wants to see a +5 volt potential for high and zero volts for low. However, it is possible for the output of the comparator to swing negative under some circumstances with disastrous results for the 7400! To prevent negative excursions of the 7400 input, it is necessary to clamp the output of the comparator with D1 (1N914). The maximum negative voltage will be the pn junction drop of this diode, which is about 0.6 to 0.7 volts. In the situation where the comparator output is positive, the diode is then reverse biased and therefore becomes inert.

A full-scale adjustment is provided through the use of voltage divider R2/R6. Resistor R2 is a potentiometer that will allow adjustment of E_2 to any fraction of analog input voltage E_1. Voltage E_2, then, is a fractional sample of E_1.

Three sections of a 7400 quad NAND gates are used in this ADC circuit. Gates G1 and G2 form an RS flip-flop. Gate G3 is the main gate and controls the clock circuit. When pin 13 of the 7400 is low, pin 11 is jammed high (no clock pulses can pass through G3). When pin 13 is high, however, the output will follow the clock impulses. This admits pulses into the clock terminal (pin. 4) of the ZN425E.

The set input of the RS flip-flop is pin 5. When an active-low start pulse is applied to this input, the RS flip-flop goes into the set condition in which Q is high and $\overline{Q}$ is low. The Q output is used as a status line, while the $\overline{Q}$ is a not-status line (i.e., active-low). During the time when the converter is making its conversion, the status line will be high. Because this line is the control signal to the main gate, the gate is opened and the clock pulses enter the DACs internal counter. The counter had been reset to zero by the start pulse.

Opening the main gate causes the binary counter in increment, and this in turn causes DAC output voltage E_3 to ramp upward in a staircase fashion (Fig. 14-2). As long as E_3 is less than E_2 (the sample of the analog input voltage), the comparator output is high. It will remain in this condition until the counter has incremented the DAC output enough to make $E_2 = E_3$. At that instant, the output of the comparator drops low, and this applies a reset pulse to the input of the RS flip-flop (pin 1 of the 7400). The RS flip-flop immediately goes to the condition in which Q is low and $\overline{Q}$ is high, shutting off the flow of clock pulses to the counter.

The state of the counter, which appears on the B1 through B8 lines, reflects the value of the analog input voltage applied (E_1). The count remains on these outputs because no new reset pulse has been issued.

The speed of this circuit is limited by the operational amplifier used as a voltage comparator. If the ZN424P is used, then the speed is 100 kHz or less. Replacing this operational amplifier with either a higher frequency operational amplifier or a high-speed IC comparator will result in operation up to 250 kHz.

The conversion time of this circuit depends upon the clock frequency. For a full-scale conversion, the value of T_c is:

$$t_c = \frac{256}{f} \qquad\qquad \textbf{12-1}$$

The conversion time, t_c, is in seconds, and f, the frequency of the clock, is in hertz.

Example: Calculate the conversion time, T_c, if the clock frequency is 150 kHz.

$$
\begin{aligned}
t_c &= 256/f \\
&= 256/(1.5 \times 10^5 \text{ Hz}) \\
&= 1.71 \times 10^{-3} \text{ seconds} = 1.71 \text{ milliseconds}
\end{aligned}
$$

The outside world needs to know when the output data is valid. During the active conversion period, the output lines (B1 through B8) will have a continuously changing binary number which is valid only when the incrementing of the counter ceases. The status and not-status lines can be used for this purpose. If an external device, such as a computer, is used, it can interrogate these lines. It would, for example, not accept any data from the ADC when it finds that the status line is high or the not-status line is low.

Alignment

Two adjustments are permitted in this circuit: *zero adjust* and *full-scale adjust*. The best accuracy is obtained when the input voltage is known to four decimal places of resolution using a 4½-digit or better voltmeter or a precision reference source with output resolution to 100 microvolts. The procedure is as follows:

1. Apply a continuous train of clock pulses to the ADC circuit.

2. Apply an analog input potential equal to the full-scale potential, less 1.5-LSB. In this case, the full-scale input voltage is 4.00 volts. The 1-LSB voltage of the circuit, then, is 4.00 V/256, or 15.63 mV. 1.5-LSB then is 23.45 mV. The applied input voltage then is (4.00 − 0.02345)V, or 3.9765 volts.

3. Adjust potentiometer R2 until all bits except the LSB are high (i.e., the output is 11111110), and the LSB bobbles back and forth between high and low.

4. Apply a voltage equal to the ½-LSB potential (7.82 mV) to the analog input.

5. Adjust potentiometer R5 (zero adjust) until all bits are low—except the LSB (00000001)—and the LSB is bobbling back and forth between high and low.

6. Repeat all adjustments until no further improvement is possible. Most simple ADC circuits have full-scale and zero adjustments that are somewhat interactive.

The full-scale input voltage can be changed by varying the resistor voltage divider between the analog input and the noninverting input of the operational amplifier.

This type of circuit can be implemented using any of several different DAC/comparator combinations. In the case of DACs other than the ZN425E, however, an external 8-bit binary counter must be connected to the DAC inputs. A pair of 7493 TTL counter chips (each four bits) connected in cascade should provide this counter. Also, in the case of a current output DAC (PMI DAC-08 or Motorola MC1408), it will be necessary to either operate the comparator in the current mode or convert the DAC output to a voltage.

Figure 14-3 shows the case where the current output, I_o, from the DAC is converted to an equivalent voltage, E_1. The voltage is created by passing the output current through a precision resistor ($E_1 = I_o R$). The amplifier is connected in the unity gain, noninverting follower configuration, so $E_o = E_1 = I_o R$.

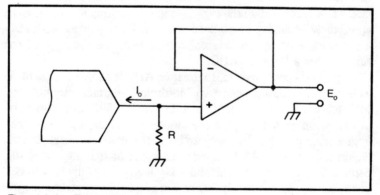

Fig. 14-3. I-to-E conversion.

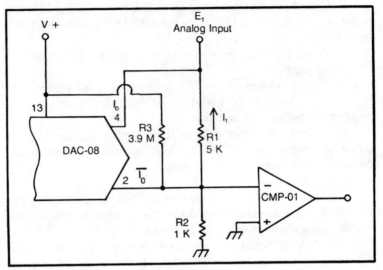

Fig. 14-4. Improved input impedance circuit.

The alternative case would be to operate the comparator in the current mode. In the circuit of Fig. 14-4, the noninverting input of a PMI CMP-01 comparator is grounded, placing the inverting input at virtual ground. The output current I_o from the DAC is applied to the inverting input. Also applied to this input current I_1, which is proportional to the analog input voltage E_1. The value of this current is $E_1/R=E_1/5000$ ohms. When $I_o=I_1$, the output of the comparator drops low.

8-BIT SUCCESSIVE APPROXIMATION ADC

Several manufacturers offer successive approximation (SA) IC registers that contain all of the logic needed to implement a successive approximation analog-to-digital converter. When wedded with a DC and (in some cases) an external comparator, the SA register (or SAR) yields a low-cost ADC.

An 8-bit successive approximation ADC is shown in Fig. 14-5. This circuit is based upon two Motorola integrated circuits, the MC1408 current-output DAC and the MCI14559B successive approximation register. For the hobby or small-scale science-engineering lab, this SA seems to be a little easier to obtain in unit quantities than the AMD device. This circuit operates from the commonly available −15-volt and +5-volt dc power-supply voltages and requires approximately 200 mW of power. The conversion rate is 2 microseconds per bit.

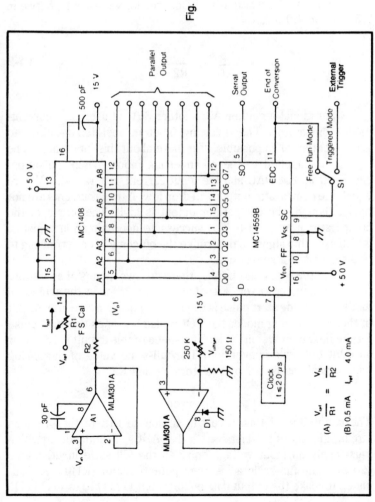

Fig. 14-5. MC-14559 SAR A/D converter.

233

Operation

As in the two previous cases, the DAC used in this circuit is a current output type. Current I_o is proportional to the reference current ($I_{ref} = V_{ref}/R1$) and the binary word applied to the digital inputs. These inputs are connected to the latched register output lines and become the ADC output lines once the data conversion is completed.

The analog input signal is applied through a unity gain, noninverting follower. The operational amplifier selection for this purpose was chosen because it has faster slew rate and shorter settling time than the 741 class of device someone might be tempted to use.

The following relationship holds true for values of I_{ref} between 0.5 mA and 4.0 mA:

$$\frac{V_{ref}}{R1} = \frac{V_{in(fs)}}{R2} \qquad \textbf{14-2}$$

Operational amplifier A2, another 301, is used as a current-mode comparator. The inverting input is operated as close to ground potential as possible. But more about this input later. The signals are applied to the noninverting input. When the output current from the DAC and the input current generated by V_{in} are equal, the comparator output will drop low. If these currents are not equal, though, the comparator output is high. The output of the comparator is applied to the successive approximation register, which uses this signal to determine the outcome of each trial and to find the end of a conversion.

As in the previous circuits, there are two modes of operation. In this circuit, however, a switch selects them. In the triggered mode, an outside start pulse is required to initiate a conversion. But in the free-running mode, the EOC pulse becomes the start pulse for the next conversion cycle. The speed of this circuit is 18 μs for an 8-bit full-scale conversion. The full-scale value of the analog input signal can be set by resistors R1 and R2.

Alignment

The calibration of this circuit is similar to that of the previous circuits; in fact, it is adaptable to other ADCs of similar design. You must apply an input voltage equal to the full-scale input, minus ½-LSB. The full-scale adjustment potentiometer (R1) is then adjusted to make the output data bobble from 11111110 to 11111111.

Next, a ½-LSB signal is applied to the input, and the zero offset potentiometer is adjusted for an output data bobble of 00000000 to 00000001. Again, make these adjustments several times until no further improvement is possible.

The zero adjust circuit in Fig. 14-5 allows the comparator bias point to be shifted slightly to account for minor differences from the ideal performance. It will also permit us to overcome the hysteresis present in all comparators, allowing more precise triggering when the two currents applied to the noninverting input of A2 are canceled out, indicating equality of the two currents.

FERRANTI ZN432

Figures 14-6 and 14-7 show the Ferranti Semiconductors type ZN432-series A/D converter chips. This device is packaged in a 28-pin DIP format. It will operate from ±5 volt dc power supplies and will provide 20-microsecond conversion times. Available are 8-, 9-, and 10-bit accuracies. The ZN432 is compatible with both TTL and CMOS logic.

The device is a successive approximation ADC circuit. It contains an internal SA register, a DAC, comparator, reference power supply, and reference amplifier. Figure 14-6 shows the block diagram of the internal circuitry.

An example circuit is shown in Fig. 14-7. The reference amplifier must be connected to the reference power supply through

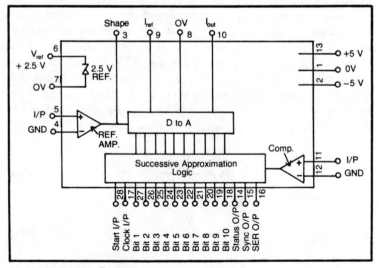

Fig. 14-6. ZN-432 (Ferranti).

235

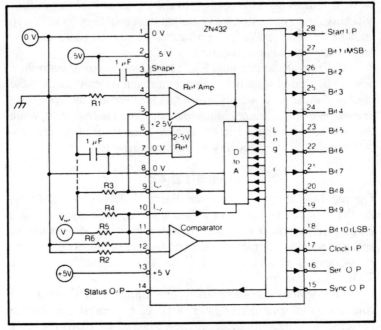

Fig. 14-7. Circuit connections for the ZN-432.

external connection. Although this method of applying the reference requires external connections, it makes the IC more versatile by allowing external reference sources to be used.

Resistors R3 and R5 must be of high quality to allow gain and offset stability. R1 and R2 are used to compensate for the amplifier input bias currents. It is necessary, therefore, that R1 = R2 and these be equal to the parallel combination of R3, R4, and R5. This is standard operational amplifier practice. The reference current is 0.5 mA, so the value of resistor R3 is $V_{ref}/0.005$ A. Current I_{out} is four times the reference current. The values of the other two resistors are given by Equations 12-3 and 12-4.

$$R4 = \frac{-V_{ref}R5}{V_{in(min)}} \qquad \textbf{12-3}$$

$$R5 = \frac{V_{in(max)} - V_{in(min)}}{I_{o(fs)}} \qquad \textbf{12-4}$$

V_{ref} is the reference voltage, $V_{in(min)}$ is the analog input voltage to make output code 00000000, $V_{in(max)}$ is the analog voltage required to make output code 11111111, and $I_{o(fs)}$ is the full-scale output current.

The calibration of this circuit is pretty much the same as in the previous case. Place an input voltage on the analog terminal that is 1½-LSB less than the maximum input voltage.

INTERSIL ICL7109

Figure 14-8 shows the Intersil ICL7109 12-bit binary output A/D converter specifically designed for interfacing with microprocessor circuits. This circuit offers 12-bit binary, with polarity and over-range bits. It uses the noise immune dual-slope integration technique. This device will permit as many as 30 conversions per second.

Timing is supported by an on-chip internal oscillator that can be connected with an RC network that sets the clock frequency. It is also possible to use a standard 3.58-MHz crystal (standard because it is the color subcarrier crystal oscillator frequency from television receivers). This device will permit as many as 30 conversions per second.

Timing is supported by an on-chip internal oscillator that can be connected with an RC network that sets the clock frequency. It is also possible to use a standard 3.58-MHz crystal (standard because it is the color subcarrier crystal oscillator frequency from television

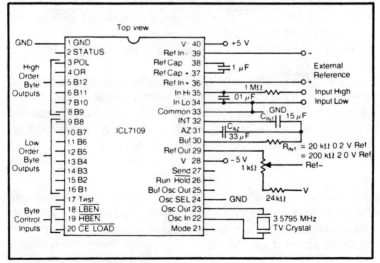

Fig. 14-8. ICL-7109 A/D Converter.

receivers). This arrangement allows seven to eight conversions per second and is less susceptible to 60-Hz interference.

One thing that makes this converter microprocessor compatible is that it has TTL, three-state data outputs. This is a necessary feature, regardless of whether I/O or memory-mapped organization is selected. If the ADC did not have three state outputs, it could not be connected directly to the data bus, or it would load the bus down. A low condition on one of the data bits would effectively short out that data line, even when the ADC is not being addressed. But in the ICL7109, the outputs are three-state. This means that the third state, which allows the outputs to float across the data bus, creates a high impedance to both the +5-volt supply and ground. Normal TTL outputs are a low impedance to +5 volts in the high condition and a low impedance to ground in the low condition.

There are two basic sections to the ICL7109 device: analog and digital. The digital section contains a conversion control logic section, oscillator/clock circuit and handshake logic (LBEN, HBEN, and CE/LOAD). There are also a 12-bit binary counter, 14 latches, and 14 three-state outputs (12 for the output data bits, with one each for polarity and overrange).

LBEN. This is the low-byte enable terminal. If the mode pin (21) is low and the CE/LOAD pin (20) is low, then making this pin low will activate the low order byte (B1 through B8). If the mode pin is high, the HBEN pin serves as a flag output bit for handshaking with the computer.

HBEN. This pin is the high-byte version of the LBEN pin. If this pin and the CE/LOAD pin are low, then making HBEN low will activate bits B9 through B12 and the polarity and overrange bits. With a high on the mode pin, this pin will become the high-byte handshake output.

CE/LOAD. This is the chip-enable/load pin. If the mode pin is held low, then the CE/LOAD is the master output enable. It turns on the three-state outputs. If this pin is high, then the 12 output bits, overrange bit, and polarity bit are three-stated. If the mode is high, this pin is the load strobe for handshake operations.

Analog Section

The analog section uses three operation phases: auto-zero, signal integrate, and de-integrate (or reference integrate). The auto-zero phase initializes the circuit. The two analog inputs are disconnected from the pins and are then shorted to the analog common ground.

Next, the reference capacitor is charged to the reference voltage. Finally, a feedback loop is closed that will charge the auto-zero capacitor. This will compensate for the normal offset voltages in the buffer amplifier, integrator, and voltage comparator. The offset can be nulled to 10 μV.

The signal integration phase causes the input of the integrator to be connected to the analog input signal for a fixed time period. Exactly 2048 clock pulses are occupied by the signal integrate phase of operation. The polarity of the input signal is determined in this phase of operation and this sets the polarity bit.

The reference integrate phase is the second slope of the conversion cycle. In this phase, the charge in the integrator capacitor is discharged by applying a reference signal to the input of the integrator. The polarity of the reference is selected to de-integrate the charge. The rate of the de-integration is fixed by the reference voltage value, so the time required to make the integrator charge zero again is determined by the level of the charge. This level is, in turn, set by the value of the analog input signal. The timer period occupied by the de-integrated phase is then directly proportional to the analog value applied to the ADC. The time is measured by the binary counter, which supplies the digital output to the computer through the three-state section.

Digital Section

The digital section contains the 12-bit counter, 14 output latches, and 14 three-state TTL outputs. It sends four signals to the analog section, namely auto-zero, integrate, and de-integrate (plus/minus). The particular de-integrate signal that is used will depend upon the polarity of the integrator voltage at the end of the signal integration period. The analog section will return the comparator output to the digital section. The inputs to the digital section that are available to the outside world are compatible with several logic families, as defined in the ICL7109 spec sheet. But for TTL compatibility, use a 3 to 5 K pullup resistor.

Mode Input. This terminal is used to select direct output or UART modes. When the mode input is held low, the ICL7109 is in the direct mode. The output data is then directly controlled by the chip-enable and byte-enable pins. When the mode input is high, the converter is placed in the UART mode. This mode allows handshaking with the outside world and will output the data in two independent bytes. If the mode input is pulsed high, this transfer occurs once, and then the chip returns to the direct mode. But if the mode is held high, the ADC will output data at the end of each conversion cycle.

The mode input is considered low when left open, in distinct contrast with other chips. The ICL7109 contains an internal pull-down resistor that will set the input low on open.

Status Output. The status output tells the outside world when the new data is available on the output latches. This terminal will go high when the ADC enters the signal integrate phase and will remain high until after the new data is stored in the output latches. The time period required for this is roughly one-half clock period after the end of the de-integrate period.

The status output is used to signal interrupts to the microprocessor, or to strobe data into some other digital circuit. The conditions are high for conversion in progress and low for conversion completed.

Run/Hold. The run/hold controls the conversion cycle. If this input is left high, the converter will continuously cycle; it performs a new conversion as soon as the old conversion is completed. The conversions will each require 8192 clock periods. Bringing the run/hold low causes the ADC to become dormant. If the converter is in the middle of a conversion, then the conversion is completed, and new data is stored in the output latches. The ADC then jumps to the auto-zero mode and stays there until the run/hold goes high again.

Direct and Handshake Modes. The direct mode allows ordinary parallel output operation of the data converter. When the mode control is left low, the outputs remain under control of the chip-enable and byte-control bits. In the handshake mode, the ICL7109 can be connected directly to the industry standard UART (universal *asynchronous* receiver-transmitter) chips. The ADC sends the CE/LOAD signal to the UART and receives back SEND, RUN/HOLD and MODE signals.

ANALOG DEVICES AD7570

The Analog Devices model AD7570 is a 10-bit monolithic sive approximation analog-to-digital converter. The internal circuitry (Fig. 14-9) contains the 10-bit DAC, successive approximation register/control logic and the three-state output logic. The use of three-state outputs permits direct interface with microprocessor buses. One feature of this circuit makes it more useful than some

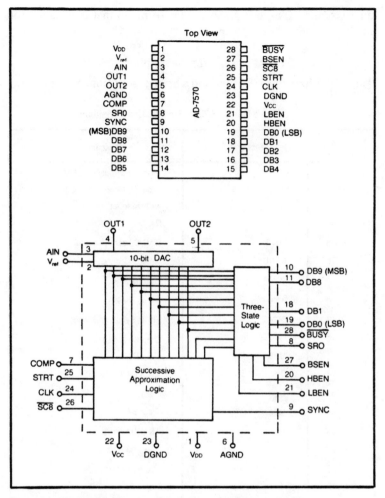

Fig. 14-9. AD-7570 A/D converter pinouts and internal circuitry.

others: there are two enable controls. One of them will control the two MSBs, while the other controls the lower eight bits. This arrangement allows it to be interfaced directly with eight-bit microprocessor data buses.

The AD7570 is capable of serial output. The serial output (SRO) is used in conjunction with the serial synchronization line to output data. The internal sync clock will operate as high as 600 kHz or can be driven externally. The frequency of the internal clock is set by an external RC time constant. At a 600-kHz clock rate, and AD7570 can perform an eight-bit conversion in approximately 20 microseconds. There is a short-cycle terminal that is used to stop the conversion after eight bits.

Pin Function Description

Table 14-1 lists the 7570 pins and a brief description. Several of the

Table 14-1. AD7570 Pin Function Definitions.

Pin	Mnemonic	Function
1	VDD	Positive Supply (+ 15 V)
2	Vref	Voltage Reference (± 10 V)
3	AIN	Analog Input
4	OUT1	DAC Current Output 1
5	OUT2	DAC Current Output 2
6	AGND	Analog Ground
7	COMP	Comparator
8	SRO	Serial Output
9	SYNC	Serial Synchronization
10	DB9	Data Bit 9 (MSB)
11	DB8	Data Bit 8
12	DB7	Data Bit 7
13	DB6	Data Bit 6
14	DB5	Data Bit 5
15	DB4	Data Bit 4
16	DB3	Data Bit 3
17	DB2	Data Bit 2
18	DB1	Data Bit 1
19	DB0	Data Bit 0 (LSB)
20	HBEN	High Byte Enable
21	LBEN	Low Byte Enable
22	VCC	Logic Supply (+ 5 V to + 15 V)
23	DGND	Digital Ground
24	CLK	Clock
25	STRT	Start
26	SC8	Short Cycle 8 Bits
27	BSEN	Busy Enable
28	BUSY	Busy

key pin functions are discussed in the following text.

Convert Start (pin 25-STRT). When the start input goes to logical 1, the MSB data latch is set to logic 1 and all other data latches are set to logic 0. When the start input returns low, the conversion sequence begins. The start command must remain high for at least 500 nanoseconds. If a start command is reinitiated during conversion, the conversion sequence starts over.

High-Byte-Enable (pin 20-HBEN). This is a three-state enable for bit 9 (MSB) and bit 8. When the control is low, the output data lines for bits 9 and 8 are floating. When the control is high, digital data from the latches appears on the data lines.

Low-Byte-Enable (pin 21-LBEN). Same as high-byte-enable pin, but it controls bits 0 (LSB) through 7.

Busy Enable (pin 27-BSEN). This is an interrogation input which requests the status of the converter; i.e., conversion in process or conversion complete. The converter status is addressed by applying a logic 1 to the busy enable.

Short Cycle 8 Bits (pin 26-SC8). With a logic 0 input, the conversion stops after 8 bits reducing the conversion time by 2 clock periods. This control should be exercised for proper operation of the version. When a logic 1 is applied, a complete 10-bit conversion takes place (L version).

Clock (pin 24-CLK). With an external RC connected, as shown in Fig. 14-10, clock activity begins upon receipt of a Convert-Start command to the A/D and ceases upon completion of conversion. An external clock (CMOS or TTL/DTL levels) can directly drive the clock terminals, if required. If V_{CC} is <4.75 V, the internal CLK will not operate.

V_{DD} (pin 1). V_{DD} is the positive supply for all analog circuitry plus some digital logic circuits that are not part of the TTL compatible input/output lines (back-gates to the p-channel devices). Nominal supply voltage is +15 V.

V_{CC} (pin 22). V_{CC} is the logic power supply. If +5 V is used, all control inputs/outputs (with the exception of comparator terminal) are DTL/TTL compatible. If +15 V is applied, control inputs/outputs are CMOS compatible.

Fig. 14-10. Input filtering.

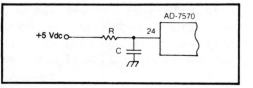

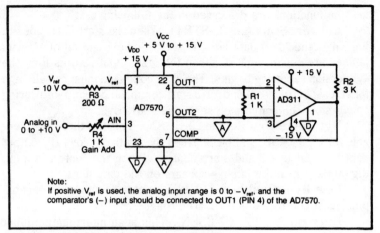

Fig. 14-11. Unipolar operation of the AD7570.

Busy (pin 28-BUSY). The busy line indicates whether conversion is complete or in process. Busy is a three-state output and floats until the busy-enable line is addressed with a logic 1. When addressed busy will indicate either a 1 (conversion complete) or a 0 (conversion in process).

Serial Output (pin 8-SRO). Provides output data in serial format. Data is available only during conversion. When the A/D is not converting, the serial output line floats. The serial sync (see next function) must be used along with the serial output terminal to avoid misinterpreting data.

Serial Synchronization (pin 9-SYNC). Provides 10 positive edges which are synchronized to the serial output pin. Serial sync is floating if conversion is not taking place. Note that all digital inputs/outputs are TTL/DT1 compatible when Vcc is +5 V, and CMOS compatible when Vcc is +15 V.

Operation

Figure 14-11 shows the circuit needed for unipolar operation. In the particular configuration shown, the circuit will operate over the range 0 to +10 volts. If the input is always positive, the reference potential must then be negative. Similarly, if the input range is negative, the reference must then be positive. It will also be necessary in the negative-input version to reverse the connections to the voltage comparator (AD311). The digital data and control lines are not shown in Fig. 14-11 and must be inferred.

The range of the ADC input can be changed by varying the reference voltage input. In the case shown, it is −10 volts, so the input range is zero to +10 volts. Reference voltages in the 1-volt to 10-volt range are useful, following the polarity rules given above.

Unipolar Alignment. The calibration procedure for this device is similar to the usual calibration procedure for this category of devices.

1. Apply a continuous start command to the STRT input of the AD7570.

2. Apply an analog to potentiometer R4 (or use the reference voltage) until the LSB bobbles back and forth between high and low. This can be seen on the SRO terminal.

The circuit in Fig. 14-12 shows what is needed to offer bipolar conversion with the AD7570. This circuit uses a resistor voltage divider (in this case, a monolithic IC containing four 20 K resistors), the AD1805LH/20 K by Analog Devices. The 741 operational amplifier is used in the inverting follower configuration. A current applied to the inverting input from the reference potential biases the amplifier to a midpoint. The analog input signal will then modulate this fixed point, causing the 741 output to vary up and down from the quiescent point in response to the +10-volt analog input signal.

Bipolar Alignment. The following is the calibration procedure for this device:

1. Apply continuous start command to the STRT terminal of the AD7570.

2. Apply an analog input voltage equal to 1½-LSB less than full-scale ($V_{fs} = V_{ref}$) to the bipolar input of the AD7570.

3. Adjust gain potentiometer for the LSB bobble between high and low. This can be seen on the SRO terminal.

The output codes for the AD7570 are shown in Tables 14-2 and 14-3. Both unipolar and bipolar versions are shown. The unipolar circuit uses straight binary in which the zero input voltage creates an output code of 0000000000. This means that the maximum allowable input signal will be 1-LSB less than the reference voltage (i.e., 9.96 volts in an eight-bit device).

The bipolar code is the offset binary, which means that the zero input voltage condition is represented by the code, 1000000000.

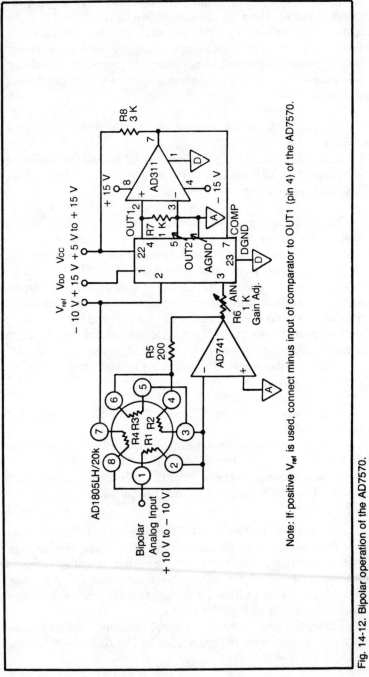

Fig. 14-12. Bipolar operation of the AD7570.

Note: If positive V_{ref} is used, connect minus input of comparator to OUT1 (pin 4) of the AD7570.

Table 14-2. Output Coding for Unipolar Operation.

Analog Input (AIN) Notes 1, 2, 3	Digital Output Code MSB									LSB
FS - 1LSB	1	1	1	1	1	1	1	1	1	1
FS - 2LSB	1	1	1	1	1	1	1	1	1	0
3/4 FS	1	1	0	0	0	0	0	0	0	0
1/2 FS + 1LSB	1	0	0	0	0	0	0	0	0	1
1/2 FS	1	0	0	0	0	0	0	0	0	0
1/2 FS - 1LSB	0	1	1	1	1	1	1	1	1	1
1/4 FS	0	1	0	0	0	0	0	0	0	0
1LSB	0	0	0	0	0	0	0	0	0	1
0	0	0	0	0	0	0	0	0	0	0

NOTES:
1. Analog inputs shown are nominal center values of code.
2. "FS" is full scale, i.e., $(-V_{ref})$.
3. For 8-bit operation, 1LSB equals $(-V_{ref}) (2^{-8})$; for 10-bit operation, 1 LSB equals $(-V_{ref}) (2^{-10})$.

The +1-LSB voltage is then 1000000001, and the −1-LSB is 0111111111. The code of $+V_{fs}$ (FS-1LSB) is 1111111111, while that for $-V_{fs}$ is 0000000000.

HYBRID ADCs

Monolithic circuits are true ICs. Hybrid circuits are built along slightly different lines and may include ICs (in chip, rather than packaged, form) along with discrete components such as resistors

Table 14-3. Output Coding for Bipolar Operation.

Analog Input (AIN) Notes 1, 2, 3	Digital Output Code MSB									LSB
+(FS - 1LSB)	1	1	1	1	1	1	1	1	1	1
+(FS - 2LSB)	1	1	1	1	1	1	1	1	1	0
+(1/2 FS)	1	1	0	0	0	0	0	0	0	0
+(1LSB)	1	0	0	0	0	0	0	0	0	1
0	1	0	0	0	0	0	0	0	0	0
−(1LSB)	0	1	1	1	1	1	1	1	1	1
−(1/2 FS)	0	1	0	0	0	0	0	0	0	0
−(FS - 1LSB)	0	0	0	0	0	0	0	0	0	1
−FS	0	0	0	0	0	0	0	0	0	0

NOTES:
1. Analog inputs shown are nominal center values of code.
2. "FS" is full scale; i.e., (V_{ref}).
3. For 8-bit operation, 1LSB equals $(-V_{ref}) (2^{-7})$; for 10-bit operation, 1LSB equals $(-V_{ref}) (2^{-9})$.

and capacitors. But the components will not look like those you are familiar with from ordinary discrete component electronic construction. They will be thick film, chip form and are microcircuits in their own right. We discussed some of these devices in Chapter 1.

Also in this class, for purposes here, are analog function modules. Some function modules are hybrid devices, while others are made from individual discrete components.

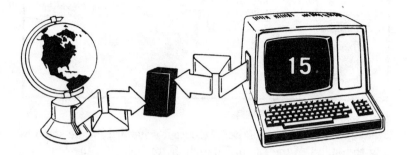

Interfacing to Microcomputers

Before the data converter can be used in practical situations, it must be interfaced to a microcomputer or microprocessor. In this chapter, we will discuss both DAC and ADC interface problems. We will consider both the case where an I/O port is available and when no port is to be found (pun!).

DAC INTERFACING

The DAC will provide an output voltage or current that is proportional to a reference voltage/current and an applied input binary word generated by the computer.

External Circuitry

Figure 15-1 shows the block diagram of a digital-to-analog conversion scheme connected to a computer. This circuit might use any of the interface techniques that will be discussed later in the chapter, so we will show the DAC's digital input as merely data from the computer. The DAC might be either a current output type or a voltage output type. If the circuit is voltage output, then this scheme can be used unmodified.

A low-pass filter is needed at the output of the DAC to smooth the step function ramp output. Recall that the output of any DAC is a staircase waveform in which each step is the 1-LSB voltage of the DAC, but the outside world will want to see a smoothly rising output ramp. The low-pass filter is selected to pass the low-

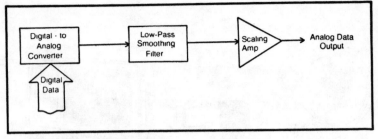

Fig. 15-1. Typical DAC interface

frequency components of the DAC output waveform, while smoothing the stairs of the ramp. The cutoff frequency of the low-pass filter is selected according to the rule given in an earlier chapter regarding the highest frequency component of the waveform.

In general, you can set the cutoff frequency to some value between the highest Fourier component of the output waveform, and twice that frequency. Some latitude is given here because you might want to use a predesigned filter circuit that has a cutoff frequency a little different from the one specified. In general, though, try to set the cutoff frequency as close to the upper passband limit, as decreed by the highest Fourier component of the desired output waveform.

You may also provide an output amplifier. In some circuits this will be a scaling amplifier, while in others it will be a unity gain output, buffer amplifier. The amplifier is built from operational amplifiers, as these are the easiest to implement. Since most DACs require a bipolar power supply of their own, it is no hardship to use the op amp. Sometimes, if all the other circuits use a monopolar supply, it is simpler to use a discrete amplifier so that the dual power supply demanded by the op amp is avoided. The voltage gain of the output amplifier is expressed by Equation 15-1 and 15-2.

$$A_v = \frac{\text{Desired Output Scaling Factor}}{\text{DAC Output Scaling Factor}} \qquad \textbf{15-1}$$

$$A_v = \frac{\text{Desired } E_{fs}}{\text{DAC } E_{fs}} \qquad \textbf{15-2}$$

The scaling factor is the 1-LSB voltage of the DAC/output. *Examples.* Calculate the scaling amplifier gain necessary to make an output scaling factor of 40 mV/LSB if the DAC output is 2 mV/LSB.

$$A_v = \text{Desired scale factor/DAC scale factor}$$
$$= (40 \text{ mV/LSB})/(2 \text{ mV/LSB})$$
$$= 40/2 = 20$$

Calculate the scaling amplifier gain if the desired output is 10.00 volts and the maximum DAC output voltage is 1.26 volts.

$$A_v = \text{Desired } E_{fs}/\text{DAC } E_{fs}$$
$$= 10.00 \text{ V}/1.26 \text{ V}$$
$$= 10/1.26 = 7.94$$

Either inverting or noninverting amplifiers can be used for the output stage. The selection choice will depend upon the required polarity and the polarity of the DAC output circuit.

Some DACs that are in common use are current output devices. The output terminal is a high impedance, generally looking back into a high-impedance R-2R ladder and bank of current sources. But most external devices and circuits that you will drive with a DAC are voltage input devices. Some means must be provided that will convert DAC output current to a voltage. Figures 15-2 and 15-3 show how this can be accomplished. The circuit in Fig. 15-2 uses an inverting follower amplifier, based on an operational amplifier circuit. Current I_o is the DAC output current, and resistor R_f is the feedback resistor in the op amp circuit. The output voltage is calculated by Equation 15-3.

$$E_o = I_o R_f \qquad \qquad \textbf{15-3}$$

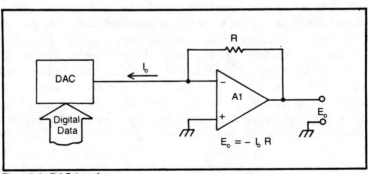

Fig. 15-2. DAC interface.

251

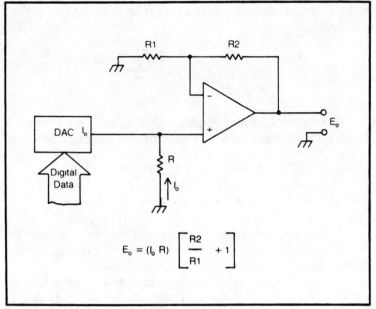

Fig. 15-3. Noninverting DAC interface.

E_o is the output potential in volts, I_o is the DAC output current (which could be − or + in polarity), and R_f is the feedback resistor.

Example. Calculate output voltage E_o in the circuit of Fig. 15-2 if the feedback resistor is 10 K and the maximum output current of the DAC is 1 milliampere.

$$\begin{aligned}
E_o &= -I_o R_f \\
&= -(0.001 \text{ A})(10^4 \text{ ohms}) \\
&= -10 \text{ volts}
\end{aligned}$$

The noninverting amplifier can also be used for this application, but a resistor must be provided to ground to sink the current from the DAC output. This circuit is shown in Fig. 15-3. The operational amplifier is connected in either the unity gain, noninverting follower or noninverting follower with gain circuits. Current I_o passes through resistor R to ground, creating voltage E at the noninverting input of the operational amplifier. The output voltage for a unity gain output amplifier is given by Equation 15-4 and for a noninverting gain output amplifier in Equation 15-5.

$$E_o = \pm I_o R \qquad\qquad \textbf{15-4}$$

$$E_o = E\left(\frac{R2}{R1} + 1\right)$$

15-5

$$E_o = I_o R\left(\frac{R2}{R1} + 1\right)$$

DAC Computer Outputs

Digital-to-analog converters can be interfaced to microcomputer/ microprocessor devices in either of two ways: I/O-port or memory-mapping. If the computer is equipped with latched output ports with the same bit length as the DAC then interfacing is almost childishly easy. It is merely necessary to secure the right parallel format connectors and connect the computer output port lines to the DAC input terminals. In order to avoid confusion, keep the bit format the same; i.e., B0 on the computer connected to B0 on the DAC, etc.

An example of I/O-port interfacing is shown in Fig. 15-4. This technique presupposes two factors: the computer output port has at least as many bits as the DAC and the output port is latched. In other words, the data appearing on the output port is stable, except during updating by the computer. Some single-board computers have unlatched output ports, which means that the DAC has to grab the data as it goes by.

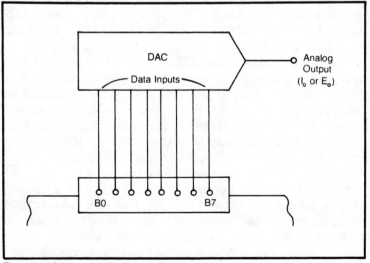

Fig. 15-4. Connecting DAC to parallel output port.

The other technique, memory-mapping, treats the DAC as if it were a location in memory. This has the advantage in some microprocessors of allowing you to use some of the memory-to-memory or register-to-memory instructions that bypass the accumulator.

DAC Select Pulses

When dealing with memory-mapped systems or unlatched I/O situations, it might be necessary to generate select pulses that tell the DAC when the data appearing at its input is valid. Since in a typical eight-bit microcomputer there is a 16-bit address bus and an eight-bit data bus, it is possible that you will be asked to discriminate between 256 different I/O port addresses, or 65,536 different memory locations, only one of which in each case is the correct address!

When discussing the device select, or I/O-memory address decoder circuits if you prefer, Z-80 microcomputer terminology will be used for the examples. If you want to use one of the other microprocessor chips, then study the chip manual and determine which signals are similar to the Z-80 signals described here. If you have a ready-built microcomputer, then determine if there are I/O pulses, or memory read/write, pulses already available on the bus.

Z-80 Signals

The Zilog Z-80 microprocessor integrated circuit is a computer central processing unit (CPU) that uses an eight-bit data bus (B0 through B7) and a 16-bit address bus (A0 through A15). The address bus also carries the I/O port addresses when an appropriate I/O instruction is being executed. In that case, the lower eight bits (A0 through A7) of the address bus contain the I/O port address (000 through 256). There are separate read and write signals (RD and WR) that are active low. In other words, when data is being read from memory or an I/O port then the $\overline{RD}$ output terminal drops low.

These signals are used for both memory and I/O operations and are designated from the CPU point of view. In other words, a data transfer from the accumulator to memory is a write, so the $\overline{WR}$ would drop low. If data is being transferred from a memory location to the accumulator, then the operation is classified as a read (from the CPU point of view), so the $\overline{RD}$ is active. In I/O operations, an input is a read, and an output operation is a write.

There are two additional signals used in conjunction with read/write signals that differentiate between memory operations and I/O operations. The $\overline{\text{MREQ}}$ is a memory request and is active whenever a memory read or write is taking place. In other words, if a memory read operation is commanded, then both $\overline{\text{MREQ}}$ and $\overline{\text{RD}}$ will be low. The I/O operation is indicated by an $\overline{\text{IORQ}}$ (input/output request) signal going low. So, if the operation is an input operation, then the $\overline{\text{IORQ}}$ and $\overline{\text{RD}}$ lines from the Z-80 go low. These designations will be used in the sections to follow for purposes of explaining the circuitry.

Address Decoders

All of the addresses that we will use are contained on the address bus. The memory addresses can occupy the entire 16 bits of the bus, while I/O addresses will always occupy the lower eight bits of the bus. We need circuits that will determine when the required address is present. Since the DAC will be placed at only one I/O port or memory location, we will need only those bits of the address bus that uniquely determine that address. In some microcomputers, which have less than the full complement of memory, we can sometimes get away with using one-bit, or up to four-bit address decoders. If the computer has less than 32 K of memory, a memory-mapped data converter could be located somewhere in the upper 32 K.

If the selected location is on a boundary, then fewer bits are needed to specify it. For example, the unique address 1000000000000000 addresses location $32,768_{10}$, the boundary between the upper and lower 32 K of memory. In this case, if you are positive that no other upper 32 locations would be needed, you can use bit A15 of the address bus as a device select pulse for the DAC, with no additional circuitry.

Figure 15-5 shows how this can be accomplished. The DAC is not connected directly to the data bus, but is buffered by an eight-bit latch. Although the microcomputer manufacturers also offer several good data latches uniquely applicable to their own products, the standard 74100 device from the TTL logic family will work fine. The 74100 is a dual quad-latch. It contains two banks of type-D flip-flops. The D-inputs are the data inputs connected to the eight-bit data bus, and the Q outputs of the 74100 are connected to the DAC inputs. The clock line, usually designated strobe input when dealing with latch ICs, is connected to bit A15. Since this is a dual quad-latch, it is necessary to strap the strobe lines from the two 74100 sections together, forming a strobe line for the entire device. Bit A15 will go high only when an address is in the upper 32 K. By using the

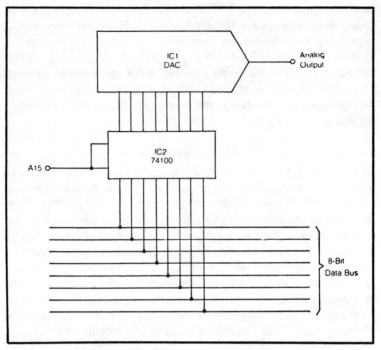

Fig. 15-5. Interfacing DAC directly to data bus.

boundary address of 32,768, you can use only one bit to select the data converter. When A15 goes high, the data on the data bus is transferred to the outputs of the 74100. This data will remain latched on the DAC input when A15 goes low again. This circuit can be used only when no other address in the upper 32 K is being used. If other addresses in that range are selected, then the DAC output will be changed every time an upper 32 K address is called for by the CPU.

The solution to this problem is to place the DAC at a boundary in which only one of the top four to eight bits are active, or to make a 16-bit address decoder. In the four-bit and eight-bit examples to follow, the input bits are specified A0 through A7, indicating the lower eight bits (as would be needed if an I/O port is addressed). But these same circuits are useful in the high range of memory if only the bit designations are translated.

Table 15-1 is the 4 K boundaries in the upper 32 K. You can generate tables for 8 K boundaries using only the upper three bits of the address bus, or 1 K boundaries if the upper six bits of the address bus are used. Such might be desirable if only 1 K of onboard

RAM/ROM are used in the computer; a likelihood if small single board computers are used.

Two-Bit to Four-Bit Decoder Circuits. The simplest decoder circuit is the simple NAND gate. In the TTL line, we find the 7400 (two input), 7410 (three input) and 7420 (four input) devices. These can be connected to the correct address line bits to form an active-low output that indicates when the correct address is being called for. Recall the rules of operation for a NAND gate: if any input is low, then the output is high; and it requires all inputs high to make the output low. All of the boundaries called for in Table 15-1 can be selected with 1, 2, 3, or 5 bits high.

Say, for example, that you want to locate the DAC at memory location $49,152_{10}$ (the 48 K boundary). According to Table 15-1, bits A14 and A15 will be high at this address. If there are no higher addresses, then you can use a 7400 NAND gate to decode the address. This device has two inputs. One each is connected to A14 and A15, respectively. The output of the 7400 will drop low only when the correct address is on the address bus, provided that you are careful to not use any address higher than the specified address (note in Table 15-1 that several other combinations result in A14 and A15 high).

The 7420 TTL device is a four-input NAND gate. If the 60 K boundary address is selected, then the inputs will be 1111 at the boundary address. Of course, these bits are high for the 60 K through 64 K addresses. Also, be sure to not address anything in that range.

How can you generate four-bit addresses that are unique? Whether you place the addresses in the upper 32 K or in the lower 256 locations (as in the I/O sectors shown in figures to follow), you can use the same four-bit decoders. Figure 15-6 shows a circuit based on the 7420 NAND gate. The NAND gate wants to see all

Table 15-1. Address Boundaries.

Boundary	Decimal Address	A15	A14	A13	A12
32 k	32768	1	0	0	0
36 k	36964	1	0	0	1
40 k	40960	1	0	1	0
44 k	45056	1	0	1	1
48 k	49152	1	1	0	0
52 k	53248	1	1	0	1
56 k	57344	1	1	1	0
60 k	61440	1	1	1	1

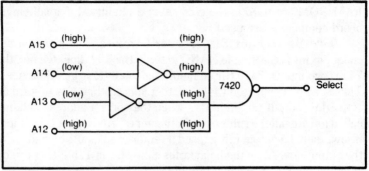

Fig. 15-6. Typical 4-bit address decoder.

inputs high before it will produce a low output. If you want an address other than the 60 K boundary, then you must fool the 7420 into thinking an input is a one when it is actually a zero. This is done in Fig. 15-6 using inverters. In this example, specify address 36964—the 36 K boundary. You can do this by noting from Table 15-1 that the correct address is 1001 (A15 = 1, A14 = 0, A13 = 0, and A12 = 1). This means that you must connect the A15 and A12 inputs of the NAND gate directly to the address bus and invert the A13 and A14 address bus inputs. The only address in this range that will turn on these bits (1001) is 36964_{10}.

This same circuit is useful for specifying the I/O port number 9

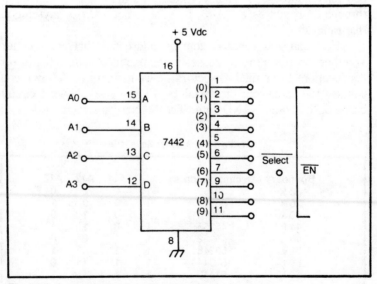

Fig. 15-7. Active-low 7442 address decoder.

$(1001_2 = 9_{10})$. The A0 and A3 inputs are connected directly to the NAND inputs, while A1 and A2 are connected through the inverters.

There are other TTL chips that can be used to make a four-bit decoder. The 7442, 7485 and 74154 devices are examples. The use of a 7442 is shown in Fig. 15-7. This IC is a BCD-to-1-of-10 decoder. A four-bit (BCD) input will cause one of 10 possible output lines to drop low. If, for example, the binary number 1001 is applied, indicating decimal 9, then output number 9 of the 7442 (pin 11) will drop low. You can then use the 7442 to select any of 10 different devices, any of which could be a DAC or ADC circuit. The inputs to the 7442 are weighted in the binary fashion: A=1, B=2, C=4, and D=8.

If you want to select up to 16 channels of data conversion or 16 other devices then a 74154 binary-to-1-of-16 decoder is used, as shown in Fig. 15-8. This 24-pin DIP IC is similar to the 7442 in

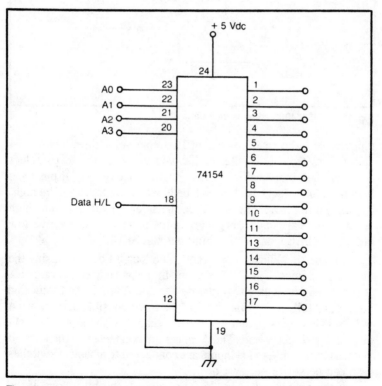

Fig. 15-8. Active-low/active-high four-bit address decoder will select 16 different banks.

259

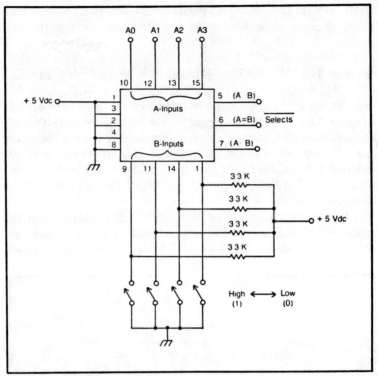

Fig. 15-9. 7485/4083 address decoder.

function, but allows 16 instead of 10 output selections. The 74154 also differs from the 7442 in that you can use pin 18 to select whether the output will be active- high or active-low. If pin 18 is low, then the selected output will be low and all others will be high. If, on the other hand, pin 18 is high, the selected output will be high and all others are low. It is generally the practice to call active-low outputs $\overline{\text{SELECT}}$ and active-high outputs SELECT.

Figure 15-9 shows a programmable four-bit decoder using the 7485 TTL device. The 7485 is a four-bit magnitude comparator IC. It examines two four-bit words, designated A and B, and issues an output that tells their relationship. The three possible outputs are A = B, A is less than B, and A is greater than B. Use the A=B output as a device selector line. The A inputs are connected to the four-bit address line, while the B inputs are connected to a bank of switches than can be set to either 1 or 0.

If the switches in Fig. 15-9 are closed, the bit is low. If the switches are open, the bit is high. The address desired can be selected by setting the switches. Of course, if you want to hard wire the address, it is merely necessary to either ground the proper input for a low or connect it to +5 volts (through a pullup resistor of 1 K to 4 K) for a high. The only time the A=B output (pin 6) goes high will be when the address present at the A inputs is the same as the address programmed onto the B inputs.

Eight-Bit Decoder Circuits. Figures 15-10 through 15-12 show three ways to make an eight-bit decoder. The circuit in Fig. 15-10 uses two four-bit, active-low decoders, such as were shown in Figs. 15-7 and 15-8. The NOR gate will produce a high output only when both inputs are low. We can therefore use one input to sense the output of one four-bit decoder on the low-order half-byte of the bus, and the other to sense the output of the decoder on the high-order half-byte. Each decoder will decode either a BCD (7442) or hexadecimal (74154) half-byte. For example, consider a circuit that will decode address 10010110. The high-order half-byte is 1001 (9_{10}), while the low-order half-byte is 0110 (6_{10}). If you connect the inputs of the NOR gate to the 9 output of the high-order decoder, and the 6 output of the low-order decoder, only address 1001 0110 will turn on the output. A high will indicate the SELECT condition.

If you use the 7485 chips, they can be cascaded to form a single output line (Fig. 15-11) that goes high only when the high-order and low-order half-bytes on the address lines contain the same binary number that is programmed into the respective 7485 device. The cascade inputs of the high-order byte are connected to the outputs of

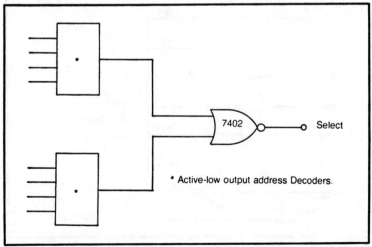

Fig. 15-10. Banking address decoders to cope with higher order address lengths.

261

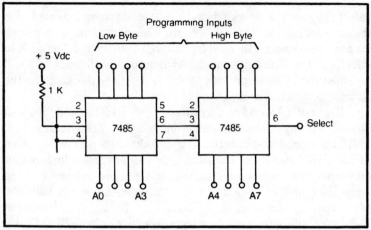

Fig. 15-11. Cascaded 7485 decoders.

the low-order 7485. The A=B cascade input of the low-order 7485 is connected high, and the other two cascade inputs are made low.

You can use the 7430 eight-input NAND gate to make a decoder similar to the one shown in Fig. 15-6 (the four-bit version). This circuit is shown in Fig. 15-12. Once again, we connect the address lines that will be high when the correct address is present directly to a 7430 input. The lines that will be low in the address are first inverted and then are connected to the 7430 inputs. The decoder in Fig. 15-12 is set for address 10010111.

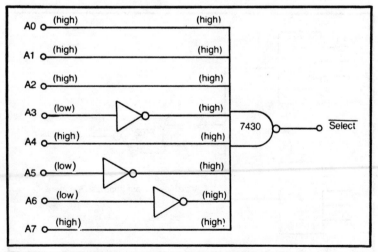

Fig. 15-12. Eight-bit address decoder based on 7430 device.

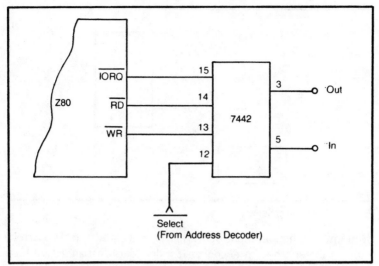

Fig. 15-13. 7442 used to generate in and out signals.

Device-Select Pulses

In either I/O or memory operations with the Z-80, it takes three or four pulses to determine memory/I/O-RD/WR status. It is not sufficient to simply know that the correct address is present on the address bus. You must also know whether it is a memory operation, I/O operation, or whether it is a read or write. The circuits discussed in this section will use the output of the address decoders of the previous section and the CPU control signals to generate the actual device select pulse.

The circuit in Fig. 15-13 shows the use of a 7442 for this purpose. The $\overline{\text{IORQ}}$, $\overline{\text{RD}}$ and $\overline{\text{WR}}$ outputs of the Z-80 are connected to the A, B, and C inputs of the 7442, respectively. The $\overline{\text{SELECT}}$ output of an address decoder circuit is applied to the D input of the 7442. The D input will then be low only when the correct address is present on the bus. This circuit responds to the binary codes shown in Table 15-2. The only time the 4 output of the 7442 is caused to

Table 15-2. Binary Equivalent Addresses.

Operation	Binary Code	Decimal Code	Op-signal
Input	0100	4_{10}	In
Output	0010	2_{10}	Out

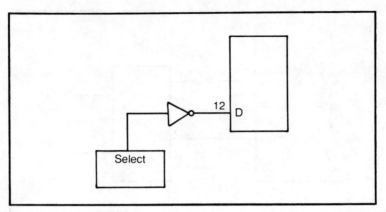

Fig. 15-14. Inverting Select.

drop low is when an input operation is requested and the correct address is seen by the decoder. If a decoder with an active-high SELECT pulse is used, then an inverter must be placed in the D-line to the 7442 (Fig. 15-14). If this circuit is to be used for a memory operation, then connect the A input of the 7442 to $\overline{\text{MREQ}}$ instead of $\overline{\text{IORQ}}$.

Figure 15-15 shows a circuit based on the 74154 that will allow you to generate both memory and I/O control signals. One feature of the 74154 device is a chip enable, active-low, input. The $\overline{\text{MREQ}}$, $\overline{\text{IORQ}}$, $\overline{\text{WR}}$ and $\overline{\text{RD}}$ signals from the Z-80 are applied to the binary inputs of the 74154, as shown in the figure. The $\overline{\text{CE}}$ line is connected

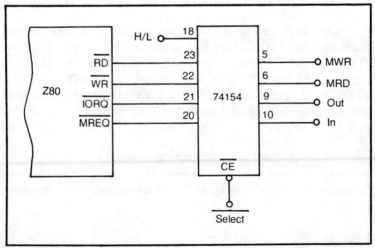

Fig. 15-15. System signals generation (In, Out, MWR and MRD).

264

Table 15-3. Binary Equivalent Addresses.

Operation	Binary Code	Decimal Code	Op-Signal
Input	1010	10_{10}	In
Output	1001	9_{10}	Out
Memory Read	0110	6_{10}	MRD
Memory Write	0101	5_{10}	MWR

to the $\overline{\text{SELECT}}$ output of the decoder. The 74154 will not become active unless this line goes low. If pin 19 is low, then the outputs will follow the binary word applied to the ABCD inputs. The output code is shown in Table 15-3. You can select whether the output op-signal is active-high or active-low by applying a high or low (respectively) to pin 18 of the 74154.

DAC Output

You now have several address decoder circuits and several device select circuits. How do you connect them to the DAC in order to effect an output? Remember that there are two techniques: I/O-port and memory mapping. Both can use the circuit of Fig. 15-5, an output latch of the 74100 type (or one of the special circuits). Instead of the A15 bit being used for turning on the *strobe* line, you would use one of the outputs of the select circuit. If you want to make an I/O-port based circuit, then the address decoder is connected to the lower eight bits of the address bus, and the OUT signal from either Fig. 15-13 or 15-15 is connected to the strobe line. In both cases, the inputs to the data latch are connected to the eight-bit data bus. If you want memory mapping, then you must use the MWR output of the select circuit. The address decoder will have to be connected to the address bus bits that will select the correct address. In most cases, this will be a boundary address.

Greater than Eight-Bit DACs

The circuit shown in Fig. 15-16 will allow you to transfer up to 16 bits to a DAC. In the circuit as shown, a 10-bit DAC is connected to the output ports of a computer. Two latched output ports are needed here. We have arbitrarily designated the ports as 4 and 5. We will output the lower eight bits of the 10-bit word through port 4, which becomes latched with the correct value. Next, the upper bits (in this case, 2) are output through port 5. Now that both output ports are active, data is transferred to the DAC. At this point, we could have used another port to provide the strobe for the latches. However, if we sacrifice the MSB of port 5, then we can arbitrarily set MSB high and the lower bits to the level required for the desired DAC word. If that is done, then the data is strobed into the 74100s during the port 5 output operation.

The circuit in Fig. 15-17 also shows how to interface a greater-than-eight-bit DAC to a microprocessor. The eight-bit data bus must be used twice, once to output the low order eight bits, and a second time to output bits B8 through B15. Only 10 bits are shown here, so only bits B0 and B1 are used in the second output operation. Three I/O or memory mapping decoders are needed. Latch A is an eight-bit 74100, and latch B is a four-bit 7475 latch. On the first output operation, eight bits are loaded into the 74100 (latch A). On the second go around, two more bits are loaded into the four-bit 7475 (latch B). When both latches are loaded, a third output operation is performed, and decoder C is addressed. This loads the outputs of A and B into latches C1 and C2. The outputs of C1 and C2 are applied directly to the DAC inputs. If this circuit is to be extended beyond 12 bits, a second 74100 latch will then be used in place of the 7475 shown.

ADC INTERFACING

Earlier in this chapter, interfacing digital-to-analog converters (DACs) with microprocessors and microcomputers was discussed.

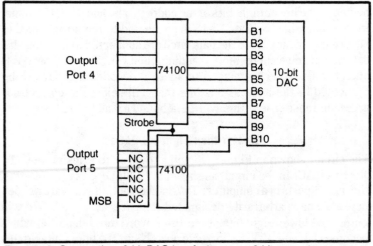

Fig. 15-16. Greater than 8-bit DAC interfacing to an 8-bit computer.

266

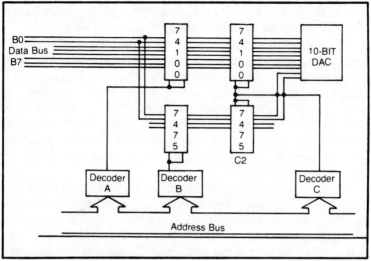

Fig. 15-17. Double-buffered DAC interface.

Two basic techniques are known, I/O-port and memory-mapping. Additionally, an address decoder and a select pulse circuit are needed before interfacing is possible. When interfacing ADCs, the same techniques are used. ADCs can be memory-mapped or treated as input ports. The same reasoning holds true for DACs, but the data flows in the opposite direction.

Three-State Logic

The output of an analog-to-digital converter must be applied to the data bus of the computer. This bus must be used at times when the ADC is not active, however, and the ADC must be connected to the bus in a manner that will not load down the bus at inappropriate times. The key is the three-state output logic device. In digital electronics, the output level is either high (a low resistance to the =5 volt line) or low (a low impedance to ground). There is a third state available on some devices that is a high impedance to both the +5 volt power line and ground. In those devices, when the outputs are three-stated, the outputs float at a high impedance that is neither high nor low.

Several devices are available that offer three-state outputs. In the TTL line, for example, there is the 74125 device. This is a quad, noninverting buffer (also known as the DM8093). Specialized devices offered by microprocessor manufacturers can be used in conjunction with their own products. Intel offers the 8212 device and the 8216. The 8212 is an eight-bit, three-state, bidirectional I/O chip, while the 8216 is a four-bit three-state buffer.

Figure 15-18 shows an interface using the 74125/DM8093 three-state buffer. Because each can handle only four bits, it is necessary to use two of the devices. The 74125 has one $\overline{CE}$ (active-low chip enable) line for each buffer. This means that you must bring all four lines, from both chips, to a common line that becomes the enable line for the input port. When this line goes low, data on the inputs of the 74125 is transferred to the outputs. The outputs are connected to the eight-bit data bus. A similar circuit can be built using the 8216 device.

Another circuit is shown in Fig. 15-19. This circuit uses Intel's 8212 I/O buffer chip. This device is a specialized chip that is intended for use as a bidirectional I/O port. Again, a $\overline{CE}$ (active-low chip enable) is used to turn on the chip. The input side is connected to the eight-bit output of the ADC, while the outputs are connected to the data bus.

Either of these circuits can be used in either I/O or memory-mapped applications. Of course, the proper address decoding and select pulse generators are required. When the correct set of circumstances exists, the chip enable pulse is generated.

Start and EOC Pulses

An ADC has a start pulse input and an *end-of-conversion* (EOC)

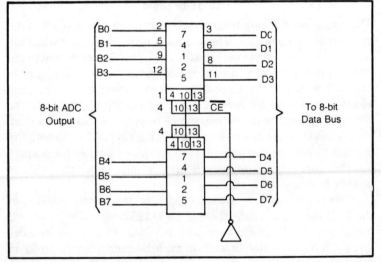

Fig. 15-18. 74125 three-state buffers.

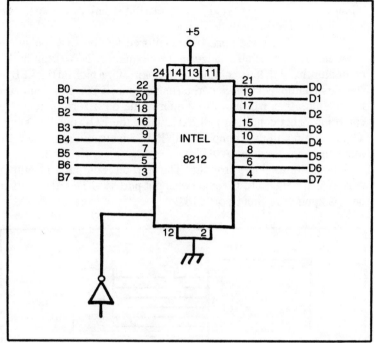

Fig. 15-19. Intel 8212.

output pulse. The start command tells the ADC to begin the conversion. But since the ADC cannot make an instantaneous conversion, there is some time delay. The data on the ADC output may be either data that was once valid or trash data that is generated in the conversion process. The EOC pulse is used to tell the outside world that the data at the output of the ADC is valid. We will consider three basic configurations for inputting data to the CPU: I/O-port (latched), I/O-port (unlatched), and memory-mapped. Several different circuits are used.

Figure 15-20 shows a system for use when the ADC has latched output. The output lines from the ADC are connected to an input port on a computer. In this case, for purposes of this discussion, port 5 is designated, but we also have to account for the EOC and start pulses. We pick one bit of another I/O port, in this case the least significant bit (LSB) of I/O port 4. The start pulse is generated by bringing the LSB of port 4 high for a brief instant. This becomes the start pulse. This is accomplished by outputting 00000001 from port 4, and then immediately resetting the LSB by outputting 00000000 from the same port. Some microprocessors, incidentally, allow you to set and reset any particular bit in any given port. The Z-80 Bit instruction will do this job.

The LSB of input port 4 is monitored for the EOC pulse. In most cases, an assembly language program must be written in the computer that will loop continuously looking for a high on the LSB of the designated port. Again referencing the Z-80, this chip has instructions that will jump to a subroutine on a zero or nonzero condition. This condition will exist when the EOC pulse is seen. The program will then jump to an INPUT 5 instruction and thereby input the data from the ADC.

Consider a sample program. The start bit is output from output port 175, and the EOC is sought on input port 175. The ADC output data is applied to input port 176.

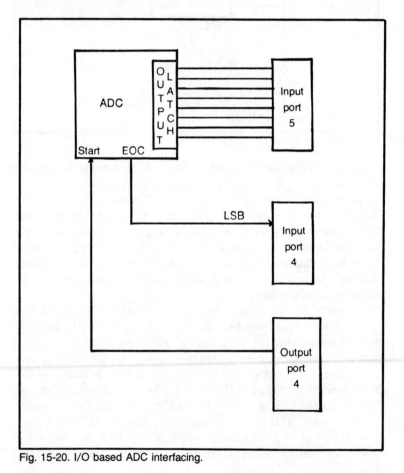

Fig. 15-20. I/O based ADC interfacing.

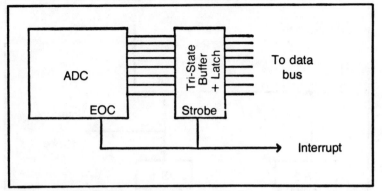

Fig. 15-21. ADC interfacing with a three-state buffer.

00 01	3E	Load accumulator with N
00 02	FF	N (guarantees Bit 7 high)
00 03	D3	OUT 175_{10}
00 04	AF	175_{10} in hexadecimal
00 05	DB	IN 175_{10}
00 06	AF	175_{10} in hexadecimal
00 07	CB	Test bit-7 of port 175_{10}
00 08	7F	
00 09	20	JR NZ (jump on nonzero)
00 10	86	(jump −4)
00 11	DB	Input 176_{10}
00 12	60	176_{10} in hexedecimal
00 13		
00 xx		
00 xx		(program to process ADC data once in computer)
00 xx		
00 xx	C3	JP 00 01 (jump immediate to 00 01)
00 xx	01	
00 22	00	

Another circuit is shown in Fig. 15-21. In this case, the ADC does not have latched outputs, and it is our job to provide such an output. We could use a 74100 TTL dual quad latch to latch the data and then feed this data to a three-state buffer. The EOC pulse could be used to gate the data into the latch. If the three-state buffer were immediately used to input ADC data to the CPU, then it would also be driven by the EOC pulse. But in most cases, we would use either

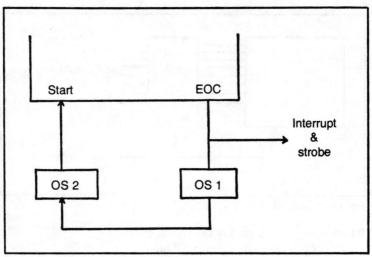

Fig. 15-22. Introducing a short delay.

an IN or MRD op signal from a device selector to gate onto the data bus from the three-state buffer.

For some applications, we might want to make the ADC convert the data applied to its analog input continuously. We can merely connect the EOC back to the start input, and this will achieve continuous conversion. But it is also nonsynchronous. We can use a pair of one-shot pulse delay circuits to synchronize the operation. The EOC pulse will tell the computer or data latch that the data is valid. However, the two one shots prevent the EOC pulse from immediately starting another conversion. OS2 is a short duration

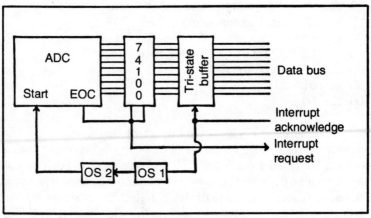

Fig. 15-23. Double buffered latching with delay.

one shot and is used to directly fire the start pulse. OS1 is a longer duration one shot that will introduce the needed delay. See Fig. 15-22.

In still other cases, we could use the interrupt capability of the CPU to input the data. The EOC pulse will be applied to the interrupt line simultaneously with the ADC output latch. When the CPU is ready to service the interrupt, it then issues an interrupt *acknowledge signal.* Figure 15-23 shows how this circuit is implemented. The EOC output from the ADC is connected to the input of the 74100. The outputs of the 74100 are connected to a tri-state buffer. The EOC pulse is also connected to the interrupt line of the CPU. In the Z-80, the $\overline{NMI}$ (nonmaskable interrupt) line could be used, which is a program-controlled restart. When the CPU begins the next instruction cycle, it will issue an interrupt acknowledge pulse. This pulse is used to strobe the 74100 output data onto the data bus by turning on the three-state buffer. The interrupt acknowledge signal could also be used to generate the next start pulse, again via the one-shot circuit shown.

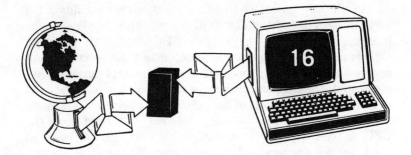

Microcomputer Control of
External Circuits and Devices

I f we want to control external devices or circuits other than ordinary digital peripherals (printers, disk drives, etc.), then we have to use special interfacing techniques. Among the external circuits that might be controlled are those which are properly considered part of the analog subsystem of the computer. We may wish to control dc motors, servo systems, lamps, stepper relays and ac-powered equipment. In this chapter, we will consider some of the methods used to control these external devices.

RELAY CONTROLS

The relay is an electromagnet-controlled switch whose origins date back a century or more. The relay was invented, some claim, by the brillant Siemens brothers of Germany during the nineteenth century. A relay consists of a movable contact and a stationary contact in close proximity to a coil of wire that forms an electromagnet. The pieces are positioned such that the movable contact mates with the fixed contacts when the coil is energized. The magnetic field surrounding the coil pulls the armature carrying the movable contacts into the piece carrying the fixed contacts.

The electromagnet may seem a little antiquated compared with the wonderful computer technology, but in some cases it is the component of choice. The primary uses are for either high voltages or high currents. Although there are other devices which will do this job, the relay retains a certain charm and simplicity. The relay can be turned on and off with a single bit of a microcomputer output port.

One possible solution to the problem is shown in Fig. 16-1. Here we use a magnetic relay to control the high ac potential from the power mains to a lamp. Transistor Q1 is a relay driver and can be almost any npn silicon type that will handle the voltage and current levels present. Types 2N3906 and 2N2907 are often suggested for this service. In this example we are assuming that TTL compatible output ports are available in which logic 0 is 0 volts, and logic 1 is +5 volts. Resistor R1 is selected for those levels. If a higher output voltage is used, then scale the value of R1 upwards proportionally.

When bit 1 is low, then transistor Q1 is cut off and no current flows in the coil of relay K1. Since K1 is deenergized, the circuit to the lamp is open and the bulb is turned off. When bit 1 goes high, on the other hand, transistor Q1 is forward biased and conducts collector current. The collector of Q1, then, goes to ground, turning on K1. In the energized position of K1 the contacts controlling the lamp are closed, so the lamp turns on.

Diode D1 is used to suppress voltage spikes generated by the inductive kick produced by the coil of K1. Diode D1 can be almost any rectifier diode in the 1N4000 series. Since the spike that is

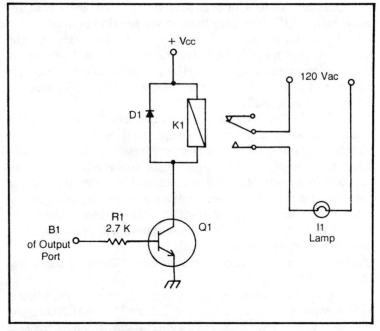

Fig. 16-1. Interfacing relay or solenoid to computer.

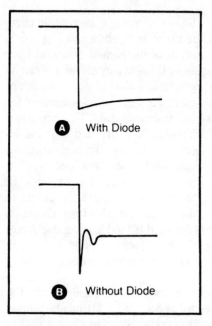

A   With Diode

B   Without Diode

Fig. 16-2. Effects of diode D1.

generated can be quite high, only 1N4004 through 1N4007 are recommended; IN4001 through 1N4003 have too low a peak reverse voltage (PRV) or peak inverse voltage (PIV) rating.

If you doubt the need for diode D1, then examine the waveforms shown in Fig. 16-2. The waveform of Fig. 16-2A shows the situation when a step-function (i.e., switch turn-off) potential is applied to K1 with D1 present and doing its job. Notice that the waveform is essentially clean.

In Fig. 16-2B, however, diode D1 has been disconnected and that has allowed a high-amplitude negative-going voltage spike at turnoff. This spike, which had been suppressed by D1, is actually larger than shown here because of space limitations. Such spikes can, and frequently do, damage electronic circuitry (i.e., Q1 is vulnerable) and can also cause spurious pulses in digital circuitry. Even where the circuitry can absorb the pulse, there is the possibility that such a pulse will reset counters and flip-flops, or be propagated through gates, at exactly the wrong time. Experienced troubleshooters will recognize that as one of the most unnerving situations that can occur.

We can also turn on a relay, as in the above example, using a logic IC instead of a driver transistor. Certain TTL and CMOS logic devices are designed with an open-collector bipolar output transis-

276

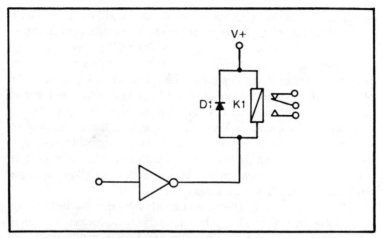

Fig. 16-3. Open-collector interfacing of relay.

tor, and in normal operation require a pull-up resistor between each output terminal and the +5-volt dc supply. This resistor will have a value in the 1 K to 2 K range. An example from the popular TTL series of devices is the 7406/7416 hex inverter. These devices are essentially the same type of IC, both being designed as relay or lamp drivers, and can connect to supplies of +15 volts and +30 volts, respectively.

To use either the 7406 or 7416, connect an appropriate relay coil between the output of one inverter section and a positive supply voltage. See Fig. 16-3.

The main advantage of the electromagnet relay is that it will handle high voltages and/or high currents while at the same time providing isolation required for safety of the computer and possibly the personnel using the equipment. We can, however, use optoisolator and silicon-controlled rectifiers (SCR) or triacs (both SCR's and triacs are examples from a class of device called Thyristors).

SCR CONTROLS

An optoisolator is a special IC that contains a light-emitting diode (LED) and a phototransistor configured such that the transistor is on if the LED is lighted. An SCR (i.e., silicon-controlled rectifier) is a rectifier diode that remains turned off unless a current is injected into the gate terminal. In the circuit of Fig. 16-4A, if the input to inverter 1 is low, then the output of inverter 2 is also low. This condition grounds the cold side of the LED, thereby turning it on.

277

The LED, then, remains turned on, and that keeps the phototransistor conducting. The collector of Q1, therefore, remains at, or near, ground potential, and that keeps the SCR turned off.

Applying a high to the input of inverter 1 places a high on the output of inverter 2, turning off the LED and Q1 and turning on the SCR. When the collector voltage of Q1 goes high, a current is set up in the gate of the SCR that is sufficient to cause it to turn on.

Once gated on, an SCR will remain on until the anode-cathode current drops below a certain critical threshold, or holding current. In the circuit of Fig. 16-4A, a commutation of the SCR is done manually by opening switch S1. This arrangement allows a single pulse to start and hold the lamp in operation.

The circuit of Fig. 16-4B, on the other hand, must be continuously pulsed in order to keep the lamp turned on. As long as a pulse train is applied to the circuit, then the SCR remains in the on

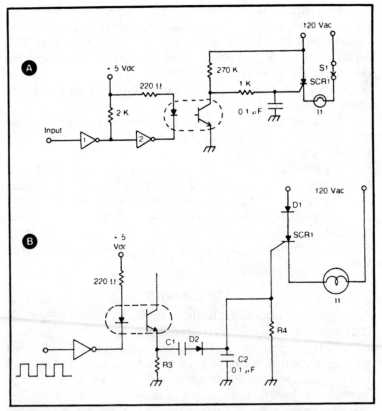

Fig. 16-4. Single-pulse turn-on SCR circuit (A), and turn-offable version (B).

condition. Diode D1 rectifies the 120-volt ac, so once every half-cycle the SCR anode-cathode current drops to zero. If the SCR gate is not excited when the next half-cycle begins, then the SCR remains turned off.

In some cases, the SCR gate can be pulsed directly by the computer output port, but since 120 volts ac is involved, the isolation provided by the optoisolator is very necessary.

The SCR gate circuit in Fig. 16-4B is controlled by RC network R4C1C2 and diode D1. If the LED is pulsed through the inverter, then the phototransistor is also pulsed, and these pulses appear across emitter resistor R3.

Pulses across R3 are coupled through C1 and D2, which charge capacitor C2. As long as the pulses continue, C2 remains charged, which keeps the SCR gate excited. But if the pulse train ceases, then C2 discharges. The SCR will remain turned off after the first zero-current half-wave cycle that the gate voltage is below the turn-on threshold.

MOTOR CONTROL

Both ac and dc motors can be controlled with a computer, provided that the proper interface circuitry is supplied. The relay, SCR and Triac circuits will provide on-off motor control. In this section, we will expand our methods to handle motors.

Let's consider an example in which several motors are used in a system and operate from the same output port. We want to design a circuit in which the motor will turn on only when its code is present (in this case 01100111_2).

Previously, a single bit was used to turn on the circuit, but in this example an entire output port is needed. Selective decoding can be done using an eight-input NAND gate and any needed inverters. Figure 16-5 shows how an eight-bit address decoder can be built from a 7430 eight-input NAND gate and an inverter.

A TTL NAND gate output will remain high if any of the eight input lines are low. To make a 7430 output high requires a code of 11111111.

But the desired code is 01100111, so we must invert bits 4, 5, and 8 (see Fig. 16-5). If this is done as shown, then the 7430 output will drop low when the code 01100111 appears on the input.

This technique is used whenever you want to use a single output port to control several devices, each of which is assigned its own unique code. The eight-bit parallel lines can be bussed together, and only the device addressed will respond.

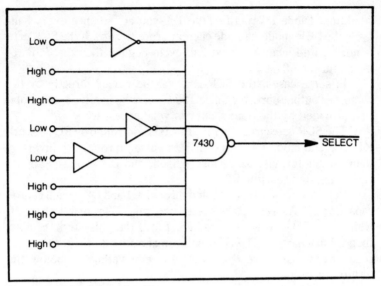

Fig. 16-5. 8-bit address decoder.

Suppose we want to perform the same job as above, except that now we require a means for the computer to verify the desired action has taken place. A computer can verify the action using only one bit of an input port, provided that an appropriate transducer or other indicator is used. The verification can be provided, with varying degrees of reliability, by any of the following: relay contact closures, detection of the output state of a gate, driver, or inverter, or a tachometer ganged to the shaft of the motor.

The relay used to turn on a motor can be specified to have one more contact pair than is otherwise necessary. These can be connected to a +5-volt dc source through a pull-up resistor and ground, such that a high is applied to an input port when the relay is energized. This scheme does not give an absolute indication of motor operation, but only that the relay has been energized and is telling the motor to operate. A defective motor would not be detected by this method. It is, however, very low cost.

Detection of the output state of one of the inverters or drivers can also yield the data but, again, it is possible for the command to be given, yet the motor be defective.

The use of a tachometer on the motor shaft is the most reliable method for detection of motor operation. This device will produce a dc or ac (most common) output that can be detected by an appropriate electronic circuit and used to tell the computer that the motor has indeed started. Since the frequency of the ac tachometer and amplitude of the dc type is proportional to motor speed, then it is also possible to use these devices in a feedback control circuit.

Other related problems can be similarly solved, with the constraint that a suitable transducer be provided.

A furnace controller, for example, ignites the flame in a burner. A photoresistor or phototransistor looking into the spy-flame hole will detect whether or not the flame is actually turned on. The output of the detector could then be fed to a TTL output comparator such as the LM311 or the Precision Monolithics, Inc., CMP-01 and CMP-02. The comparator output will then serve to tell the computer that the flame is on.

Other transducers that provide a voltage output can be similarly applied to a comparator to supply verification.

Thus far, all of our applications have involved step-function control; a device is either on or off. A continuously variable control circuit is possible if a digital-to-analog converter is used.

CONTROLLING SMALL DC MOTORS

Many control system projects require the use of a small, fractional horsepower dc motor as the prime mover. These can be used in several ways: on-off or continuously variable, in either closed-loop or open-loop configurations. Turning a motor on and off is the most

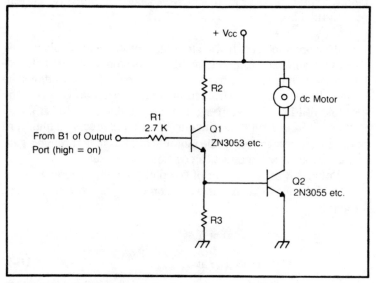

Fig. 16-6. Controlling a dc motor.

trivial problem and is an example of a simple open-loop system. The definition of an open-loop system is that there is no controlling negative feedback; the output causes no effects at the input. Any of the methods used for ac loads earlier in this chapter will also work for dc motors, but we can also use a regular power transistor to control the motor (see Fig. 16-6).

Transistor Q1 in Fig. 16-6 serves as a driver for Q2. If Q1 is a 2N3052, and Q2 is a 2N3055, then motors drawing up to 8 or 10 amperes can be accommodated by this circuit. We do not want to drive the 2N3055 directly from the output port of a computer because the transistor may not have sufficient beta gain to drive the motor to full output with the current levels typically available from TTL output ports.

For the TTL compatible output port (those with +5 volts) the value of R1 shown will suffice. Scale R2 according to the level of Vcc. The operation of this circuit is as follows:

1. A low on the output port turns off both Q1 and Q2, so nothing happens.

2. A high on the output port bit used to control this circuit forward biases Q1 to saturation, making the voltage at its emitter high. This condition turns on Q2.

3. Q2 is now forward biased to saturation, so it turns on the motor. (Note: Resistor R3 must have a value that limits the current flow in the base of Q2 to a safe value.)

In an open-loop control system the motor would simply turn on and off by command from the input, i.e. the computer. In a closed-loop system, on the other hand, the motor control commands can be modified by data received from the action of the motor. Consider the example of Fig. 16-7. Here we are using a dc motor to lift a load suspended from a rope from height Y_0 to Y_1. A precision multiturn potentiometer is ganged to the motor shaft, possibly through a gear train, so that it is, in effect, a position transducer.

Voltage E at the output of the potentiometer represents the height of the load (Y), and is a fraction of E_{ref} proportional to that height:

$$E = 0 \text{ at } Y_0 \qquad \textbf{16-1}$$

$$E = E_{ref} \text{ at } Y_1 \qquad \textbf{16-2}$$

$$E = E_{ref} (Y - Y_0)(Y1 - Y0) \qquad \textbf{16-3}$$

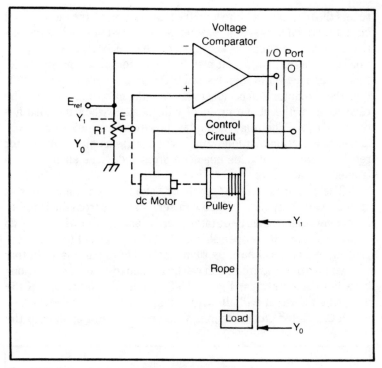

Fig. 16-7. Example of controlling a system.

Both E and E_{ref} are connected to an operational amplifier voltage comparator that will produce an output level according to the following rules:

Condition	Comparator Output	
E = 0	Low	**16-4**
E = E_{ref}	High	**16-5**

The comparator output is connected to a single bit of the computer input port, while the motor is connected through a circuit such as Fig. 16-6 to a single bit of the computer output port.

The idea here is to write a program into the computer that will turn on the motor by setting the control bit of the output port high, then periodically test the Y_1 position-indicating bit of the input port for a high condition. As long as that bit of the input port remains low, then the program keeps the motor running. But when a high is detected, indicating that the load is at position Y_1, then the program resets the output port bit to low, thereby turning off the motor. This circuit is trivial for several reasons, not the least of which is the fact that the load cannot be lowered once it has reached the high position. Of course, another bit may be wired to a relay driver. If the relay is connected in the classic DPDT double-cross or X circuit, then the computer will be able to reverse the motor. In that case the reverse from the above protocol will indicate when the load has returned to Y_0. The relay method is, however, too inelegant—even tacky. In a section that follows we will discuss an electronic motor reversal circuit that does not need archaic devices such as electromechanical relays.

The circuit in Fig. 16-7 could be used for such applications as an automatic flagpole or window raiser. It suffers from the inability to recognize more than two states, i.e., Y_0 and Y_1. But what if you do not want your window open all of the way, or you want to mourn the passing of a national hero by running the flag to half-mast? In that case you will need a circuit that can be trained to recognize positions between the extremes. Figure 16-8 shows a modification of the original circuit that will allow the computer to dictate height Y at which the motor stops turning. Voltage E_{ref} is still applied to the

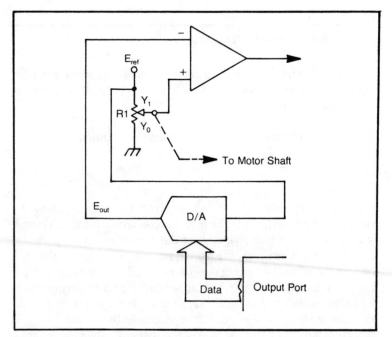

Fig. 16-8. Alternate control circuit.

284

position potentiometer as before, but only a fraction of E_{ref} is applied to the comparator. You have learned that the output voltage from a D/A converter is:

$$E_{out} = \frac{A}{2^n} \times E_{ref} \qquad \textbf{16-6}$$

E_{out} is the D/A converter output potential, E_{ref} is the reference voltage, n is the number of bits at the D/A converter's digital inputs (usually eight in microcomputer systems), and A is the value of the digital word applied to the D/A converter input.

Example. Find the output voltage from an 8-bit D/A converter if E_{ref} is 10.00 volts and A is 10000000_2. (Note: $10000000_2 = 129_{10}$).

$$E_{out} = \frac{(128)(10.00 \text{ V})}{2^8}$$

$$E_{out} = \frac{(128)(10.00 \text{ V})}{(256)} = 5.00 \text{ V}$$

Since Y is proportional to E and a fraction of E_{ref}, and E_{out} is also a fraction of E_{ref}, we can set the height at which the comparator output goes low (telling the computer to halt the motor), by setting A in Equation 16-6.

$$Y_1 = 255/256 \qquad \textbf{16-7}$$

$$Y = A/256 \qquad \textbf{16-8}$$

$$Y_0 = 0/256 \qquad \textbf{16-9}$$

Note that some D/A converters can give bipolar output voltages. They will produce a negative or positive output potential depending upon the digital code applied to the inputs. This feature opens up both the possibility of the controlling motor direction and speed.

Figure 16-9 shows the type of motor drive amplifier required to electronically reverse the motor. This circuit is based on the complementary symmetry circuit used in high-fidelity amplifiers. Note that bipolar, +VCC and −VCC, power supplies are required for this circuit to operate properly.

A positive potential applied to the input, i.e., point A in Fig.

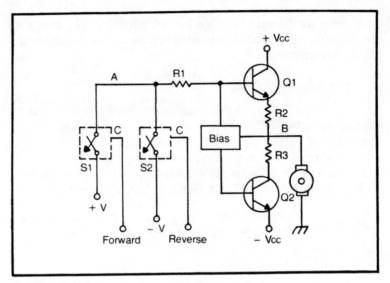

Fig. 16-9. Control circuit using an electronic switch.

16-9, will reverse bias transistor Q2 and forward bias transistor Q1, making the potential applied to the motor (i.e., point B) positive.

To reverse the motor's direction of rotation it is necessary to reverse the polarity at point B. This is done by applying a negative potential to point A. In that case, Q1 is reverse biased and Q2 is forward biased.

In the example of Fig. 16-9 we have used CMOS electronic switches such as the 4016 and 4066 to supply positive and negative inputs on command. The positive input is connected when the control line from S1 is high, while the negative potential is applied if the control input of S2 is made high.

Continuously variable motor speed control is available if the output of a D/A converter is applied to point A in Fig. 16-9 instead of a +V or −V source. If the D/A converter is a bipolar type, then both speed and direction of rotation can be dictated by the digital command from a computer output port.

Figure 16-10 shows analog and digital versions of a continuously controlled servomechanism using a dc motor. This circuit uses negative- feedback control techniques. Any such system can be described by Equation 16-10.

$$\frac{E_{out}}{E_{in}} = \frac{H}{1 + HB} \qquad \textbf{16-10}$$

E_{out} is the output voltage, E_{in} is the input in voltage, H is the gain of the forward path, and B is the gain of the feedback loop.

In the examples of Fig. 16-10, the value of H is the gain of the servo amplifier, while B is unity (there is neither gain or attenuation in the feedback loop).

The analog version of the circuit is constructed of operational amplifiers and power transistors. The summer is merely a multiple input operational amplifier stage such as an inverting follower with more than one input source. If only two inputs are needed to produce a difference signal, as in Fig. 16-10A, then a simple dc differential amplifier will suffice.

The motor is driven by the output of the servo amplifier E_M. This voltage, E_M, is the product of the servo amplifier gain A_v and error voltage E_E,

$$E_M = A_v E_E \qquad \textbf{16-11}$$

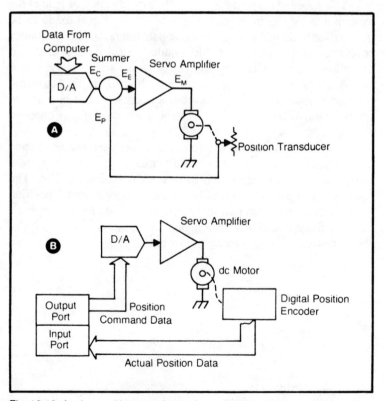

Fig. 16-10. Analog position transducer (A), and digital position transducer (B).

287

E_E is the difference between the position signal E_P from the transducer and the control signal E_C that indicates what the position should be. E_C can be supplied from a computer-controlled D/A converter.

$$E_E = E_C - E_P \qquad \textbf{16-12}$$

$$E_M = A_v (E_C - E_P) \qquad \textbf{16-13}$$

If the position is correct, then $E_C = E_P$; by Equation 16-13, E_M is zero and the motor is turned off. But if $E_C \neq E_P$, then the motor is turned on. Since the motor is a dc type, its operating speed is a function of E_M. Clearly, then, the greater the difference between the actual and correct positions, the greater the value of E_M, so the faster the motor speed.

The speed of response is set by the amplification or gain of the system and by the frequency response. If the signal tends to be overcritically damped, i.e., too sluggish, increase the frequency response of the system. But if it is undercritically damped, i.e., it overshoots, then reduce the frequency response of the system.

A digital version is shown in Fig. 16-10B. In this case the position transducer is shown as a block because it may be a potentiometer and A/D converter, or it can be one of the digitally encoded transducers.

In the digital version the comparison between the actual and correct position data is made in software. In an eight-bit system there are 256 different states to represent position points. The computer compares the eight-bit word indicating actual position with the eight-bit word indicating correct position by performing a binary subtraction that is analogous to Equation 16-12. Both of these systems are essentially self-regulating.

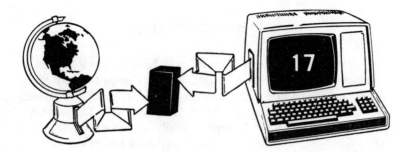

Projects

This chapter contains several practical projects that interface analog subsystems to computer data acquisition systems. For the most part, these projects are amplifiers that are used ahead of analog-to-digital converters and so forth. Keep in mind that this book is both theoretical and practical. This particular chapter is the practical end of the subject. All of these projects have actually been built either by myself or close associates. The designs are not necessarily the be-all and end-all of electronic design, but are well-behaved and capable of being built by persons whose expertise is in areas other than electronics.

Caution Notice

Some of the projects in this section are biomedical amplifiers. These are intended for animal use only. The reader is responsible for testing each circuit for human use, and is assumed to have studied medical electrical safety issues beforehand.

SINGLE-ENDED AMPLIFIER

A single-ended amplifier is one in which there is a single input line with respect to ground (a differential amplifier uses two inputs with respect to ground). These amplifiers are used in a lot of different applications. The circuit shown in Fig. 17-1 is a single-ended amplifier with a gain of 100. The gain is derived from the following equation:

$$A_v = (R2/R1)(R4/R3)$$

For the values shown R1 = R3 = 10 K, and R2 = R4 = 100 K, the gain is (−10) (−10) or (+100). We can change the gain of the stage by changing the value of any of these resistors. Be careful, however, when changing the value of resistor R1. The input impedance of this circuit is dependent totally on the value of R1, and in fact, Z_{in} = R1. For practical purposes, limit the lower value of resistor R1 to 10 times the output or source impedance of the driving stage or device. In most cases, this means that R1 must be 1000 ohms or more, with 10 K being a more practical limit.

We can adjust the gain by using a potentiometer for R4. If a 100 K, linear taper potentiometer is used for R4, then the gain will be adjustable from 0 to 100 with the potentiometer. Similarly, a 10 K potentiometer at resistor R4 would give us a gain of 0 to 10, and a 1 K potentiometer yields a gain of 0 to 1.

The operational amplifiers used in Fig. 17-1 are 741 devices. The 741 is a low-cost, common, garden variety operational amplifier and is almost universally available. Some readers might like to replace both operational amplifiers (A1 and A2) with a single 1458 operational amplifier. That device contains a pair of 741 devices in a single 8-pin DIP.

All 741-family devices are said to be *frequency compensated*, or *unconditionally stable*. Both terms mean the same thing: the frequency response is limited severely in order to prevent oscillation at high frequencies. As a result, these devices will not behave as operational amplifiers above frequencies of a few kilohertz.

The stability of the amplifier circuit in Fig. 17-1 is not greatly diminished when the capacitors are deleted provided that the other devices in the system are not operated from the same dc power supplies. In that case, there might be stage-to-stage coupling (feedback) that produces a deleterious effect on the operation of the circuit. That effect is eliminated by the use of the decoupling capacitors. Since these capacitors don't harm anything when present, it is good engineering practice to always include them.

The 0.1 μF capacitors in Fig. 17-1 (C2 and C3) are used to decouple high frequencies. They should be mounted as close as possible to the body of the operational amplifiers. The 4.7 μF

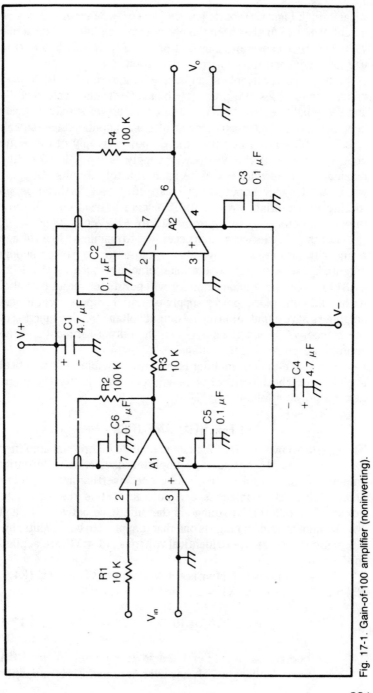

Fig. 17-1. Gain-of-100 amplifier (noninverting).

291

capacitors (C1 and C4) are for low frequency decoupling, and may be mounted a little further from the operational amplifiers. The actual values of these capacitors may be from 1 μF to 10 μF. It is best to use tantalum capacitors for this application.

The dc power supplies can be anything from ±6 volts to ±15 volts. In most cases, it is prudent to make the absolute values of V− and V+ equal to each other. When selecting power supply voltages keep in mind that the maximum permissible output voltage (signal) is 2.5 to 3.5 volts lower than the dc power supply of the same polarity. Hence, if the V+ power supply is +6 Vdc, then the maximum output voltage will be approximately 3 volts. Clipping will result if higher output potentials are attempted. In that case, go to a higher potential. A voltage of 15 Vdc for V− and V+ will allow the output voltage to swing from −12 to +12 Vdc.

For those cases where it is necessary to maintain a low voltage along with an output voltage that is close to the power supply potential, use a BiMOS operational amplifier such as the RCA CA3140. That operational amplifier will permit an output potential within 0.5 volts of the power supply potential. Bipolar operational amplifiers have a limitation on the output voltage that is a function of the number of pn junctions between the output terminal and the appropriate power supply voltage.

The single-ended amplifier is of limited usefulness in practical applications. The majority of users will need a differential amplifier. Several projects follow.

DIFFERENTIAL AMPLIFIER

The circuit shown in Fig. 17-2 is a simple dc differential amplifier based on a single operational amplifier device. A differential amplifier is one that has two inputs, one inverting and the other noninverting. Both inputs see a voltage that is referenced to ground. The differential voltage is the difference between V2 and V1. A common mode voltage is one that is applied to both inputs, or, alternatively, a case where identical voltages (V1 = V2) are applied to the two inputs.

The gain of this amplifier is set by the ratio R3/R1, or, (R4 + R5)/R2, provided that R1 = R2, and R4 + R5 = R2.

$$A_v = R3/R1 \qquad\qquad \textbf{17-1}$$

The operational amplifier used in this circuit is the RCA CA3140 device. Unlike the 741, however, this operational amplifier

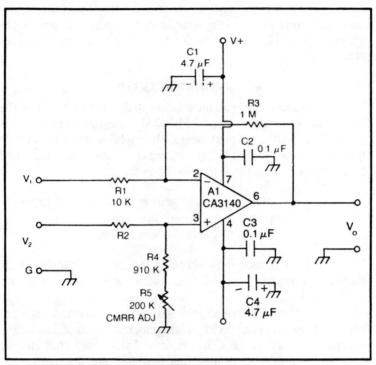

Fig. 17-2. Gain-of-100 dc differential amplifier.

is not frequently compensated, so may oscillate if not treated properly. The decoupling capacitors are absolutely necessary, and cannot be deleted. The same discussion applies for these capacitors as applied to the previous project, so will not be repeated here.

The CMRR Adj control is used for adjustment of the Common Mode Rejection Ratio. This control is used to balance the circuit, and is adjusted as follows: short together the two inputs (V1 and V2), and then apply to the common junction a signal of approximately 1000 Hz@ 1-volt peak-to-peak. Monitor the output on either a sensitive ac voltmeter, or, an ac-coupled oscilloscope (the preferred method). Adjust the vertical sensitivity on the oscilloscope for a signal of several divisions amplitude. Next, adjust R5 for minimum signal. Then readjust the input sensitivity of the oscilloscope for a larger signal and repeat the adjustment of R5. Keep repeating the process, using ever-increasing sensitivity on the oscilloscope until no further reduction is possible.

The simple dc differential amplifier of Fig. 17-2 is useful for a large variety of applications, including one which we will examine later in this chapter in a slightly modified form. There are limitations, however, including the same limitation on input impedance as existed in Fig. 17-1. There is also a practical limitation on gain of around 500.

INSTRUMENTATION AMPLIFIER

Figure 17-3 shows a circuit for a differential amplifier based on the National Semiconductor type LM-363AD integrated circuit. This device is a multigain instrumentation amplifier that can provide gains of ×10, ×100 and ×1000. Setting of the gain is accomplished by strapping two or three pins as follows:

pins 2,3,4 open: gain = 100
pins 3 & 4 shorted: gain = 10
pins 4 & 2 shorted: gain = 1000

Switch S1 is used for controlling the gain, with the settings shown in the inset of Fig. 17-3 determining the gain provided by the amplifier.

Notice that there are no gain-setting resistors in the circuit of Fig. 17-3. An integrated circuit instrumentation amplifier (ICIA) normally uses only one resistor, or none. In the case of this circuit, none is required—all gain setting resistors are internal to the amplifier.

The decoupling capacitors are absolutely essential in this circuit. Like the circuit of Fig. 17-1, the 0.1 μF capacitors are used for high frequency decoupling and must be mounted as close as possible to the body of the LM-363AD. The 4.7 μF capacitors are used for low frequency decoupling. As in the previous case, the 4.7 μF capacitors are tantalum electrolytics, and can have a value of 1 μF to 10 μF.

Frequency compensation is provided by the capacitors C_a and C_b, and by resistor R_a. The values of these components can be set to provide the frequency response required for the specific application.

The input circuit is a little different from what you might expect if you are only familiar with operational amplifiers. The two differential inputs are pretty much straightforward, but there are also guard shield terminals on this device (pins 8 and 9). These terminals are connected to the shields of the respective inputs; pin 8 to the shield of the inverting input, and pin 9 to the shield of the noninverting input). The case shown here is where both shield terminals

294

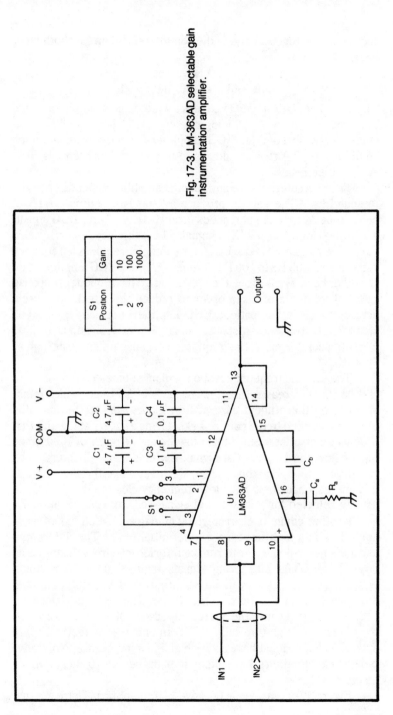

Fig. 17-3. LM-363AD selectable gain instrumentation amplifier.

295

are connected together and to the common shield around both input lines.

ECG BIOELECTRIC AMPLIFIER

The term *bioelectric amplifier* covers a wide range of amplifiers used in medicine and medical/biological research. These amplifiers include electrocardiograph (ECG) amplifiers, electroencephalograph amplifiers (EEG) that are designed to pick up biopotentials from surface electrodes.

The characteristics of any specific amplifier depends upon the intended use. The gain to produce a "standard" output of 1-volt peak-to-peak, for example, needs to be 1000 for a 1-mV ECG signal, and 10,000 for a 100-μV EEG signal. The frequency responses also vary. The *diagnostic grade* ECG, for example, requires a frequency response of 0.05 Hz to 100 Hz. *Monitoring grade* ECG amplifiers, on the other hand, want to see the upper end of the frequency response reduced to 40 Hz or so in order to reduce the effects of muscle artifact from an active patient. EEG amplifiers normally have a 0.05 Hz to 30 Hz frequency response. In amplifiers designed to pick up EMG (muscle) signals, the frequency response might be as high as 2000 Hz.

The low end frequency response of most bioelectric amplifiers is 0.05 Hz. The reason that it is not made equal to dc (which might seem to be the prudent case at first glance) is that the metallic electrode applied to the patient's skin forms a *battery* at the site that produces a dc offset. Since this offset is on the order of 1000 times higher than the biopotential signal, the dc offset will saturate the amplifier output. For this reason, we must make the low-end frequency response some very low frequency close to dc; 0.05 Hz is usually selected for practical and signal-shaping considerations.

Another common characteristic among almost all biopotential amplifiers is a high impedance differential input. The differential aspect is needed in order to reduce interference from the 60 Hz ac power lines. The interfering signals tend to affect both inputs equally, so the result will be suppressed in the output of the amplifier (common mode rejection ratio). The high impedance aspect is needed because the source impedance of electrodes applied to skin is very high (typically 10 K). In order to correctly amplify such signals, we must have a very high input impedance. Normally, bioelectric amplifiers have input impedances of 10 megohms or more.

Figure 17-4 is a special purpose ECG amplifier. There are two

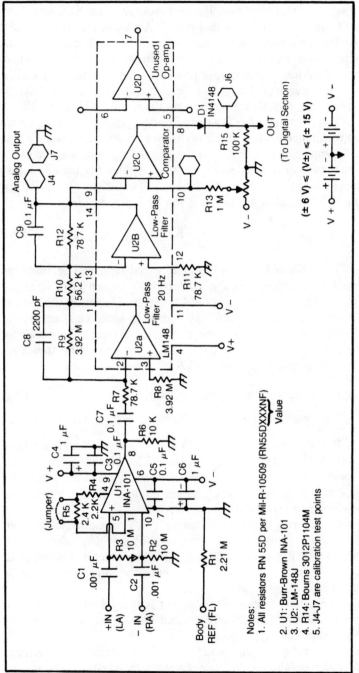

Fig. 17-4. ECG amplifier/QRS detector.

Notes:
1. All resistors RN 55D per Mil-R-10509 (RN55DXXXNF)
2. U1: Burr-Brown INA-101
3. U2: LM-148J
4. R14: Bourns 3012P1104M
5. J4–J7 are calibration test points

297

outputs from this amplifier. The analog output is the ECG waveform itself, while the digital output (OUT) is a pulse that is coincident with the sharp spike-like feature of the ECG waveform. The digital output can be used to drive circuits such as a cardiotachometer, or to control other instruments or processes that are linked to the ECG signal (such as in cardiac output computers). For those users that do not need the digital output, truncate the circuit at U2C and U2D.

The input amplifier is a Burr-Brown type INA-101. This device is programmable with a single resistance between pin 1 and pin 4. In the example shown in Fig. 17-4 the gain setting resistance takes the form of two series-connected resistors. A jumper is shunted across one of the resistors for high gain and left out of the circuit for low gain. The equation for gain is given by Equation 17-2.

$$A_v = ((40 \text{ K}/R) + 1) \qquad \textbf{17-2}$$

The INA-101 device has differential inputs. The inverting input is on pin 10, while the noninverting input is on pin 5. The input circuit of the amplifier in Fig. 17-4 is designed to permit the low end frequency response of 0.05 Hz required by bioelectric amplifiers. The input resistors and capacitors (C1, C2, R2 and R3) are used for this purpose. The −3 dB point in the low end of the frequency response is given by Equation 17-3.

$$F = 1/6.28RC \qquad \textbf{17-3}$$

This equation requires that R2 = R3 = R, and C1 = C2 = C

Resistor R1 is connected in series with the common signal electrode applied to the patient's body. This 2.21 megohm resistor is used to limit the current applied to the body in the event of a catastrophic failure of the electronic circuits. This is a matter of patient safety and should not be ignored.

Output from the INA-101 (amplifier U1) is applied to the input of an inverting follower operational amplifier (U2A), which in turn drives another inverting follower, U2B. The upper end −3 dB point of the frequency response curve is set by the combination of R9C8 and R12C9, using Equation 17-3.

The analog output of the project is taken from the output of operational amplifier U2B. This signal will take on a value of around 1-volt when the input voltage is 1-millivolt.

The analog output drives the digital section of the circuit, which also consists of operational amplifiers. Amplifier U2C is used as a comparator. Such a circuit is essentially an amplifier with too much gain. Note that there is no feedback resistor on U2C. This means that the gain of the stage is essentially the gain of the operational amplifier, which could be as much as 1,000,000. As a result, the output will be either near V+ or near V− if the two input voltages are not equal. As soon as the two input voltages differ by more than a couple of millivolts, the output will be high with a polarity that indicates the relative polarity of the two input signals.

In this particular circuit, the output is limited to positive voltages by diode D1. This means that the output will be zero when the two inputs see equal voltages, or, when the inverting input is more negative than the noninverting input. Only when the ECG signal passes a certain threshold will a positive pulse be generated.

The operational amplifiers in this project are all part of a single IC which contains four internal operational amplifier devices: LM-148.

ANOTHER ECG BIOELECTRIC AMPLIFIER

Another version of the same sort of circuit is shown in Fig. 17-5. This circuit is essentially similar to the previous circuit, with the exception that the operational and instrumentation amplifiers are changed.

The front end of this circuit is a National Semiconductor LM-363-500 device, which provides a fixed gain of 500 in a 10-pin metal IC package. This type of construction makes a small package and easy circuit construction. The amplifier replaces the INA-101 of the previous design.

The input circuit is essentially the same as in the previous case. The series-connected input capacitors are used to limit the low-end frequency response of the amplifier to something in the neighborhood of 0.05 Hz. The resistors serve to keep amplifier input bias currents and other charges from charging the capacitors and thereby latching-up the amplifier. It is important in both circuits to keep these resistors balanced; therefore, it is recommended that only 1 percent or better tolerance resistors be used.

Again, the 2.2 megohm resistor in series with the common signal return from the patient is used for purposes of safety. The purpose of the resistor is to limit the current flow to a safe value in the event of a catastrophic failure. You are cautioned that humans should not be connected to any instrument that is also connected to the ac power lines unless you are thoroughly familiar with electrical safety problems in medical instruments and have the capability for

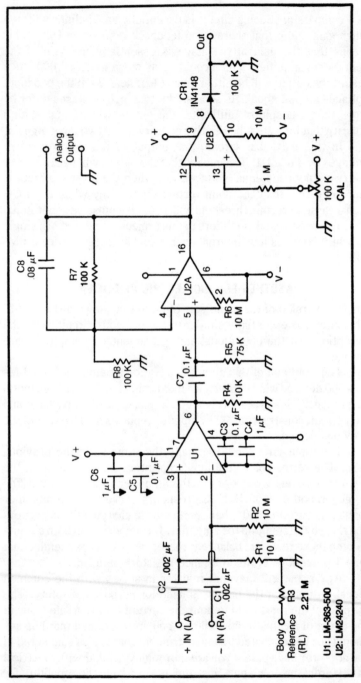

Fig. 17-5. Alternate ECG amplifier.

testing the device for hazards. Although it is beyond the scope of this book to delve into that topic, we can tell you that, in general, bioelectric amplifiers for human use should employ isolated amplifiers. None of the projects in this book use these amplifiers. As a result, the publisher and I recommend that all of these projects be limited to animal use only.

The remainder of the circuit is analogous to the circuit of Fig. 17-4, so the relevent discussion will not be repeated. It must be noted, however, that for many patients the ×1000 gain will be insufficient. This gain can be increased by decreasing the value of resistor R8 according to Equation 17-4.

$$R8 = R7/(A_v - 1) \qquad \textbf{17-4}$$

R7 is 100 K, R8 is the new value of R8 in kohms, and A_v is the gain required of amplifier U2A (presently 2).

WHEATSTONE BRIDGE TRANSDUCER AMPLIFIER

Perhaps one of the most common forms of instrumentation transducer is the Wheatstone bridge. This form of simple four-armed bridge uses resistances in each arm. It is ideal for use when a transducible property of some physical parameter is a change of dc resistance. In a pressure or force-displacement transducer, for example, the property of *piezoresistivity* is used. The piezoresistive element is placed such that it can be deformed by an applied pressure which in turn produces resistance changes. Similarly, there are temperature transducers in which the resistance will change as a function of temperature. All of these transducer types may find themselves used in a Wheatstone bridge circuit.

One principal advantage of the Wheatstone bridge is that it can be adjusted to produce a zero voltage output when the applied stimulus (e.g., pressure, temperature, etc.) is also zero. Figure 17-6 shows a typical Wheatstone bridge transducer. This one is a form of force-displacement transducer used in physiological studies. The transducer will be shielded, and will have some sort of connector at one surface.

The excitation and the common are the power supply connections. The voltage applied to the transducer must be regulated and precisely known or there will be an error term in the output data. Since many researchers use these transducers with battery power, I suspect that there has been a lot of unnecessarily bad data taken because of errors in the excitation potential. In addition to the

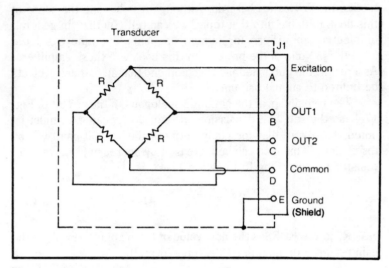

Fig. 17-6. Typical Wheatstone bridge transducer.

regulation of the potential, it is also necessary that the voltage be kept less than a certain critical value. There will be a maximum voltage specification above which the transducer may not be operated without danger to the device. In most cases, I would recommend that one not use more than two-thirds the maximum voltage in order to control self-heating and thermal drift. These twin problems are especially acute in low sensitivity instruments.

The sensitivity of a Wheatstone bridge transducer is given by a specification in the form microvolts (or millivolts) per volt of excitation per unit of applied stimulus. For a pressure transducer, for example, the spec might be 50 μV/V/torr (note: 1 torr = 1 mmHg). This means that the output voltage will be 50 microvolts per volt of excitation per torr. Let's look at an example. Suppose that the above transducer is excited with +5 volts, and the applied stimulus is 100 torr. The output voltage is:

$$V_{out} = (50 \ \mu V/V\text{-}T)(5 \ V)(100 \ T)$$

$$V_{out} = 25,000 \ \mu V$$

$$V_{out} = 25 \text{ millivolts}$$

A principal problem with these transducers is that the signal output may be quite small, so interference from the 60 Hz ac line and other sources might overwhelm the signal. We can improve the signal-noise ratio by boosting the signal at the input end of the line to the oscilloscope, chart recorder, computer or whatever other device receives it.

Figure 17-7 shows an amplifier that can be used at the transducer end of the system in order to boost the signal per the requirement above. The transducer amplifier is built inside of a small metal shielded box that is mounted directly onto the body of the transducer through a mating connector.

This particular circuit is designed to fit inside of one of the small blue Pomona boxes that are normally used for instrumentation connections, rf patch cords and the like. These boxes are small enough to not burden the transducer too much, while at the same time are sufficiently large to house the circuit. The boxes are also strong enough to survive the normal rigors of laboratory and shop environments.

Connector J1 is the connector on the transducer, while P1 is the exact mate for J1. For the sake of simplicity, the transducer internal circuitry is not shown (refer back to Fig. 17-6 if you need to look again). Connector P2 is a small five-pin female connector that will take the signal from this amplifier to either the instrument or a control box, and will bring dc power to the transducer amplifier.

The amplifier (A1) is a National Semiconductor LM-363-x, where x is the gain and will be either 10, 100 or 500. In most normal situations, the gain will be either 10 or 100 in the transducer amplifier with additional gain made up in the control box to follow. There is no reason why you must adhere to that, however. If your particular application requires the gain of 500, then specify an LM-363-500 instead of LM-363-10 or LM-363-100.

The dc power is brought into the amplifier housing from the control box or some other outside power source. Connector P2 supplies the power. For most applications, use 12 volts for both V− and V+ (i.e., V− = −12 Vdc, and V+ = +12 Vdc). This power should be regulated, if possible, even though the circuit will work without regulation. There are several capacitors in the power supply lines which seem to duplicate the functions of capacitors in the power supply. Keep them in the circuit despite this fact, however, as they will improve the stability and the rejection of noise from outside of the amplifier. The two 0.1 μF units (C5 and C6) are used to decouple high frequency signals. These capacitors should be mounted as close as possible to the body of the amplifier, although keep in mind that such standard advice is difficult to achieve in the

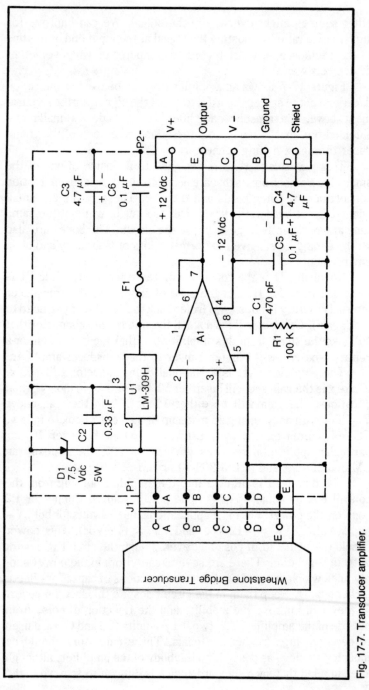

Fig. 17-7. Transducer amplifier.

cramped space allowed to this amplifier. The two 4.7 μF units are for lower frequency decoupling, and these should be tantalum electrolytics.

The excitation potential for the transducer is +5 volts and is developed from the +12 volt line in a three-terminal IC voltage regulator (U1), an LM-309H. If the excitation potential were not regulated, then there would be an error term in the output signal. Recall from the equation for the output voltage of a Wheatstone bridge transducer that the excitation voltage is one of the factors. We must, therefore, regulate the excitation voltage.

The LM-309H is a +5 volt, 100 milliampere voltage regulator. The current capacity is suitable for almost all normally encountered transducers, which means a looking back or *Thevinin's resistance* of 50 ohms or more. The way to tell the looking back resistance of a Wheatstone bridge is to look at the element resistances. In this limited case, the looking back resistance is the same as each element resistance. The H suffix denotes a metal TO-5 package for the regulator, making it easy to install inside the housing with the amplifier. I don't trust some of the plastic package H devices.

If a higher current is required or if the heat generated by U1 is too great for comfortable operation of the amplifier, then relocate the regulator in the main box (of which, more in a moment) and use a six-pin connector for P2 to accommodate the extra wire.

Zener diode D1 is not used to regulate the excitation voltage, as one might surmise from a quick look at the circuit. The zener potential of D1 is selected to be less than V+, and less than or equal to the maximum voltage that the transducer will tolerate, while also being greater than the excitation voltage. The purpose of D1 is to protect the transducer (which might cost hundreds of dollars) in the event U1 fails catastrophically. In that event, the +12 volt input potential on pin 1 of U1 will appear on the output where it could damage the transducer. Diode D1 will clamp that voltage, and then blow the fuse. That fuse, incidentally, should have a current rating approximately 1.5 times the normal operating current of the transducer, and the fuse should be of the *picofuse* variety (or some other axial lead, fast blowing fuse).

The two projects that follow are used with the transducer amplifier in some instances. The universal rear-end can be tacked onto almost any electronic project that must drive an output device such as an oscilloscope, strip-chart recorder, or A/D converter input on a computer. The dc power supply, of course, can be used for a variety of other projects.

UNIVERSAL REAR-END

The *rear end* of an electronic instrument is the output section. The circuit in Fig. 17-8 is a so-called universal rear-end, in that it will accept signals in the 50 millivolt to approximately 10 volt range, and prepare them for delivery to the outside world. Both sensitivity and position control are provided.

The heart of this circuit is simple dual operational amplifiers of the 741-family of devices. These particular amplifiers are both part of 1458 devices (two are used, A1 and A2). Since the circuit consists of four (an even number) inverting followers in cascade, the overall circuit is noninverting.

Each stage of the circuit is designed as unity gain, so the overall gain of the circuit is also unity. If for any reason you want a different gain, select a value for resistor R2 that will net the gain you require. The equation is the usual for this type of circuit. R2 is specified in ohms.

$$A_v = R2/10$$

If R2 is 10 K, then the gain of the rear-end circuit will be 0 to 1. If, however, we want a gain of 0 to 10, then we can make R2 = 100 K. A sometimes overlooked application of operational amplifiers is to make a gain of less than unity. If we want the gain to vary from 0 to 0.1, for example, we could make R2 = 1000 ohms (1 kohm).

Control over the gain of the circuit is provided by potentiometer R6, which is connected as the feedback resistor for amplifier A1B. Since the input resistor for this stage (R5) is 10 K, and the maximum resistance of R6 is also 10 K, the overall gain of this stage is 0 to 1.

There are two similar circuits using potentiometers to provide an offset potential to the circuit. Potentiometer R10 is used as a position control, while potentiometer R4 is an offset null control. In some applications, both of these controls might prove optional, but they are nonetheless recommended. In both cases, an offset voltage is created at the output of their respective stages by injecting a current into the input summing junction. The controls differ as follows:

Offset Null. This control is used to null the output voltage to zero. It has the effect of cancelling both the offset potentials of this circuit, and also the cumulative offset of the previous stages or other input signal source. This adjustment is usually a screwdriver adjustment.

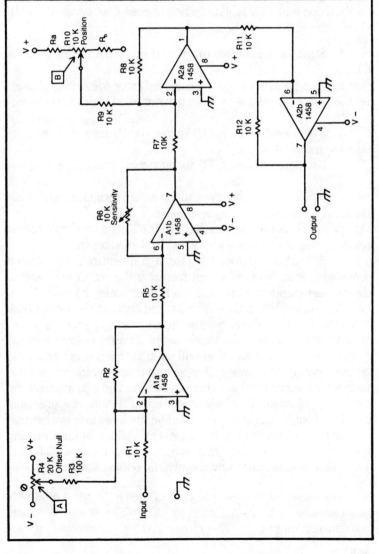

Fig. 17-8. Universal rear-end for instrumentation projects.

Position. This control is used to control the position of the signal baseline on a strip-chart recorder or oscilloscope that displays the signal appearing at the output.

The position control can be custom tailored to the application by limiting the range to exactly that required to push the signal off the screen. This job is done by adjusting the values of R_a and R_b.

Adjustment of this circuit is simple, but does require some instrumentation. Required are either a 3-1/2 digit digital voltmeter, an analog voltmeter with a 0 to 0.5 volt scale (or better), or, an oscilloscope with dc coupling (which is almost all oscilloscopes!). Follow the steps given here.

1. Short the input leads together (i.e. ground the input end of R1.

2. Using a sensitive dc voltage indicator (described above), set the voltage at point A to 00.00 volts ± 10 mV using potentiometer R4.

3. Use potentiometer R10 to set the voltage at point B to 00.00 volts ± 10 mV.

4. Set potentiometer R6 to maximum resistance (highest gain).

5. Connect the dc indicator to the output terminals, and adjust the scale to produce the highest on-scale reading.

6. Adjust potentiometer R4 for 00.00 volts ± 10 mV output reading; readjust the indicator sensitivity if necessary.

7. Adjust potentiometer R6 through its entire range several times while watching the output meter. If the output level shifts, then repeat step 6 until there is no further improvement.

8. Unshort the input terminals, and connect the input to the anticipated signal source. Set the signal source to produce a zero output value, and check the output meter. If there is a dc component to the signal, the output offset will shift. If this test is impossible because the signal source cannot be conveniently reduced to zero, then set the signal level at a convenient point and adjust sensitivity control R6 through its range several times. If there is appreciable shift in the output signal level or baseline, then you may assume that the input signal contains a dc component. Adjust R4 until running the sensitivity through its entire range no longer shows a baseline shift. This test is most conveniently run on an oscilloscope.

The universal rear-end can be packaged to fit into a relatively small area, so it is easily incorporated into almost any electronic instrumentation project. This circuit gives a professional appearance and operational capability to the project, not to mention increasing its flexibility.

UNIVERSAL INSTRUMENTATION POWER SUPPLY

The circuit shown in Fig. 17-9 is a dual-polarity dc power supply for use in small instrumentation projects. Although designed as part of the transducer amplifier shown earlier, this power supply is given separate treatment because of its utter universality. The power supply will provide ± 12 volts dc at currents up to 500 milliamperes per voltage (1 ampere total). In addition, with a little modification the circuit can double the output current.

Transformer T1 reduces the 115 Vac line voltage down to a level that can be used for the power supply. In this case, the transformer is rated at 25.6 Vac *center-tapped* (emphasis added because many transformers in this voltage are not center-tapped), at a secondary current of 1 ampere. Rectifier BR1 converts the ac from the secondary winding of T1 to pulsating dc, which is in turn filtered by C1 (for V+) and C2 (for V−). Note that, although a single fullwave bridge is used for both sides of the supply, each side uses half, so BR1 operates as two parallel half-wave rectifiers. The rule of thumb for selecting the values of C1 and C2 are 2000 μF/ampere. If the current rating is doubled, then increase the values of C1 and C2 to 2000 μF.

Devices U1 and U2 are fixed output three-terminal IC voltage regulators. The LM-340T-12 and LM-320T-12 are positive and negative regulators, respectively. These regulators are housed in TO-220 packages, which are tab-mounted plastic "transistor" cases. The tab is a heatsink, so make sure that it is mounted to the metal chassis, if such is provided.

Caution! The pinouts for the negative regulator (U1) are different from the positive regulator! If this fact is not noted, then you are likely to burn out one or the other—probably the negative regulator. Since pin 3 is normally connected to the tab, it is necessary to use a mica insulator underneath U1.

Parts List

   P3 ac power cord
   F1 1/4-ampere fuse and fuse holder, chassis mounted
   S1 SPST or SPDT ac power switch, chassis mounted
   T1 25.6 Vac, center-tapped, 1-ampere transformer
   BR1 100 PIV (or more), 1-ampere bridge rectifier
   C1,C2 1000 μF/50 WVdc electrolytic capacitor

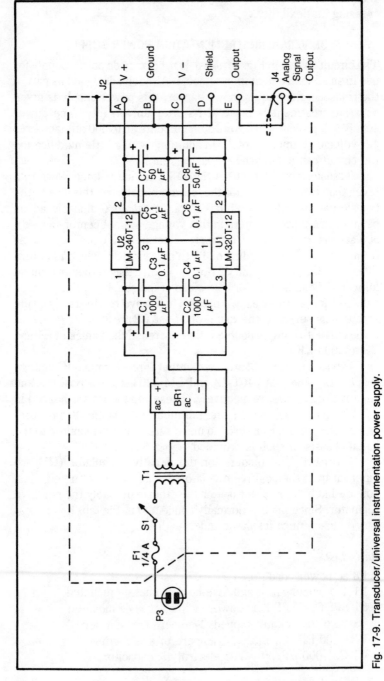

Fig. 17-9. Transducer/universal instrumentation power supply.

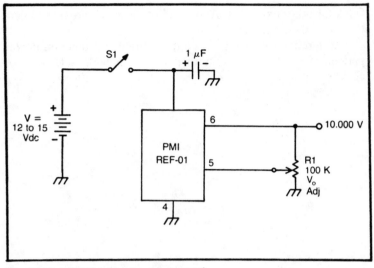

Fig. 17-10. REF-01 reference power supply.

C3,C4 0.1 μF/50 WVdc capacitor
C5,C6 0.1 μF/50 WVdc capacitor
C7,C8, 47 μF/35 WVdc tantalum electrolytic capacitor
U1 LM-340T-12 regulator IC
U2 LM-320T-12 regulator IC
J2 Output connector to suit application, 5-pin or more
J4 BNC female chassis-mounted connector (or other type that matches the instrument receiving the transducer signal). This component is deleted when the transducer amplifier is not built.
Chassis or cabinet to suit application

If it is desired to increase the output current to 1-ampere per voltage, then increase the values of C1 and C2, increase the rating of T1 to 2-amperes and the rating of BR1 to 2-amperes.

PRECISION 10.00 VOLT REFERENCE POWER SOURCE

Figure 17-10 shows a precision reference source. This particular circuit outputs 10.00 volts, and is adjustable. The reference regulator is a Precision Monolithics, Inc. *REF-01* device. Adjust the output voltage for precisely 10.00 volts using potentiometer R1. Do not adjust the circuit until it has been operating for 15 minutes.

There are also a number of other devices on the market, and you are referred to the National Semiconductor Linear IC Data

Book for other examples. Almost all of these ICs are as simple as this circuit, or simpler.

Reference sources are used to calibrate instruments, in comparison circuits and measurements, and in both A/D and D/A converters.

Appendix

Appendix

Excess-three Code

DECIMAL DIGIT	XS 3 CODE	BINARY VALUE
0	0011	3
1	0100	4
2	0101	5
3	0110	6
4	0111	7
5	1000	8
6	1001	9
7	1010	10
8	1011	11
9	1100	12

Gray Code

DECIMAL	BINARY	GRAY
0	000	000
1	001	001
2	010	011
3	011	010
4	100	110
5	101	111

Standard ASCII Codes

HEX	MSD							
	BITS	0	1	2	3	4	5	6	7
LSD		000	001	010	011	100	101	110	111
0	0000	NUL	DLE	SP	0	@	P	`	p
1	0001	SOH	DC1	!	1	A	Q	a	q
2	0010	STX	DC2	"	2	B	R	b	r
3	0011	ETX	DC3	#	3	C	S	c	s
4	0100	EOT	DC4	$	4	D	T	d	t
5	0101	ENQ	NAK	%	5	E	U	e	u
6	0110	ACK	SYN	&	6	F	V	f	v

		0	1	2	3	4	5	6	7
7	0111	BEL	ETB	'	7	G	W	g	w
8	1000	BS	CAN	(	8	H	X	h	x
9	1001	HT	EM	)	9	I	Y	i	y
A	1010	LF	SUB	*	:	J	Z	j	z
B	1011	VT	ESC	+	;	K	[	k	{
C	1100	FF	FS	,	<	L	\	l	|
D	1101	CR	GS	-	=	M	]	m	}
E	1110	SO	RS	.	>	N	^	n	~
F	1111	SI	US	/	?	O	_	o	DEL

317

IBM Standard 8-bit EBCDIC Codes

HEX (LSD)	BITS	0	1	2	3	4	5	6	7	8	9	A	B	C	D	E	F
(MSD) →		0	1	2	3	4	5	6	7	8	9	A	B	C	D	E	F
0	0000	NUL	DLE	DS		SP	&	-						{	}	\	0
1	0001	SOH	DC1	SOS				/		a	j	~		A	J		1
2	0010	STX	DC2	FS	SYN					b	k	s		B	K	S	2
3	0011	ETX	TM							c	l	t		C	L	T	3
4	0100	PF	RES	BYP	PN					d	m	u		D	M	U	4
5	0101	HT	NL	LF	RS					e	n	v		E	N	V	5
6	0110	LC	BS	ETB	UC					f	o	w		F	O	W	6

Hex	Bin	0	1	2	3	4	5	6	7	8	9	A	B	C	D	E	F
7	0111	DEL	IL	ESC	EOT					g	p	x		G	P	X	7
8	1000	GE	CAN							h	q	y		H	Q	Y	8
9	1001	RLF	EM						`	i	r	z		I	R	Z	9
A	1010	SMM	CC	SM		¢	!	¦	:								
B	1011	VT	CU1	CU2	CU3	.	$	,	#								
C	1100	FF	IFS		DC4	<	*	%	@								
D	1101	CR	IGS	ENQ	NAK	(	)	_	'								
E	1110	SO	IRS	ACK		+	;	>	=								
F	1111	SI	IUS	BEL	SUB	|	¬	?	"								EO

Index

A

Absorption, dielectric, 139
Addition, binary, 150
Address decoder, 255
Advanced Micro Devices, 202, 207
Alphanumeric code, 159
Amplifier, 46
Amplifier, bioelectric, 7
Amplifier, common emitter, 53
  ac, transistor, 55
  common base, 53
  common collector, 53
Amplifier, current difference, 85
  Norton, 85
Amplifier, isolation, 75
  differential, 76
  positive-negative, 75
  user of feedback in, 75
Amplifier, log-antilog, 105
Amplifier, motor drive, 285
  complementary symmetry, 285
Amplifier, noninverting, 72
Amplifier, operational transconductance, 98
Amplifier, sample-and-hold, 141
Amplifier, scaling, 250
Amplifier, summer, 287
  bioelectric ECG, 296, 299
  differential, 292
  instrumentation, 294
  single-ended, 289
Amplification, voltage, 48
Analog, definition of, 2
Analog Devices, Inc., 191
Analog instrumentation, need for, 1

Analog reference source, accuracy of, 109
  generation of, 110
Analog reference source, integrated circuit, 115
Analog refrence source, temperature effects, 113
  calibration of, 113
Analog signal, 2
  domain of, 2
  inference of opposite, 2
  range of, 2
Analog signal, sources of, 5
Analog subsystem, "front end" of, 5
Analog-to-digital converter, 4, 181
  dual-slope integrator, 187
  quadslope, 191
  single-slope integrator, 182
  triple-slope, 191
Analog-to-digital converter, microcomputer-compatible, 223
  application of, 223
  bit length, 224
Analog-to-digital converter, microcomputer interface, 266
  three-state logic, 267
Analog-to-digital converter, parallel, 191
  binary ramp, 193
  flash, 191
  output latch, 196
  servo, 193
  successive approximation, 197
Analog-to-digital converter, speed of, 225

AD7570, 240-247
alignment of, 230
current to voltage converstion, 231
8-bit binary ramp, 226
8-bit successive approximation, 232
hybrid, 247
ICL7109, 237
ZN425E, 27
ZN432, 235
Analog-to-digital converter, start pulse, 268
continuous conversion, 272
end-of-conversion (EOC) pulse, 268
Intel 8212 I/O buffer, 269
Aperture time, 135
Aperture time, data conversion, 167
Arithmetic, binary, 150
Arithmetic, two's complement, 151
ASCII, 157, 159

B

Band-gap regulator, 116
Base, transistor, 45
Base resistor, 523
Baudot code, 159
Bias, transistor, configurations of, 50
Bias network, transistor, 47
Binary-coded decimal (BCD) code, 158
Binary number system, 144
Bioelectric amplifier, 7
Bit, 145
Boltzmann's constant, 25, 107
Bridge, Wheatstone, 15

C

Code, ASCII, 157
Code, binary-coded decimal (BCD), 158
Alphanumeric, 159
ASCII, 160
Baudot, 159
EBCDIC, 160
Excess-3, 159
Gray, 159
Code, digital, 156
Code, hexadecimal, 157
Code, split-octal, 158
Collector, transistor, 45
Collector current, maximum, 51
Common mode rejection ratio, 77
Comparator, voltage, 100
hysteresis in, 102
Continuous signal, mathematical representation of, 3

Control system, open-loop, 282
closed-loop, 282
Conversion time, data conversion, 166
Converter, data, 161
Converter, digital-to-analog (D/A), 161, 170
analog-to-digital (A/D), 161
Current difference amplifier, as reference bias regulator, 94
comparator, 95
Current difference amplifier, input configuration, 85
simplified, 87
Current difference amlifier, inverting ac, 88
ac coupled, 89
as linear signal mixer, 92
differential, 91
noninverting, 90
quiescent output voltage, 89
Current mirror, 88
Current regulator, bipolar transistor, 127
Current regulator, precision, 123
Current source, constant, 15

D

DAC-08 (D/A converter), 207
ac operation, 220
external control of, 222
logic protocol compatibility, 211
negative output operation, 219
negative reference operation of, 213
pin-out for, 209
positive unipolar operation of, 210
slew rate of, 221
voltage output, high impedance, 214
voltage output, low imepdance, 218
Data converter, output states of, 5
Data representation, binary, 156
Decoder, address, 255, 280
Decoder, two-bit to four-bit, 257
binary to 1-of-16, 259
eight-bit, 261
programmable four-bit, 260
Depletion zone, 43
Differential amplifier, 76
Differential amplifier, IC, 62
Differentiator, 104
high-pass filter, 104
op amp, 105
Differentiator, op amp, 34
Digit, binary, 145

Digital-to-analog converter, 170
  amplifier settling time of, 177
  binary weighted, 171
  block diagram, 171
  multiplying, 171
  nonmultiplying, 171
  output voltage of, 176
  R-2R ladder, 171
Digital-to-analog converter, greater
    than eight-bit, 265
  double-buffered interface, 267
Digital-to-analog converter, I/O-port
    interface, 253
  direct data bus interface, 256
  memory mapped interface, 253
  select pulses, 254
  Z-80 output signals, 254
Digital-to-analog converter, mic-
    rocomputer interface, 249
Digital-to-analog converter,
    microcomputer-compatible, 203
  DAC-08, 207
  ZN425E, 204
Diode, constant-current, 123
Diode, semiconductor, 43
Diode, temperature dependence of,
    25
Diode, zener, 59, 110
Droop, 136

E

EBCDIC, 159
Electrocardiograph (ECG), 4, 6
Electrode, 5, 6
Electrode, Ag-AgCl, 7
  circular disc, 8
  column, 8
  flat plate, 8
  needle, 8
  tower, 8
Electrode, biomedical, 6
Electrode, mutual resistance of, 7
Electroencephalograph (EEG), 6
Emitter, transistor, 45
Emitter resistor, 51
End of conversion pulse, 190
Error, quantization, 163, 165
Error, sampling, 133
Excess-3 code, 159

F

Feedthrough, 138
Ferranti Semiconductor Division, 116
Field effect transistor, advantages of,
    59
Fourier series, 3
Frequency response, transistor, 56

G

Gain, 46
  alpha, 46
  beta, 46
  current, 46
  voltage, 46
Gate, multiple transmissions, 61
Gauge factor, 12
Gray code, 159

H

Half-bridge, 15
Half-cell potential, 7
Hexadecimal code, 157
Hexadecimal number system, 146
Hole, semiconductor, 42
Hollerith card, 160
Hooke's Law, 34

I

Inductance, 28
Inductive reactance, 28
Integrated circuit, 61
  linear, 61
Integrator, 102
  low-pass filter, 103
  op amp, 103
Intersil, Inc., 118
Inverting follower, op amp, 68
  variable gain, 71

J

JFET, applications of, 60
JFET, as current regulator, 123
JFET, n-channel, 56
  p-channel, 56
JFET, use as amplifier, 59
Junction, pn, 43
  depletion zone of, 43

K

Kirchhoff's Law, 46

L

Least significant digit (LSD), 148
Logic, three-state, 267
Logical operation, 156
  symbols for, 156
Logical operation, NOT, 156
  AND, 156
  exclusive-OR (XOR), 156
  NAND, 156
  NOR, 156
  OR, 156

M

Mixer, audio frequency, 93

MOSFET, applications of, 60
MOSFET, operation modes of, 58
MOSFET, single gate, 57
  dual gate, 57
MOSFET, use as amplifier, 59
Most significant digit, (MSD), 147
Motor, computer control of, 279
Motor, dc, computer control of, 281
Motor reversal, electronic, 285
Motorola Semiconductor Products, Inc. 202
Movement artifact, 8
Multiplication, binary, 154
Multivibrator, monostable, 34

N

Noninverting follower, op amp, 73
N-type semiconductor, current flow in, 42
Number system, 142
  decimal, 143
  positional notation in, 143
  radix of, 143
  weighted, 143
Number system, binary, 144
Number system, conversion of, 147
Number system, hexadecimal, 146
Number system, octal, 145
Nyquist's Theorem, 164

O

Octal number system, 145
Op amp, problems of, 79
  offset null terminals, 81
  use of compensation resistor, 79
Operational amplifier (op amp), 64
  circuit symbol, 65
  gain of, 65
  ideal, 67
  inverting input, 65
  power supply for, 66
Operation, logical, 156
Operational transconductance amplifier, 98
Optoisolator, 277
Output section, instrumentation, universal, 306

P

Passband, 4
Photodiode, 39
Photoresistor, 38
Phototransistor, 39
Photovoltaic cell, 39
Picofuse, 305
Piezoresistivity, 10, 301

Pn junction, forward biased, 44
  reverse biased, 44
Position transducer, single-quadrant, 32
  two-quadrant, 32
Potentiometer, as position transducer, 31
Power supply, instrumentation, 309
  reference, 311
Precision Monolithics, Inc., 121, 207
P-type semiconductor, conduction in, 42

Q

Quantization, 5
Quantization error, 163, 165
Quantization error, effects of, 165
Quantization, inherent error in, 5

R

Radix, 143
Reference power supply, ICL-8069, 120
Reference source, analog, 109
Regulator, band-gap, 116
Regulator, op amp buffered, 114
Regulator, shunt, 112
Relay, electromagnetic, 274
Resistance, electrical conductor, formula, 9
Resistivity constant, 9
Resistor, base, 52
Resistor, emitter, 51

S

Sample-and-hold amplifier, 141
  buffered input, 141
  floating switch, 141
  integrator, output, 141
Sample-and-hold circuit, 4, 128, 132
Sampling error, 133
  aperture time, 135
  during sampling, 134
  sample-to-hold, 135
  settling time, 134
Sampling error, acquisition time, 139
Sampling error, dielectric absorption, 139
  hold-to-sample, 139
Sampling error, feedthrough, 138
Sampling error, switching transient, 135
  droop, 136
  during hold, 136
  sample-to-hold offset, 136
Sampling rate, minimum, 4, 164

Scaling amplifier, 250
Seebeck effect, 24
Semiconductor, 40
  covalent bonding in, 41
  definition of, 40
  impurity in, 40
  n-type, 40
  p-type, 40
  types of, 40
Servomechanism, continuously controlled, 286
Settling time, D/A converter, 169
Shunt regulator, 112
Signal, 1
  analog, 2
  continuous, 3
  sampled, 2, 5
Signal, digital, 5
Signal, digitized, 4
Signal, types of, 162
Signal processor, 100
Silicon-controlled rectifier (SCR), 277
Sine wave, 4
Skin, impedance of, 6
Solar cell, 39
Split-octal code, 158
Strain gauge, 9
Strain gauge, bonded, 14
  circuitry for, 15, 16
  linearity of, 14
  unbonded, 14
Strain gauge, effects of displacement on, 31
Strain gauge, full-bridge, 17
Strain gauge, piezoresistive, 11
Strain gauge, sensitivity factor of, 19
  calibration of, 20
  offset voltage of, 20
Subsystem, analog, 5
Substrate, semiconductor, 61
Subtraction, binary, 151
Subtraction, two's complement, 152
Successive approximation register (SAR), 198
Switch, FET, 128
  low-enable, 132
  MOSFET, 129
  positive-enable, 131
Switch, solid-state, 61

T
Tachometer, 34, 280
Temperature coefficient, of material, 22
Temperature probe, diode, 25
  bipolar transistor, 26

Temperature transducer, semiconductor, 25
Thermistor, 21
Thermistor, response of, 23
  self-heating of, 23
  time constant of, 23
Thermocouple, 23
Three-state logic, 267
Thevinin's resistance, 305
Thyristor, 277
Transconductance, formula for, 98
Transducer, 5, 8
  definition of, 9
Transducer, inductive, 28
Transducer, light, 38
Transducer, position displacement, 29
Transducer, pressure, 34
  Bourdon tube, 37
  cantilever force, 36
  fluid pressure, 37
  force, 34
  force-displacement, 36
  LVDT, 38
Transducer, temperature, 21
Transducer, velocity, 32
  acceleration, 32
Transducible property, of material, 10
Transfer function, 5
Transformer, linear variable differential, 29
Transistor, 44
Transistor, bipolar, 56
  field effect, 56
  junction and field effect (JFET), 56
Transistor, insulated gate field effect (IGFET), 58
  metal oxide semiconductor field effect, (MOSFET), 58
Triac, 279
Trigger, comparator, 34
  Schmitt, 34
Trigger, Schmitt, 97
Two's complement, 151

V
Voltage divider, 15

W
Waveform, harmonic content of, 4
  pure, 4
Wheatstone bridge, 15
  output voltage of, 18
Wheatstone bridge, inductive, 28

Z
Zener diode, 110

OTHER POPULAR TAB BOOKS OF INTEREST

| TAB | TAB BOOKS Inc.

Blue Ridge Summit. Pa. 17214

Send for FREE TAB Catalog describing over 750 current titles in print.